DUSTIN HOFFMAN

Iain Johnstone

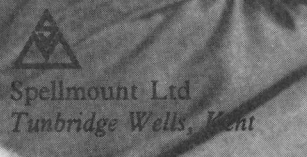
Spellmount Ltd
Tunbridge Wells, Kent

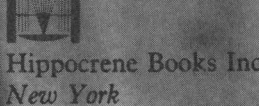
Hippocrene Books Inc
New York

First published in the UK in 1984 by
SPELLMOUNT LTD
12 Dene Way, Speldhurst
Tunbridge Wells, Kent TN3 ONX

ISBN 0-946771-25-1 (UK)

British Library Cataloguing in Publication Date
Johnstone, Iain
Dustin Hoffman. –(Film and Theatre Stars)
1. Hoffman, Dustin 2. Actors –
United States – Biography
1. Title 2. Series

First published in the USA in 1984 by
HIPPOCRENE BOOKS INC
171 Madison Avenue
New York, NY 10016

ISBN 0-88254-899-3 (USA)

All rights reserved. No part of this publication may be reproduced, stored in a retrieval system, or transmitted in any form or by any means, electronic, mechanical, photocopying, recording or otherwise, without prior permission in writing from Spellmount Ltd, Publishers.

Commissioning Editor: Sue Rolfe
Series Editor: John Latimer Smith
Cover Design: Peter Theodosiou

Printed & bound in Great Britain
by Anchor/Brendon Ltd, Tiptree, Essex

Contents

Chapter One	11
Chapter Two	20
Chapter Three	30
Chapter Four	41
Chapter Five	54
Chapter Six	71
The Films of Dustin Hoffman	87

List of Illustrations

Alfredo, Alfredo (1973)
Alfredo exhausted by the demands of his wife.

Straw Dogs (1971)
David begins to take control.

The Graduate (1967)
Benjamin's classic view of Mrs Robinson's right leg.

The Graduate (1967)
Benjamin removes the newly married Elaine Robinson (Katharine Ross) from the church.

Midnight Cowboy (1969)
Ratso Rizzo and the innocent Joe Buck (Jon Voight)

Midnight Cowboy (1969)
Ratso caught shoplifting.

Straw Dogs (1971)
David is threatened by Scutt (Ken Hutchinson) and Venner (Del Henney)

Straw Dogs (1971)
David asserts himself against Cawsey (Jim Norton).

Papillon (1973)
Louis Dega discusses the escape with Papillon (Steve McQueen) against the advice of the trusty.

Papillon (1973)
The getaway: maybe prison was preferable to this.

All the President's Men (1976)
Bernstein and Woodward (Robert Redford) discuss tactics with director Alan J. Pakula.

Marathon Man (1976)
Babe Levy in training round Central Park.

Marathon Man (1976)
Babe asserts himself.

Kramer vs Kramer (1979)
Ted Kramer plays mother and father to his son Billy (Justin Henry)

Marathon Man (1976)
Babe escapes the ordeal in his bathroom into a friendless city.

Tootsie (1982)

On the following page: *The Graduate* (1967)
Benjamin's classic view of Mrs Robinson's right leg.

Chapter One

It is not an easy thing to become a film star; there is no prescribed route to the job. Attendance at an acting academy may give you a head's start but it is more often a passport to poverty than a stepping stone to stardom. Even the old studio training schemes turned out a thousand nonentities for every one who found his name in lights. Some people have appeared in a hundred films and nobody knows their names. Others have appeared in just one and gained an instant screen reputation. Such a person is Dustin Hoffman.

How did he manage it? Undoubtedly he was and is possessed of a formidable acting talent – but that is not an essential ingredient for the job. Many men and women have become stars who were less than brilliant actors and actresses. The reasons for their popularity are diverse but they are united by one common blessing. Luck. And, as Pasteur said, luck favours the prepared mind.

Hoffman's luck began about five years before he was born when his parents, Harry and Lilian, left Chicago in the wake of the depression seeking a brighter future in California. Harry harboured hopes of becoming a movie producer but found work in the studios as a prop man. His sons therefore grew up in the ambience of the movies. Dustin was born on the 8th of August 1937 and named after the cowboy actor, Dustin Farnum. His brother Ronald had also been named after a film star, more likely Colman than Reagan. When Dustin was two, Ronald was already in the movies, as an extra in Frank Capra's *Mr Smith goes to Washington*. It was his first and last screen appearance. Dustin had to wait nearly three decades before he stepped in front of a camera.

In fact he got off to a slow start; he didn't even speak until he was three and a half. After that, said his mother, 'he was a clown from the word go.' His first recorded stage performance was in the seventh grade at John Burroughs Junior High School in Charles Dickens' *A Christmas Carol*. Hoffman was cast as Tiny Tim, he recalls, 'because I was the shortest in the class. Because a ninth grader dared me, in front of all the parents at the

Christmas show, I said: "God bless us every one, Goddamit." I got suspended for that. In high school the other guys had hair on their chests and played football. I played tennis, had a big nose and acne so bad my face looked like a rifle range.'

Although known to his mother as Dustala – a Jewish endearment – at school he collected the epithet Dustbin. In spite of his acne and lack of inches, perhaps because of them, he became a ringleader. He would always dance with the ugliest and fattest girl in the class to get a laugh and draw attention to himself. He would engineer minor pranks, like getting everyone in the class to cough at exactly 2.05 p.m. The teacher was in no doubt who was behind the ruse – 'go to my office, Hoffman.'

Home life was less fun. California is a place most Americans want to escape to; paradoxically, even as a child, Hoffman wanted to escape from it. He told me when I first met him: 'I never really liked it there very much. Even as a kid I always wanted to be living in New York. I used to see the Leo Gorcey OUR GANG comedies, the Dead End Kids. I always wanted to be like them. We didn't live in a movie star section, but you'd see a movie star now and then – it never meant much. I think one time I was playing baseball, when I was about 11 years old and Robert Young passed by. I'd hit a ball that had gone over the fence and he threw it back. I remember thinking: "Gee, Robert Young threw the ball back." '

His mother realised early on that he had an artistic bent, but not as an actor. 'Both my parents wanted me to be a concert pianist and I studied piano from the age of 6 until about 16. And then I went into playing jazz and I was just playing jazz, not very well, and started college. I didn't know whether I wanted to go into music or medicine but it was decided for me because I was flunking both.'

So he abandoned his medical ambitions after a year at Santa Monica City College (where his mother was taking a course at the same time) and his parents' musical ambitions at the Los Angeles Conservatory of Music and, in 1957, took an acting course at the Pasadena Playhouse. 'I think I probably went into acting out of negative reasons. I never thought about being an actor as a child. The first time I thought about acting was when I was taking that course. It was the first subject I ever felt I could concentrate on.'

Twenty years later Hoffman rationalised the decision to Cosmopolitan Magazine. 'I did it so that I could meet girls. Pretty girls came later. In class they'd ask us to do improvisatons – to follow our impulse. My impulse was to take a girl in my arms and kiss her – which is what I did. I'd pick a certain acting class because of the girls in it. That's reason enough to be an actor. If someone says he wants to act so that he can meet pretty girls, there's more of a chance he'll become a great actor than if he says he can't live without acting. Saying you can't live without acting is just so much esoteric pretension.'

Kissing apart, his stage work was good enough for one instructor to advise him, according to Time Magazine, 'Dusty, it may take you a long time – 10 or 15 years – but you are going to have a life in the theatre.'

I asked him why he didn't look for small parts in movies when he graduated. 'I didn't feel I could get any work in Hollywood. There was no stage there; at that time it was all cowboy TV series and I wasn't the type.' And then, more tellingly, he added: 'Besides, I wanted to fail away from home.' In 1958 he embarked on a Greyhound bus for New York. He sought out an old friend from acting class – Gene Hackman – and found a place to sleep on his kitchen floor. Hackman described the character who turned up at his door: 'He had very long hair, a sheepskin vest with no shirt, leather boots and blue jeans.'

For the aspirant actor the New York theatre held many more opportunities in 1958 than it does today when Broadway largely consists of a few hit musicals and a lot of dark theatres. In the glow of major works by Arthur Miller and Tenessee Williams, many serious writers were able to get their plays performed, especially off-Broadway. Lee Strasberg's Actors' Studio was not only the place to learn but a valuable location in which to be seen by directors. Entry was by audition and it took Hoffman five attempts and two years to get in.

So, like Hackman who was working as a furniture remover,

On the following page: *The Graduate* (1967)
Benjamin removes the newly married Elaine Robinson
(Katherine Ross) from the church.

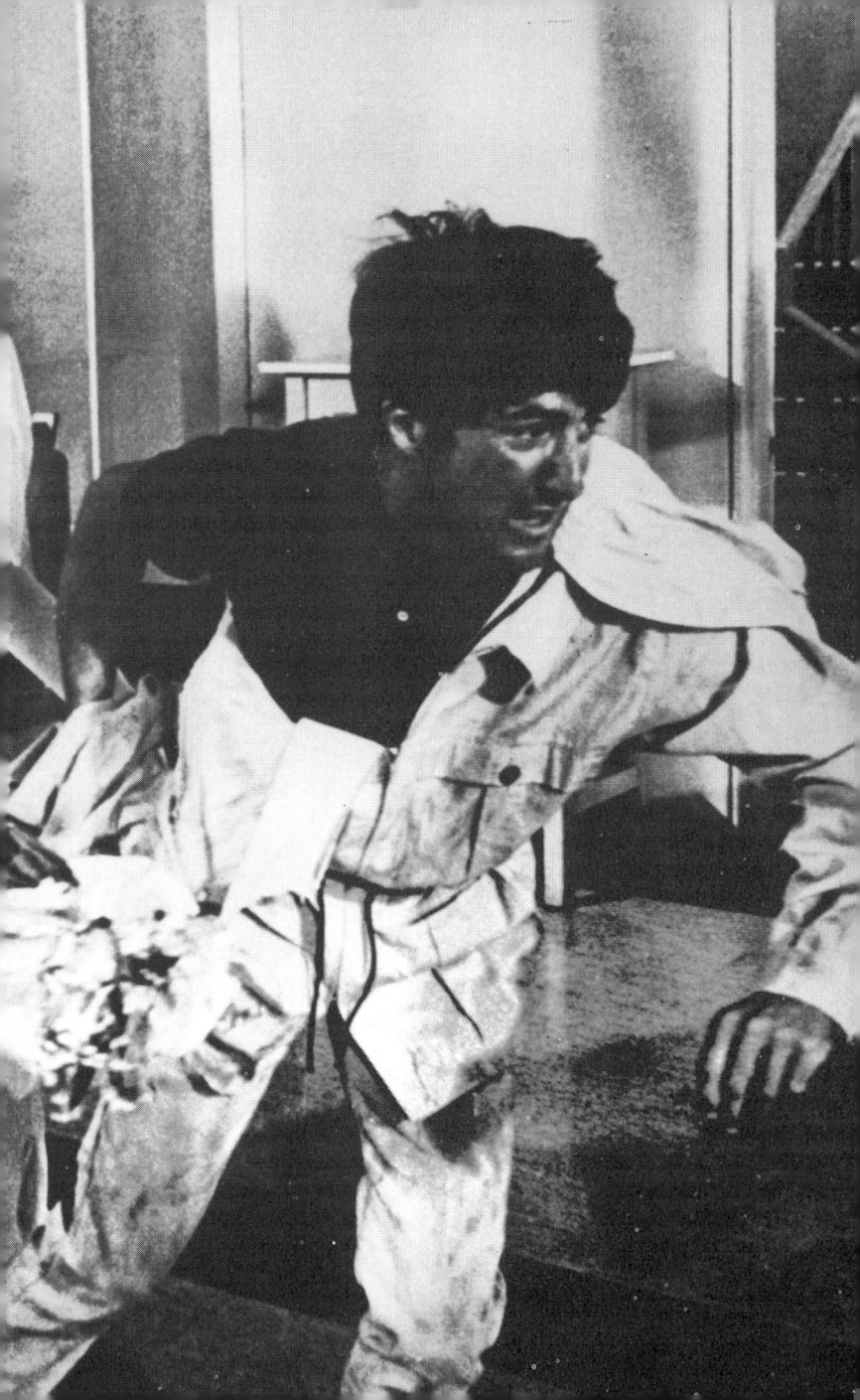

he became that New York institution: the out-of-work-actor. He was an excellent typist working at Reuben Donnelly's, sundry law firms and Yellow Pages. His medical training was put to good effect when he got a job as an orderly in a mental hospital. 'I used to hold patients for electric shock treatment. Then later on they would beat me at Scrabble.' His days as a counterman at Rudley's were shortlived: 'I wanted to get fired and finally did when I ate six steaks in a day.' Inevitably he wanted to get close to the theatre so he sold soft drinks at the Longacre theatre and one day, working in the cloakroom, he checked Eleanor Roosevelt's mink, claiming that in her presence he was, for the first time, starstruck. He appeared at the Premise as a waiter, cook and dishwasher – but never on the stage.

For the first two years he was subsidised by his parents to the tune of $50 a week and he kept his weekly budget in Mason jars on Hackman's kitchen shelf – one for food, one for rent, one for transport. The two men, yet to be ennobled by their Oscars, gave vent to their thespian frustration by acting out street dramas (Hackman would be an old tramp who would seize a young girl – a fellow employee of Dustin's from Macy's – and Hoffman would rescue her.) When the New York Times was on strike, Hoffman went out and shouted the news in Times Square.

His main hobby, at that time, was girls. He moved into an apartment with some fellow actors, including Robert Duvall who observed: 'Dustin has had more girls than anyone I've ever known and more than Joe Namath ever dreamed about. When waitresses asked him"How do you like your coffee?"He'd reply: "Black, with sugar and a kiss"and occasionally he'd get one.'

Duvall should know. One girlfriend I met remembers being serenaded to sleep in Dustin's arms by a guitar solo from Robert Duvall. It was appropriate therefore that his first East Coast stage appearance was at an all girls school. In May 1959 he took an unpaid part in Gertrude Stein's *Yes is for a Very Young Man* at Sarah Lawrence College. He needed to act and he needed the exposure. It probably led to this Broadway debut in *A Cook for Mr General*, not a memorable one; Hoffman only spoke one word.

After two years his parents stopped sending him money – 'they doubted that I'd ever become an actor and didn't want me to stay in New York when they felt I could go back to Los Angeles and live with them for nothing' – so he found himself more regular employment out of town at the Theatre Company of Boston. It was there that he met Ulu Grosbard who directed him in *Waiting for Godot*. They became friends. Grosbard later gave him a job as assistant director – *not* as an actor, the leads went to Jon Voight and Robert Duvall – in his New York production of *A View From the Bridge* and Hoffman later got Grosbard to direct him in two movies. Another friendship was struck up with the playwright Murray Schisgal when Hoffman appeared in three of his plays in Stockbridge, Massachussetts. Their collaboration, unlike the one with Grosbard, continues to this day; Schisgal co-wrote *Tootsie*.

Undoubtedly Hoffman's inventive skills as an actor were appreciated in these regional productions; he also had local star power. Whenever he came on stage in *Three Men on a Horse* the audience would squeal. But ending up as an assistant director was hardly the role he was aiming for. He felt like giving up. 'I decided that a good time to quit acting is before you get a job.'

Fortunately, he didn't. He auditioned for an off-Broadway production of Ronald Ribman's *Harry, Noon and Night* – 'I played a hunch-backed German homosexual with a limp,' he told me. 'I studied the German accent and I studied the limp and I worked a little bit on the homosexuality.' It was his first major success in his adopted city, the kind that provided an insurance policy. He could expect some sort of continuity of stage work from then on.

He soon got his first major Broadway role in the second company of Frank Gilroy's long-running drama *The Subject Was Rose*. But fate intervened in a fashion that was to prove initially cruel but ultimately lead to the decisive moment that was to make him famous.

He went round to a girl friend's apartment for dinner. A pot on the stove caught fire and as he rushed to lift it, it exploded. His arms were badly burned – he bares the scars to this day – and he was rushed to hospital. There followed a month of painful treatment with Hoffman being given powerful doses of Demerol to alleviate the agony. He entered the hospital weighing 140 pounds and left weighing 110. Worse than this, he had almost become a 'junkie' on the pain relievers. 'When I got home, I honestly didn't think I could stand it. My life was unbearable. I didn't feel pain from the burns any more but that had been replaced by pain 100 per cent worse. I felt as if hordes of people were constantly shaking me, shaking my whole insides, shaking me until I'd cry in anguish. But gradually I beat the craving.'

When troubles come, they come not single spies but in battalions. He found that the part in *The Subject Was Roses* had not been held open for him and when he found work as Sparky in John Arden's *Sergeant Musgrave's Dance* it was shortlived. He fell out with the director who fired him. But this triple bout of bad luck left him free to audition for a new Ronald Ribman play *The Journey of the Fifth Horse*. Again it was a chance to display his mastery of character acting. 'I played a 43 year old spinsterish Russian clerk,' he told me. 'It was the first time I was reviewed in New York – that was after about eight or nine years of being there. I got very good reviews and an award for it.'

What he didn't tell me was the acute agony he experienced in creating the character, Zoditch. During the rehearsals the director demanded: 'Where's the character?' 'There is no character,' replied Hoffman, 'because I haven't found him yet.' On the opening night he was still searching for the key to this hysterical clerk with a vivid fantasy life. Hoffman was so nervous when he appeared on stage he began to speak in a high-pitched voice. He continued to do so. He had found the key.

The award was the 1966 Obie for best actor off-Broadway, a prize elevated by the fact that George C. Scott and Al Pacino had also been nominated. Ribman won the Obie for Best New Play.

When the much-praised Henry Livings' comedy *Eh?* was imported from London, Hoffman was an obvious candidate for yet another vividly eccentric character, the cockney night watchman Valentine Brose.

It was directed by a fellow actor, Alan Arkin. He duly cast Hoffman in the part but then did him a much greater favour by suggesting to his friend, Mike Nichols, that he should come and see the performance. Nichols had enjoyed an acclaimed debut as a film director with his first movie *Who's Afraid of Virginia*

Woolf? starring Richard and Elizabeth Burton. Now he was looking for someone to play the lead in his second film, *The Graduate*.

Chapter Two

The Graduate wasn't Dustin Hoffman's first film. It was, in fact, his third. Thanks to his burgeoning off-Broadway reputation and because he was known to the writer, Murray Schisgal, he got the part of Hap in Arthur Hiller's film *The Tiger Makes Out* based on Schisgal's play. It starred Eli Wallach and his wife, Anne Jackson, but hardly Dustin Hoffman since he was on the screen for only thirty seconds.

However he enjoyed the experience. 'I got there at 10 am and was done by 7 pm. Then I 'phoned everybody and said: 'Well, I've just finished my first movie!'

After he was cast in *The Graduate* but before filming began he went to Rome to make *Madigan's Millions* and $5000 for himself. Originally George Raft was set to play the lead but he abandoned the ordeal to Cesar Romero who co-starred with Elsa Martinelli. It was directed by Stanley Prager and produced by Sidney Pink. Perhaps anticipating that it would not a wild success – Time Magazine was later to observe 'the movie's garish color and lighting would give an aspirin a headache' – American International Pictures prudently waited until both *The Graduate* and *Midnight Cowboy* had been released before they inflicted it on the public.

The Graduate had been intended to be Mike Nichols' first movie. 'The producer sent me the book and said "did I think it could be a movie?" and I said yes I did. We agreed to do it and then *Virginia Woolf* came up and I did that first.'

'Came up' is something of an understatement. Although Nichols had enjoyed Broadway hits as a performer *An Evening With Mike Nichols and Elaine May* and as a director with *Barefoot in the Park*, he had never set foot on a movie set until he arrived to direct the Burtons. His opportunity was entirely due to them – 'It didn't seem to me that anybody was going to give me *Virginia Woolf* with the Burtons in it, but they being loyal and, God knows, trusting friends asked for me to do it and held out till I was allowed to do it.'

Success is power in Hollywood and when Joe Levine backed Nichols to make *The Graduate* he also backed his instinct in casting. At Levine's Embassy offices in New York the most fancied candidate was Chris Connelly of *Peyton Place* who at least looked like the character described in Charles Webb's novel. Nichols however wanted a new face.

Hoffman didn't look like the character and revealed to me that he didn't think he was suitable for the part. 'When I read the book I felt I was wrong for it. Then when I was going to be screen-tested I talked to Nichols on the 'phone, because I was in *Eh?* in New York and he was in Los Angeles, and I said to him that I did not think I was right for the role. He said "Why?" and I said: "Well, he's a kind of Anglo-Saxon, tall slender, good-looking chap." And he said: "And you're Jewish." And I said: "That's right. Short and Jewish." He said: "Well, inside, Benjamin Braddock is short and Jewish."

'What did you do in the screen test?' I asked him. Hoffman paused.

'I tried to play tall and Jewish. And failed at that. I was sure I would not get the part. In fact, I dropped a New York subway token on the floor as I was leaving and one of the grips picked it up and said "Here kid, you're going to need this." And I said: "I know that." The same grip was in the film and at the end of the film he gave me 15 silver-plated tokens.'

When I interviewed Mike Nichols he concurred that they had initially searched for someone more physically appropriate for Ben.

'We were really looking for a rather more California type of man. But I couldn't find one and I kept thinking of Dustin, because I knew he was a good actor, and I brought him out to read and to test. There's been a lot of stuff about how he screwed up the test, which isn't true. He was remarkable. Although he wasn't the physical type we'd been looking for, once we saw him it seemed that, since he was playing an outsider, there was a lot to be said for his looking like an outsider. So we cast him.'

Katherine Ross was already cast as Elaine Robinson. She did the test with Hoffman and remembers his edginess: 'Here was this little guy, white as a sheet. He kept saying "I don't know why I came here, I don't want to do this. I want to go back to character parts.' At one stage he grabbed her bottom, she reacted angrily and Nichols sensed he had this man, or rather boy, since Hoffman would be obliged to shed ten of his thirty years for the part.

Hoffman's impact on Joe Levine was less impressive. 'I was asked to come up to his office in New York and meet him. I went up there and waited. The day before it had rained very hard and the windows of his office apparently were very dirty. He had asked for someone to clean them and when I came in, he said: "The windows are over there" and I said: "What do you mean?". He said: "Aren't you here to clean the windows?" I just smiled and took a handkerchief out of my pocket and went up to the windows and started cleaning them.'

The staff in Levine's office were equally suspicious, knowing that their future depended on Levine recouping much more than the $3.1 million he had raised for the picture. They were ushered into the screening room. Bob Weston, the vice-president of advertising, addressed them. 'Now I know you've all seen him around the office and you've thought "What's that ugly guy doing as lead in the picture? But look at this. Just watch.' He ran the screen test. Stuart Byron was working there at the time and recalled his first reaction in Village Voice.

'I don't want to say we changed our minds looking at that screen test; let's say our opinions were put in limbo. For then and there, watching only one small scene, we were swept by the electricity which a year later was to carry *The Graduate* to fiscal glory . . . there, in Hoffman's manner, in his performance, were the gestures, combining Jewish nightclub offhandedness with an inner core of both insecurity and strength, which were absolutely new to the screen.'

Byron also disclosed that Nichols had thought of changing the character of Mrs Robinson to a Frenchwoman so that Jeanne Moreau could play here. On this occasion Levine's opinion prevailed. 'We talked him out of that. But now Mike can have anything he wants. Who are those guys he wants to do the score? He wants Simon and Schuster, he gets Simon and Schuster.'

In the event the soft melodies of Simon and Garfunkle – especially *Scarborough Fair* – gave a dream-like quality to the picture which was brought harshly into reality by the calculating performance of Anne Bancroft as Mrs Robinson, first as a determined seductress, later as an embittered and vengeful mother. The screenplay stayed close to Webb's novel. Ben returns, cum laude, from university for an idle summer at home in California. He is nervously enticed into an affair with the wife of his father's business partner and then, against her orders, he disastrously courts and falls in love with her daughter. The Robinsons hurriedly marry her off but in a significant change from the book, Ben wrests her from the altar, not in the nick of time, but after the marriage ceremony has been concluded. 'Too late,' shouts Mrs Robinson. Not for a child of the sixties! Just as we laugh at the beginning of the picture when a party guest offers Ben one word of career advice – 'plastics' – so we are reassured at the end that a new, more liberated set of values reigns supreme.

One element of the sixties that the film ignores was the one that dominated the television news every evening: Vietnam. The campus at Berkeley is hardly a hotbed of flower-power and political ferment and the one reference to Vietnam in the screenplay was finally cut. In it Benjamin is hitching a lift and the driver who picks him up asks repeatedly, 'Why aren't you there?' Benjamin replies: 'Because I'm here.' Nichols was probably right to drop it as it would have set the film off down another less popular avenue but the absence possible explains Hoffman's cryptic remark to Time: 'If *The Graduate* were better, it wouldn't have done so well.'

That was in retrospect. When making it he was, initially, ill at ease. 'I don't know whether it was my own paranoia or what, but when I went to work on the film I thought the whole crew thought there was a tremendous farce being played, that this was a big joke. I felt very tense and uncomfortable, and it was Mike Nichols' second film and I think he was somewhat tense. I even think he was somewhat ambivalent about casting me throughout the first couple of months of shooting. I picked up that ambivalence and though we worked well together, I nevertheless continued to feel through most of the shooting that I wasn't able to give him what he wanted. Since then I've learned that films aren't supposed to be a pleasant experience. We rehearsed for three weeks, like a play, so by the time the first day's shooting came, we knew the entire script by heart. In the rehearsal we did a lot of improvisations and a character came out of it. I was 29 when I did it, and I tried to go back and remember the way I felt at 21, how funny I saw myself when I was 21. I didn't try to be the now generation.'

Hoffman's doubts and insecurities were not without foundation although he may not have realised so, even today. I asked Nichols if he found he was getting a better performance from him than he had anticipated. His answer was equivocal.

'We had to do a lot of work on Dustin because it was his first picture and he was clearly brilliant, but he didn't yet have enough technique. Let's say we would do seven takes; he would do five strange takes and one good take and one terrific one. He was really still finding his technique. He was one of those people that, when you put his scenes together, they become more.'

Hoffman was aware of the director's manipulation. 'He makes you feel like a kite. He lets you go ahead and you do your thing. And then when you've finished he pulls you in by the string. But at least you've had the enjoyment of the wind.'

But it was those moments of soaring invention that made Hoffman's performance tantalisingly original: the nervous whimper, barely audible in a cinema that was usually cacophonous with laughter, the clinical rigidity with which he placed his hand on Mrs Robinson's breast for the first time – he claimed he always fantasised doing exactly that to a girl in high school assembly – and, most notably, the scene with Buck Henry when he attempts to book a hotel room for their tryst. He communicated the fearful embarrassment of the encounter by remembering his first attempt to buy prophylactics in a drug store.

It was this scene, Hoffman told me later, that gave Nichols the first indication they had a hit on their hands. 'I didn't go to rushes – actors weren't allowed to – but he came back after viewing the hotel scene and he said: "I think we may have a decent picture." '

Nevertheless it was with relief that he left the set and the mellow ambience of California. 'The day *The Graduate* finished shooting I flew back to New York. I just couldn't wait to get

---

Midnight Cowboy (1969)
Ratso Rizzo and the innocent Joe Buck (Jon Voight.)

back.' His fate was in another's hands. 'Finally it's the director's picture, his painting and I'm just a colour in it.'

He now faced a five-month wait to find out whether or not he had a future in movies. 'After I finished the film in August I went to the unemployment offices. I got one audition before the film opened, for the Dauphin in Anouilh's *Joan of Arc* at the Lincoln Center in New York. I didn't get the part.'

Financially he was secure. He had been paid $17,000 for the film and he rented a $175 week apartment in Greenwich Village. He had no need to return to washing dishes or typing Yellow Pages. Emotionally he felt contradictory. He told Ulu Grosbard that if the previous three months experience were really what making movies was like he never intended to do another. In his heart, he knew the film would be a hit and he wandered the streets, looking at peoples' faces, imagining how it would be different when he became famous. With time on his hands he sought refuge at the psychiatrist's, often as many as five days a week.

The picture opened just before Christmas in 1967. If Hoffman turned to the review in Time first, his heart must have sunk. '*The Graduate*, Nichols' second screen effort, unfortunately shows his success depleted . . . most of the film has an alarmingly derivative style . . . Hoffman is an original, likable actor whose bag of monumental insecurities marks the truly assured comedian.'

But the despair would have been short-lived. The rest were raves. 'Excellent comedy . . . Hoffman is perfect in his role', Variety. 'Dustin Hoffman makes a sensationally attractive movie debut as the troubled, virtuous hero.' New Yorker. 'Dustin Hoffman, a young actor already known in the theatre as an exceptional talent, here increases his reputation,' The New Republic. 'A new, young actor who is nothing short of superb,' New York Times. And so on, and so on.

If Hoffman was thinking of switching his subscription from Time to Newsweek, he had further grounds for doing so when he read their notice. 'Dustin Hoffman turns Benjamin into an

---

Previous page: *Midnight Cowboy* (1969)
Ratso caught shoplifting.

endearing, enduring hero. He never seems sure of what his voice, eyes or hands are doing or whose orders they are following. He wears the world like a new pair of shoes. He nods his head whenever he doesn't quite know what he means, which is often. He is wrenchingly simple and vividly intelligent, even with his self-doubts, and his bumbling seduction scenes with the wife of his father's law partner, elegantly played by Anne Bancroft, are as funny as anything ever committed to film.'

Sometimes the views of the critics are out of kilter with the movie tastes of the masses. In this instance, they were not.

Chapter Three

Confirmation, if confirmation was needed, that Hoffman had become an instant cult that Christmas came from Ma Bell. His name was still in the Manhattan telephone book and he began to get calls from strangers. So he changed it and went ex-directory. The number was reassigned to another person who then rang the 'phone company to complain that he was getting calls all day long and, worse still, all night long. The telephonist deputed to find out from Dustin why this might be was, evidently, not appraised of his recent fame. 'Mr Hoffman,' she enquired, 'is there any explanation for this?'

The delights of being persistently recognised and accosted in the street were tempered by his ultimate desire to get back to acting and secure some privacy. He sought refuge at the shrink. 'It is probably the most important thing in my life. Some people take dope to escape pressure. Well, scrutiny is one of the most acute pressures a person can have. People come up to me in the street now all the time. Psychoanalysis is my way of escaping from this stuff and I know it has helped me.'

He also became a sex object with women clamouring for his company and more, even to the extent of turning up on his doorstep. This too was tempered by the fact that he had acquired a more regular girl friend, Anne Byrne. She was a dancer, six years younger than him and, at five foot nine, three inches taller. They had met two years previously in a Greenwich Village laundromat. Hoffman took her to the Improvisation, where he had washed dishes, and the following day on the back of his motorcycle to Jones Beach. They lost contact and she went to Philadelphia to work, where she met and married a financier, Winfried Schlote. It didn't last long but it provided her with a daughter, Karina. Before *The Graduate* opened she was back with Hoffman and went with him to the premiere.

The instant and widespread success of *The Graduate* liberated him from one set of worries and provided him with another, primarily how to follow it.

"After the film opened I was offered a lot of carbon-copy Graduate scripts and I turned them down. I really wanted to get back into plays. Or, if I was going to be a movie star, I wanted to be a movie star on my own terms."

A movie producer, Jerome Hellman, had acquired the rights to James Leo Herlihy's novel *Midnight Cowboy* and when he saw Hoffman in *Eh?* immediately thought of him for the part of Ratso Rizzo. He engaged Waldo Salt to write a script and the British director, John Schlesinger, to direct. Schlesinger was in the process of enjoying a commercial flop with his latest film *Far From the Madding Crowd* and himself acknowledged 'I was simply out of fashion. It didn't matter that I had had a previous success,' (this was *Darling* which had won Oscars for its writer, Frederick Raphael and its star, Julie Christie.) Moreover the story had failed to arouse much excitement in United Artists, where a script reader had advised against it, maintaining 'the action of the novel goes steadily downhill from the outset.'

It was offered to Hoffman and, against all advice, he accepted it. 'I was told not to do *Cowboy* because it was a supporting role and I'd already established myself as a star, and also it was an unattractive character.'

But he was hot and his acceptance of it guaranteed him a fee of $250,000 and backing from United Artists. Schlesinger had not seen Hoffman's stage work and, knowing him only from *The Graduate*, naturally thought he was wrong for the part of Ratso, a little runt of a man, tubercular, down-and-out, rejected by society. So Hoffman invited the director to meet him in Times Square. They walked 42nd street and spent the night in a diner. Schlesinger was amazed: 'He just melted into the background. I'm sure he had planned it all very carefully. There was never any question: he was Ratso.'

Hoffman told me with glee: 'Schlesinger took one look at me and said: "I thought you were wrong for this part when I saw *The Graduate*, but you're not really that healthy-looking at all." '

Finding the cowboy, Joe Buck, was less easy. Finally they narrowed it down to a short-list of five men and, to Schlesinger's delight, Hoffman rehearsed and screen-tested with all five. Eventually the director settled on one: Michael Sarrazin. But his studio pushed up his price and then said he had to do another picture for them first. That left the role open for Jon Voight, an actor the director had initially rejected as 'too baby-faced and butch looking.'

Before shooting started Hoffman had an appointment in Hollywood. He had been nominated for an Academy Award for *The Graduate*. With a perverse honesty he told reporters on the eve of the ceremony; 'I hope to God I don't win an Oscar tomorrow night. It would depress me if I did. I don't really deserve it.' His hopes were fulfilled: Rod Steiger was voted Best Actor for *In the Heat of the Night*, but Mike Nichols won the Oscar for Best Director.

Midnight Cowboy is essentially the story of Joe Buck, a Southwesterner who arrives in New York, high in sexual prowess but low in urban cunning, who has the more than credulous aim of getting rich by servicing ladies. He falls victim to the seedy underbelly of the city, personified by the hapless Ratso who indeed lives like a rat in a cellar. At first Ratso attempts to con Joe, as he does everyone else, then he finds himself, probably for the first time in his life, with a friend. He takes him in and cares for him. But Ratso is dying. Joe gives blood to get him drugs and even steals to take him to the warmer air of Miami. As their bus reaches this promised land, Ratso dies in Joe's arms.

Hoffman knew Voight from the days when he had served as his understudy and the assistant director in *A View From The Bridge*. The week before shooting they rehearsed together, in Schlesinger's words, 'to see how far the actors could go beyond the scripted material.' They improvised on how it would be like to be holed up in Ratso's tenement. Waldo Salt, the writer, recorded this and amended the script accordingly.

Schlesinger used his practised eye as a documentary film maker to recreate the bleak insanity of the shady side of New York. Everything he included he had seen for real: a body lying, unremarked, on the sidewalk; a woman on drugs running up and down 8th Avenue; a tripped-out mother and her child playing with a toy mouse. It distressed him. 'It wasn't a particularly enjoyable picture to make; in fact, I was miserable. I don't like New York enormously and somehow one was always confronted by something worse on the street than one was putting into the film.'

Hoffman was more at home on the city streets. He happily signed autographs and Anne and Karina came and visited him on the set. But most of all he knew his performance was working. 'I wanted at the outset to be bold with it. I didn't want to portray a documentary-type character. I wanted to have it, somehow, a little distorted, almost the way maybe Daumier draws. It's real and yet it's not Ratso; it's maybe a lot of Ratsos. I felt I had a hook on it. I think I felt like Ratso for many years in New York.'

They began shooting before he felt he had found the character and there are a couple of scenes, notably one in a hat shop, in which he didn't feel right. But the external image was always there. 'I looked in the mirror and tried to get a sense of what I wanted. I realised that if I put my hair straight back, it just did something. I wanted that kind of look. I wanted my nose coming out ten feet, I wanted blemishes. I wanted to dissipate myself much as I could so that I could feel that dissipation and then have as much dignity as possible.'

His spontaneity, when in character, was captured in that inspired improvised moment when he slaps the bonnet of a taxi screaming 'I'm walking here' followed by a derisive gesture and a shout of 'up yours, you son of a bitch.' His first appearance is some way into the film where he is discovered in a bar. He felt a black man should have sat on the stool beside him whereupon Ratso would get up and move away, to signal immediately how dispicable he was. Schlesinger refused to shoot this on the grounds that it would alienate the audience too much.

The scenes between him and Voight were magically taut, and then tender. 'We never thought, in acting it, of Buck or Ratso. We thought of Voight and Hoffman. And if there were moments of love between us it was because the scene was going right and at the same time "I'm gonna act better than you in this scene." It wasn't a case of upstaging each other; it was "let's see who can really act the best in this scene," – I think it's the strongest thing in the film.'

On the following page: *Straw Dogs* (1971)
David is threatened by Scutt (Ken Hutchinson) and Venner (Del Henney).

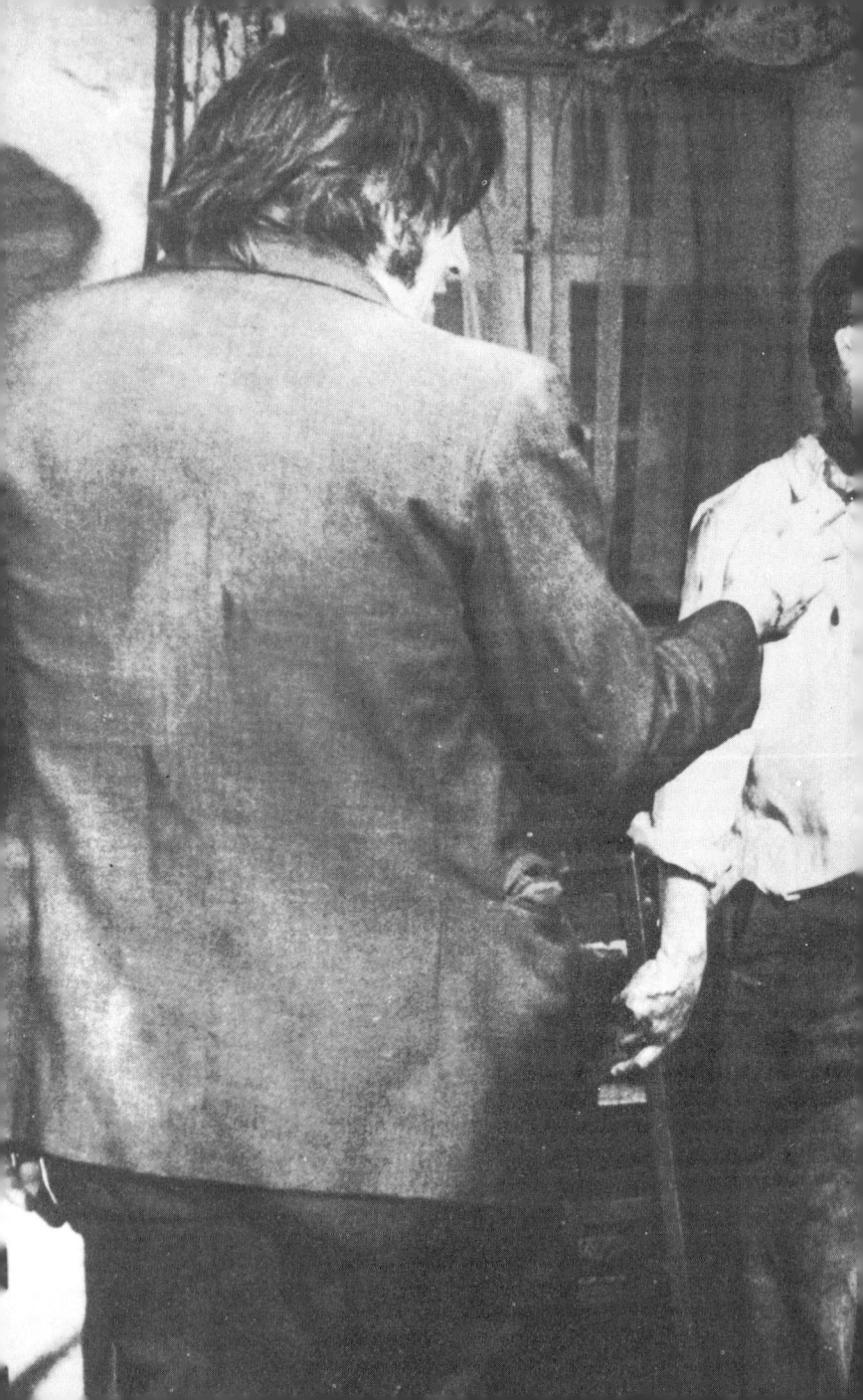

Straw Dogs (1971) David asserts

himself against Cawsey (Jim Norton).

When he saw a rough cut of the film he feared he had made a big mistake. He immediately resolved to play someone normal, signing for the part of John in *John and Mary*. But when *Midnight Cowboy* opened in June 1969 his fears were immediately allayed.

A certain schizophrenia emerged among the critics, pretty well unanimous in their enthusiasm for the film, but divided whether to rate Hoffman's mesmeric character peformance above the eponymous newcomer. Newsweek acknowledged that they were both 'remarkably good performances . . . Hoffman's work is in no way inferior but the script gives the movie to Voight.' Hollis Alpert in Saturday Review saw it the other way round: 'Hoffman emerges with top honours, proving his heady debut in *The Graduate* was no fluke but it makes it clear that he is an exciting new talent.' Alpert pinpointed the real achievement in Hoffman's characterisation of Ratso – 'He infuses him with, by the end, a totally surprising tenderness.' Time went with Voight: 'Hoffman has progressed by stepping backward – to a supporting part. It is an act of rare skill and rarer generosity. No matter how well Ratso is performed, *Midnight Cowboy* is the tale of Joe Buck. It is a mark of Voight's intelligence that he works against his role's melodramatic tendencies and towards a central human truth. In the process, he and Hoffman bring to life one of the least likely and most melancholy love stories in the history of American film.' But, perceptively, Stanley Kauffman in The New Republic realised that the film's enduring images lay with Dustin: 'I won't easily forget Hoffman shivering on the cot in their dingy room, saying fearfully to Joe, "Hey don't get sore . . . but I don't think I can walk any more." '

The Academy kept the equilibrium by nominating them both for Oscars and preserved it by awarding one to neither man. Unfortunately for them it was John Wayne's year. Once again it was Hoffman's director who actually won the Oscar. It was a time for screen chemistry between men – the 'buddy' movie – canonised by the prizes for *Butch Cassidy and the Sundance Kid* at the same ceremony.

Unfortunately chemistry and indeed anything warmly physical was lacking in Hoffman's liason with Mia Farrow in his next film, *John and Mary*. It was based on a short story by Mervyn Jones, transported to Manhattan, wherein a young man picks up a young woman in a singles' bar and in the succeeding twenty-four hours gets to know her in all but name. The film's final couplet rectifies the omission:

MARY: My name's Mary . . . what about you?

JOHN: I'm John.

The part of John might have seemed heaven-sent for Hoffman; after all he had spent much of his New York life picking up women. But he decided against using the wit and charisma that usually instantly endeared him to the opposite sex. He made John shy, diffident and weak. Even then he didn't feel comfortable in the role.

'It's funny, there are parts I feel I'm not connected with that much. I felt that way about *The Graduate* and I feel the same way about *John and Mary*! I'm very much in the director's hands and I trust, in this case, Peter Yates. But with *Midnight Cowboy* I felt very close to the role. I had a strong picture in my mind of what I was doing.'

Hoffman had seen Yates' direction of the film *Bullit* with Steve McQueen which gained more plaudits for its spectacular car-chase than its intimate moments and felt he could trust him to build something more substantial on the scaffolding of rather a frail script. This, plus the desire to play a normal male lead after Ratso and the undoubted box-office appeal of coupling his name with Mia Farrow – she had recently had a winner with *Rosemary's Baby* – made him do the film.

The two of them had never worked together before and they spent the first week rehearsing with Yates in the apartment he had rented in Park Avenue. Then they moved to the old Biograph studios in the less salubrious wastes of the East Bronx, studios used by D.W. Griffith before the First World War, for much of the shooting. Hoffman was in a play, *Jimmy Shine*, on Broadway at the time and was unable to go to Hollywood so Hollywood had to come to him. Besides, the exteriors were primarily on the Upper East Side and the film began at the 'in' singles bar, Maxwell's Plum, where John first encounters Mary and gets landed with a hideously expensive round of drinks.

Yates liked what Hoffman was doing with the part – 'he has

such vulnerability. He has an unhypocritical way of portraying a young person of today.'

Hoffman still had doubts about the enterprise. 'It wasn't the script. I'm not even sure that I understood the character. I mean his life is ordered, he's a good cook, he's aware of clothes, he has a neat apartment. I never lived that way. But when I saw *Bullit* I thought "this wasn't the script either – it was all in the director's head". With a play, it seems to me, you go for the text. With a film, you go for the director.'

At one stage Yates persuaded Hoffman to use his own hands for a close-up. It was something he was reluctant to do since his finger nails are perpetually bitten to the quick. But he agreed and it awakened a moment from his childhood. 'Do you realise my first memory was having my hands tied to the side of the crib so that I couldn't bite my nails. I've been seaching for a cure ever since.'

Emotionally at that time Mia Farrow (having once been married to Frank Sinatra) was in love with André Previn, and Hoffman was closer than ever to Anne Byrne, so both of them had to *act* their romance rather than experience it. Hoffman had been far too career-orientated ever to indulge in the hippy philosophies of the sixties but Mia Farrow had taken them all in, so there wasn't exactly a marriage of minds. On one occasion he said of her: 'She's fine, except that she talks a lot about meditation. I tend to avoid those conversations.'

The film opened at the end of 1969 to lukewarm reviews. The New York Times observed; 'The film is not without relevance. People do jump into bed together these days without much preliminary investigation, often (like John and Mary) having exchanged vague opinions on Italian movies but not their own names. Social accuracy, however, can contribute to – but not substitute for – human comedy.' Although the film was enjoyable to watch, especially because of Hoffman who, as Pauline Kael shrewdly noted 'draws upon his astute knowledge of the audience's goodwill towards him and does well' , it failed to catch the spirit of the age. While hardly a disaster for Hoffman, it showed him that he needed a stronger story to pull the crowds in and it remains one of his least successful films at the box office.

Chapter Four

On the fourth of May 1969 Dustin Hoffman married Anne Byrne. He was thirty-one and Jewish; she was twenty-five and Roman Catholic, a divorcée with a baby daughter, Karina. She was marrying a very rich man. He had just completed *John and Mary* for a reputed fee of $425,000 and was shortly to embark on *Little Big Man* for an estimated half a million dollars.

Anne's father was librarian at Columbia University. The reception for thirty-five friends was held at her family home in Westchester and then she and Dustin left for a honeymoon in Asia. He needed the rest. While he had been shooting *John and Mary* he had also been appearing on Broadway in his friend Murray Schisgal's play *Jimmy Shine*. Doing both had proved a debilitating experience. Twentieth Century Fox had had to buy out the Wednesday matinées to permit him to film, and night shooting had to await the final curtain.

Jimmy Shine was a perfect opportunity for him to demonstrate his versatility and, at the same time, shrug off the image of *The Graduate* which was his only released film. At the time he said: 'Movies, the whole narcisstic thing, *The Graduate*, the pseudo-religious experience when kids see me on the street; man, that's not real. If I can lift people, if I can make them cry, hate, do something out in front of me, live, then I mean something . . . I know I can't beat *The Graduate* experience but somehow I have to show I've grown, to connect, to get to them, to shake them up, to show them I'm not a celluloid fluke.'

Jimmy Shine is a man in his early thirties who becomes a painter because his best friend talks him into it. But the best friend is persuaded by his father to go into business while Jimmy is left to struggle in a loft, alone with his art and his fantasies. With songs by Simon and Garfunkle the play had a revue format enabling Hoffman, according to Time, to 'growl like Durante, drone like W.C. Fields, shamble like Groucho Marx and dance like a good-natured puppy.'

The out-of-town run proved painful for Hoffman; he cut his head in Philadelphia and his finger in Baltimore, bad enough to need seven stiches and a nightly announcement that he was appearing with a cut finger. The Baltimore Sun applauded him but not the plot – 'a character in search of a play' – and this was the general reaction when they opened on Broadway. Clive Barnes, then the Butcher of that district thanks to his platform in The New York Times, gave him a personal rave: 'Hoffman has the strange ability to be himself . . . or at least if that is not himself he is playing, or at least some aspect of himself, he must be so unnaturally talented that he is practically monstrous.'

But even if Barnes had cut the ground from under him, Hoffman was still an exciting new star whom everyone wanted to see in the flesh. A mob would assemble nightly at the stage door. He tried to rationalise his popularity: 'It's exciting, like an old newsreel of the Beatles from *A Hard Day's Night* but it has nothing really to do with you. You're just the thing of the moment, the image; no one knows you personally, or cares, and if it wasn't you it would be somebody else. I just wonder how soon it will be somebody else.'

After the discomfort of portraying a normal New Yorker in *John and Mary*, Hoffman knew he needed a strong character role to remind his cinema audience that he had a range that exceeded most of his peers. So from the far East he went west, to Billings, Montana, to play Jack Crabb, sole survivor of the Battle of Little Big Horn, in the film *Little Big Man*. Crabb, at the beginning of the film, is 121 years old and I suggested to Hoffman that it was a challenge many stars would resist for fear of appearing ludicrous. He disagreed. 'Any actor would have taken it. The make-up artist, Dick Smith, created a terrific make-up. In fact I said I wouldn't do it unless he did it. Put that face on – anybody can act under that thing.'

It took Smith five hours every morning to put on the fourteen piece mask that aged Hoffman ninety years but it was time the actor was content to spend. 'I like playing eccentrics. It's easy. You're freer to operate behind a mask.' He knew he could handle the part and, again, he had taken out a dual insurance policy in a proven book, Thomas Berger's epic comic novel, and a proven director, Arthur Penn, who had a quality track record culminating in the financially and critically successful *Bonnie and Clyde*. In fact, Hoffman could not have the one without the other since Penn had bought the book in 1965.

On the surface it was the remarkable story of a young white boy, captured by the Cheyennes at the age of ten and raised by them to be a brave, and his subsequent oscillations between the red men and the white men until their bloody confrontation at the Battle of Little Big Horn. But both the author and the director had a deeper intent in attacking the conventional Hollywood notions of civilised white man and savage Indian using the most potent weapon in the hand of the filmmaker: humour. Central to the Indian side of the story was the Chief, Old Lodge Skins. Originally Penn tried to get Paul Scofield or even Laurence Olivier for the part. When they proved unavailable he settled for Richard Boone who dropped out before they started shooting. Like a good general, a good film director needs, above all, luck and this chapter of refusals led to the arrival of a genuine Indian, Chief Dan George, who proved to be the finest thing in the film. Displaying the sang-froid of a Jack Benny he inquires of Little Big Man's relationship with his wife: 'Does she show a pleasant enthusiasm when you mount her?' Later he lies down to die in the traditional Indian manner and the experience proves fatally unfatal. Dan George accepts this reverse with a shrug: 'Sometimes the magic works, sometimes it doesn't.'

Hoffman got on well with Penn who permitted him to essay an unlovable side to the leading role. 'He wants characters to be human, rather than hero or anti-hero or leading man. He likes to show weak, even unattractive sides to a character that's basically sympathetic. He gives me so much freedom. I feel as relaxed as I ever have in a movie . . . What Penn likes are actors who use themselves, go for broke. He'll try anything. He likes unpredictability. He's constantly trying one way, then another. You suggest something to him and he says "let's try it". He's open.'

Penn himself was perhaps preoccupied with his own lordly aims for the film. He wanted it to be different. 'We're into another way of looking at narrative now. We've got to be willing to abandon a straight narrative line in terms of circular, cyclical narrative. The old style is not sufficient. We can't go in quest of just another story. The insights of psychoanalysis – Freud, Erikson – the stages of development, the repetitive characteristics of patterns of living have affected direct narrative so that seemingly disconnected events become meaningful. You've got to include the seemingly irrelevant. Nothing is clear and simple in a person's life.'

It was bold to experiment with a big budget movie – $6 million – *and* a major star, but unfortunately the lack of clear narrative line and an empathetic leading man led to some lukewarm reviews and only a moderate return at the box office. Variety puts its U.S. and Canadian rentals at $15 million, well below *The Graduate* ($49 million) and *Midnight Cowboy* ($20 million) but considerably above *John and Mary* ($4 million.)

At 2½ hours the film made ardous demands on the audience's attention and Vincent Canby in the New York Times pointed up the weaknesses, suggesting 'often it is not terribly funny, at just those moments when it tries the hardest, and it sometimes wears its social concerns so blatantly that they look like war paint.' Hoffman, however, survived with his reputation intact: 'Mr Hoffman is one of our two best young character actors (the other is Jon Voight) and although there are peculiar traces of both Ben Braddock and Ratso Rizzo in his Jack Crabb, he is fine.' The film got one of its best reviews from Izvestia when it was shown at the Moscow Film Festival. The paper praised it for 'debunking still another myth of the bourgeois world," saving its most fulsome words for the eponymous hero 'in this honest and courageous film we again see the wonderful American actor Dustin Hoffman.' The 'again' puzzled some Western commentators since none of Hoffman's previous films had been released in Russia.

Prudently Hoffman made his first four major films with well-established directors. After *The Graduate* he had the eminence and the power to pick and choose and he told me he felt much safer with them – 'In a film you can give a very good performance and by the time it's seen on the screen, if it's misdirected or the takes have been badly chosen in the cutting-room, you can look very bad. You can have a very bad director

Papillon (1973)
The getaway: maybe prison was preferable to this.

from a stage play and, in fact, be in a very bad play, and still come across well. The opposite is true in films.'

Imprudently, for his fifth film, he agreed to work with a stage director and an old friend, Ulu Grossbard, whose assistant he had been in *A View From The Bridge*, starring Jon Voight. Encumbered with the title *Who Is Harry Kellerman and Why Is He Saying Those Terrible Things About Me?*' the film had, as its central character, Georgie, a man with whom Hoffman was well able to empathize. His dilemma is that he is enormously successful. Georgie has written sixty songs in the past year as well as anthems for peace marches *and* the Air Force and a cancer jingle. He has made the cover of Time Magazine but when the film begins he is about to commit suicide, throwing himself off the top of the General Motors building but landing, thankfully, in his psychiatrist's couch where the tale of apochryphal Harry Kellerman spills out. There is no such person saying such things; it is a figment of Georgie's troubled mind.

It was based on a short story the writer Herb Gardner had published in The Saturday Evening Post and previously Mr Gardner had had a Broadway hit with *A Thousand Clowns*. Barbara Harris had starred in the film version of that and in *Harry Kellerman* she was cast as Georgie's girlfriend who keeps sticking to things, 'I can't seem to let go of this lamp right now,' she confesses while trying to leave him.

Hoffman had to age from seventeen to forty-two in the film, a slightly less absurd range than that for *Little Big Man* but probably a sterner challenge for a thirty-three year old. He immersed himself in the record business to research the part, deeming it 'a cross between the theatre and the garment centre' and, calling on his musical talents, learnt to play the guitar – 'I developed some nice calluses.' The main reason he chose the film was less for these external techniques than Georgie's internal angst. 'He was somewhat like myself. He was more

---

Previous page: *Papillon* (1973)
Louis Dega discusses the escape with Papillon (Steve McQueen) against the advice of the trusty.

multi-levelled than anything else I had done. I couldn't see it. I took him home with me. I didn't enjoy playing the guy and yet I enjoyed the experience more than any film I have ever done. It's a script I'm emotionally connecting with. What happens in a period of a man's life interests me. In a few years the change can be so great. People make shifts in their own role playing. He's very involved with time, staying young, keeping in shape.'

The film was rich with inventive funny ideas, the adhesive girl friend and the fact that Georgie's mother looks at his chest when she talks to him because that was where his head was when he was twelve, and funny lines. Georgie despairs 'I feel like I've just auditioned for the human race and lost the job' and when the shrink prescribes pills for his depression he retorts: 'I come to you in flames and you treat me for sunburn.' But critics and audiences alike failed to share Hoffman's empathy with a character whose problems stem from the fact that he has too much. Even the songs failed to strike any enduring chords but, inevitably, Hoffman's own talent could not be dismissed lightly. Vincent Canby in The New York Times liked his comic performance and Molly Haskell pointed out: 'Dustin Hoffman brings a dolorous, melancholy quality to the part and, by not being quite the self-pitying bastard the role seems to call for, gives Georgie a great deal more humour and sympathy than he perhaps deserves.'

Hoffman avows he is 'selfish and self-centered, particularly when I'm working' but during the shooting of *Harry Kellerman* Anne was pregnant and he did his pre-natal duty. 'I'd get home at night emotionally exhausted from acting the part of a potential suicide and then I'd go off to natural childbirth classes with Anne – protesting all the way.' On October 15th 1970 their daughter, Jennifer Celia, better known as Jenna, was born.

In February of the following year he left for England to shoot *Straw Dogs* in wintery Cornwall. This was another abrupt change of direction for Hoffman, playing a character close to himself in age and looks but far removed in temperament. I met him for the first time on the location – he agreed to let me film a profile of him at work for the BBC – and he explained that he wanted to do the part 'to examine the violence in myself which I would like to exercise or exorcise.'

Again he put his trust in a proven director, Sam Peckinpah, whose name had become a byword in screen violence after the success of *The Wild Bunch*. Although his original use of slow-motion death to heighten the brutality of the moment – a technique very different from the discreet avoidance of blood and guts by such classic Western directors as John Ford – probably caused the film to be both popular and memorable. Peckinpah, like the old masters, infused a strong sense of metaphor in the telling of the story. The first scene is of some children setting fire to a scorpion; it has two options: to burn to death or to commit suicide by stinging itself. It chooses the latter. So do the Wild Bunch, later.

The scene in *Straw Dogs* of children playing in a graveyard, shows a dire warning of the lurch from the playful to the lethal that will befall the characters in the drama. Based on the book by a Scotsman, Gordon Williams, called *The Siege of Trencher's Farm*, the appeal of the story lay in the fact that it wasn't the wild west nor, indeed, the wilder streets of Manhatten where violence lurked – but in a pastoral community in civilised England. Hoffman played David Sumner, an American mathematician, who takes a year's sabbatical to do research in a remote farmhouse there with his English wife Amy, played by Susan George. The local yobboes are bitter about this match and certainly titillated by her, a state of affairs in which she is something of an accomplice going about the village in a flighty and bra-less state. They serve notice on Hoffman that he is weak and they are physically strong by trespassing on his territory, leaving his cat hanging in his closet and, eventually, raping his wife.

The pusillaniminity of his initial response has the effect of spurring their more outrageous actions. He buys them a drink in the local pub; his response to the rape is to fire the men who are working in his house. His tenderness extends to the village idiot (played, uncredited, by the fine Shakespearean actor, David Warner) who has accidentally killed a young girl. Against Amy's wishes Hoffman gives him succour in their home and this precipitates the final onslaught by the local layabouts turned psychopaths. It is the protection of the hearth that spurs the mild Hoffman to retaliation; 'I will not allow violence against my house' he cries. Nor does he – with the aid of, among other things, a shot gun, some boiling oil and a man trap, he decimates the opposition. After this last stand the little man apparently becomes big at last; 'Jesus, I got 'em all,' he says with a smile of satisfaction.

This powerful and skillfully edited ending must be credited entirely to Peckinpah, but watching both men on location I noticed the incessant input from Hoffman at every turn. He improvised dialogue, he made suggestions to the English actors and invented additional nuances to his own character – when David is trying to make a dignified exit after he has fired the men, being American, he goes to the wrong door of his car to drive away. Peckinpah would tease him, like putting a swastika on the back of an actor who had to turn and walk away from Hoffman. Dustin allowed that a director and an actor usually have a silent war but at the same time, as in a marriage, they had to be on the same wave length.

Waiting for shots to be set up, Peckinpah presented the tough exterior of the ex-marine, by throwing knives against the stable door. 'I made a statement about violence in *The Wild Bunch*,' he told me, 'this film is another statement about violence. But in a strange way Hoffman's character incites this violence. Maybe he's waiting for them. These things have a way of happening.'

In person, Dustin Hoffman proved witty, intense and beguiling with an outrageous lease on vulgarity. When Susan George came to hear if she had got the part, he persuaded the producer and director to join him in dropping their pants in unison and 'mooning' her. In the long cold evenings, he played pranks on the staid residents of the elegant Tregenna Castle Hotel. He exhorted Ken Hutchison, one of the villagers, to jump on the dining room table and with a cry of 'want to see an Eskimo pee?' pulled down his flies, whereupon a flurry of ice cubes would fall out. He endowed the actor Colin Welland, later to collect the screenplay Oscar for *Chariots of Fire* with the label 'old frilly teeth.'

The movie attracted some critical acclaim – 'the finest film of the month' enthused After Dark magazine going on to make the questionable claim 'Dustin Hoffman's performance as David, the professor, is undoubtedly his finest' , and Time Magazine rightly noting 'a brilliant feat of movie-making' put its finger on the indisputable fact that 'Hoffman's performance is nervously cerebral and superbly realised.' At the other end of the spectrum Vincent Canby in The New York Times found the film 'a major disappointment. Why make a movie at all; why not release a greeting card instead.'

Despite the lure of Hoffman's name, a fair leavening of sex and a disproportionate dose of violence the film failed to sustain at the American box-office. Rentals of a mere four million dollars made it even less popular than *John and Mary*. He did little to redress this wane in his popularity in a madcap trip to Italy to play a bank clerk in Pietro Germi's *Alfredo, Alfredo*. Germi had already made a potent satire about the widening chasm between reality and the law in the ways of the matrimonial courts in *Divorce – Italian Style* and this was to be another poke at the system. Hoffman might have realised that things were going a bit astray when he spent a month on an Italian crash course and then, when he got to Rome, he discovered the director was going to shoot his part in English. When the film surfaced in America he was, of course, dubbed into Italian.

Germi was delighted to snare a major International star. He told Variety he sent Hoffman the script 'with about as much hope as those who put messages in bottles and toss them in the ocean.' And Hoffman professed to the same paper that he was enjoying the experience: 'The pace is very leisurely. Germi knows exactly what he wants and cuts as he goes along. He doesn't have to take as many shots and gives more time to each one he wants. Everyone round him is like a member of a family. He's worked with them for years; I was the only newcomer on this unit and felt like a new boarder in a rooming house until I settled in.'

It is Alfredo's lot to have to service his wife two or three times a day on doctor's orders and although she is the beguiling Stefania Sandrelli, the pleasure is all hers and is rent out in her howling orgasms that terrify even the local curs. It was always going to be an art-house film rather than a roadshow blockbuster and Hoffman may have found reassuring justification in his decision to do it in Pauline Rael's review (never a Hoffman fan) who deemed the first half hour 'probably the most pleasing and least self-conscious screen acting he has yet done.'

Chapter Five

Hoffman had not had a really big hit since *Little Big Man* and any film star, whatever his artistic aspirations, knows that unless he forms considerable queues at the box-office from time to time his value is going gradually to erode. So *Papillion* was, on paper, a potentially attractive project. It was based on the best seller by Henri Charrière about an escape from the inhumane prison, Devil's Island in French Guiana. It had Steve McQueen, then at the height of his popularity in the title role and Franklin J. Schaffner, with an Academy Award in his pocket as a result of *Patton*, as director.

It seemed a gift-horse. Hoffman was prepared to look it in the mouth even if the script was not right. 'I knew that I wouldn't be interested in doing the film if it was going to be one of those buddy prison pictures where Steve McQueen and I would be required to play charismatic head-to-head.'

An inventively written script by the veteran Dalton Trumbo (who played the Commandant in the film) and the highly commercial Lorenzo Semple Jr. swayed him. He was to play the part of Louis Degas, a forger who lacks Paillion's obsessive desire to escape from the hell hole, preferring instead to try and accept life there, but when committed to the break-out subverts his cowardice to an inventive desire to remain free.

To prepare himself for the part he spent several weeks in the New York Public Library. 'I read about ten or twelve books about prison life in French penal colonies. One of these books was by a former inmate, an art forger whose life had great similarities with what I thought about Degas. I drew from this man's real life experiences as a frame of reference for filling out my concept of Degas.'

Schaffner, meanwhile, was looking for a French penal colony. He ruled out French Guiana (not hotels big enough), the United States (no jungle), Nicaragua, Brazil and Mexico (politically unstable), Colombia and Venezuela (hardship areas – as Peter O'Toole and Richard Burton found when they made *Murphy's War*.) He ended up in Jamaica, using a colony of Germans who lived near Montego Bay to play the white extras and a group of Hindu Indians from the same area who were prepared to take off their modern clothes to portray the Guajiri village Indians in Charrière's book.

The crocodile came from the local African safari. The director would have preferred an alligator. 'The difference between a crocodile and an alligator is that a crocodile cannot be tamed. The one we used was staked by one leg and it could only travel in a circumference. If the tail catches you, you have a broken leg. I kept telling McQueen and Hoffman there was no danger but I had men with rifles standing around just in case. They ad-libbed most of the scene.'

Hoffman survived both the crocodile and the discomfort of the part; in fact he was comforted by the presence of his wife who played a small role as his wife in the film. It was really McQueen's movie but he brought his customery brilliant flair to the quirky character. Richard Schickel noted in Time: 'Hoffman submerges himself eccentrically and amusingly in the coward's role.' The critics, on the whole, did not warm to the film but the public did. It earned three million dollars in its first week in the United States and Canada and twenty-two and a half million in the same territories to date, making it Hoffman's fifth most popular film.

It was no accident that the producers of *Alfredo, Alfredo* opened it the day after *Papillon*. Hoffman was equally taciturn about both films. He expressed regret that he was not given time to learn Italian for *Alfredo*. His taciturnity on the subject of *Papillon* bordering on the cynical. 'It's the first time I made a movie with a superstar, I don't have to be too candid. He's fine. It was a workmanlike experience.'

By that time, at the end of 1973, his thoughts were set on a much more demanding part and project: *Lenny*, the biography of the outrageous, scatological comedian Lenny Bruce, which was due to start shooting in January in Miami. As usual he was doing his homework. 'I never saw him. I've now spent three or

---

On the following page: *All the Presidents Men* (1976)
Bernstein and Woodward (Robert Redford) discuss tactics with director Alan J. Pakula.

four months trying to make up for that. I've seen his mother and his daughter and interviewed all his friends. And then I came upon a tape, his last tape made three hours before his death and finally it all added together. Jesus, I've never played anybody this real before. You don't really know what you're getting into, especially when the guy's only been dead seven years. It's not what one wants to exploit in the wrong way.'

Already he felt an identification with the part. 'Lenny was very seductive. He negotiated for himself and had this winning way. He was up against a wall and I've felt up against a wall now for a while. I feel I haven't been putting it together the way I want in my work.' Although Hoffman had the external trappings of a well-liked, well-heeled movie star he still attended a psychoanalyst regularly to try to understand his inner dissatisfaction. 'If you become successful, become a star, it doesn't matter. I've been a star for about six years. But my feelings about myself and my work are based on the first 30 years. The feelings I had when I couldn't get a job, the way people treated me then.'

Lenny Bruce, too, was the victim of dark depressions. Although he started out in the Catskills with a relatively clean act – he even did 'you dirty rat' James Cagney impersonations – he felt the need to expand the boundaries of his humour. It was said that he was a surgeon with a scalpel for false values. He wanted to demonstrate the absurdity of people being offended by profane language, liberally sprinkling his act with the word 'fuck' and, occasionally, addressing his audience as 'cocksuckers.' He used unacceptable epithets to touch the deeply hidden nerve of racial prejudice: 'I see a nigger. And there's another nigger. And there's a kike.' He took drugs, usually uppers and amphetamines. They enabled him to keep going and the work he packed into the five short years of his greatest notoriety was prodigious. But he was arrested for obscene language and drug abuse and eventually no club would dare to engage him. He died on the third of August 1966 of an overdose of morphine. He was bankrupt and the supposition was that he had taken his own life.

His mother told Hoffman that he was like her son. He was circumspect, a listener. He wanted to figure people out. She told him that Lenny might get up in the middle of a meal in a restaurant and go into the kitchen and talk to the guy washing the dishes. As a result of these conversations Hoffman recalls: 'I tried to close in on those things in me that they said were reminiscent of Lenny.'

Julian Barry, who wrote the script, had already had a stage play about the man. He felt that in the play he mythologized him; in the film he emphasised his ultimately successful capacity for self-destruction. He worked on this new interpretation with the director Bob Fosse who had enjoyed a golden year in 1973: an Oscar for *Cabaret*, a Tony for *Pippin* and an Emmy for *Liza With a Z*. He proved an unremitting taskmaster on the set, shooting each scene again and again, sometimes up to thirty takes, until it was to his satisfaction. Tim Cahill who reported from the location for Rolling Stone noted that there was substantial animosity towards the director from some of the crew because of this exhaustive schedule. Some considered him a little hard on Valerie Perrine, who was playing Honey, Lenny's wife. To get her to break down in a court room scene Fosse invited her to think back to the death of her fiancé in a hunting accident.

Hoffman knew the risk he was taking in portraying a man whom many of the critics had seen for real. One of the first reviews in Newsweek confirmed his fears. 'Anyone who has seen Lenny Bruce perform immediately recognised something wrong with Dustin Hoffman's routines. The words are there but the demonic energy is missing. Bruce's high-voltage monologues were rambling, brilliant flights of verbal jazz, blown from the pit of the stomach. Hoffman captures the puckish charm, as if Bruce were some Peck's bad boy, a moralist and reformist, instead of the volcanic hipster with the machine-gun mouth.' John Simon in Esquire found the film 'a mess – precisely because it is neither fact not imaginative fiction.' For him Hoffman was 'too nice, cool and lucid with little of the madness and meanness that were mixed in with the messianism.'

Judith Crist, looking presumably at the same film, considered it 'brilliantly conceived and executed . . . Dustin Hoffman deserves a full credit, vanishing into the Bruce persona to simply stunning effectiveness to offer us understanding of the boyish insecurities, the infatuation with shiksa gloss and stupidities, the daring risks and downright challenges of the Establishment done with clear-eyed passion, the destructive determination to find vindication.'

Hoffman, as ever, was ambitiously self-critical. 'Some of the critics said I wasn't hostile enough; others thought I *was* Lenny. I'm never happy with any film I've ever done. I have tremendous reservations about them. There's always something more.' His fellow members of the Academy were more impressed, nominating him again for an Oscar (it was won by Art Carney for *Harry and Tonto.*) It was the ninth film he had made and to date it is his ninth most popular. It had been a draining experience and it was a cue for a change.

His friend Murray Schisgal who had enjoyed a Broadway success with *Luv* ten years previously and had also written *Jimmy Shine* which had been Hoffman's last stage appearance, had a new play, *All Over Town*. It was, Mr Schisgal told The New York Times 'a contemporary comedy about city life with eighteen characters of diverse and multifarious ethnic and social backgrounds. It is a spectrum of our country encapsulated on a single stage during an evening's performance.'

Hoffman could have guaranteed instant backing by agreeing to appear in it; by deciding to direct he found that finance was less forthcoming for so large a production. Joe Levine, the producer of *The Graduate*, came and went with his $100,000 and eventually Adela Holzer, who had done very well with *Hair* came up with most of the money, with Hoffman and another friend, Gene Hackman, dipping into their own pockets to make up the necessary $300,000.

Hoffman auditioned 1500 actors for the parts – although Cleavon Little had always been destined for the lead – and saw amateurs as well as professionals. He very nearly gave a shoe-shine man a part and he tested and rejected Meryl Streep who was to enchance one of his major film successes later on. He warmed to the task of once again directing actors, generous with advice from his own experience: 'Don't lose that paranoia. It's like when you were a kid jumping off the bed, saying "I didn't do anything." ' Schisgal observed how effective and welcome this was – 'they respond to his work as an actor, they feel as if they are privy to his acting.' Cleavon Little considered him 'the best director I've ever worked with. Most directors don't know anything about acting. They're traffic cops. The actors end up doing the work themselves. Dustin is very creative. It was very stimulating.'

Hoffman was happy. 'This is the best experience I've had yet. For the first time I feel part of something I've done.' But he was aware that his control could never be absolute. 'A director alters a writer's work, and then the actor alters it from the way a director and writer saw it. It's an uncooperative collaborative art form.' The alterations continued after the opening in Washington to generally unfavourable reviews. Hoffman got Schisgal to clarify the script and had to initiate a cast change – something every director dreads, especially if he has once been on the receiving end of such an experience himself. Anita Dangler was dropped from the part of the psychiatrist's wife and Carol Teitel replaced her. Hoffman sensed the ripple of disquiet it sent through the rest of the cast – 'any time you fire someone, it disturbs actors. They always think they're next.'

More than any critic, Hoffman was aware that the performance of a play is a fluid happening, never to be repeated. 'You get these wonderful moments, maybe from different members of the cast on different nights. But you may never get your whole cast giving the same wonderful moments on the same night. I guess that's why directors get frustrated and go into films. On film you freeze the wonderful moments from all the footage they take.' Fortunately for him the opening night on Broadway found most of the players on form. The audience responded wholeheartedly. But that was irrelevant. Clive Barnes gave it a very favourable review in The New York Times and that was enough to sustain the show.

The scenario for one of Hoffman's most telling screen performances began life on June 17th 1972. On that day two Washington Post journalists Bob Woodward and Carl Bernstein were assigned to look into the break-in at the Watergate in Washington. The rest is modern political history of the most monstrous kind. Prudently the two journalists decided to write their own account of their investigations and when it was in manuscript form Hoffman's brother Ronald, who was an economist in Washington, got hold of it and sent it to him. He saw it as an ideal movie for himself – not least because of a considerable physical resemblance between him and Bernstein – but when he tried to buy the rights he found Robert Redford had beaten him to it. Redford had paid $450,000 and then commissioned William Goldman, who wrote *Butch Cassidy and the Sundance Kid*, to do the script. His initial dialogue produced an abreaction in the reporters – 'it read like a Henny Youngman joke-book of one-liners', complained Bernstein – but being foreign to the movie industry they failed to realise that dialogue can be altered or improvised on the set; what makes Goldman one of the outstanding post-war screen-writers is his ability to structure a film. Bernstein's attempt to re-write the script was not a success.

Hoffman was too proud to ask Redford for the part but not too proud, when Redford turned up at a rehearsal of *All Over Town* to offer it, to reply: 'What took you so long?' After the play opened he immersed himself in research particularly about how reporters work, finding Timothy Crouse's excellent book, *The Boys on the Bus*, following the journalists who follow the Presidential campaign, the truest to life. He also immersed himself in the newsroom of the Washington Post itself, walking down the street every morning from the comfortable splendour of the Madison Hotel. He was obliged to wear a tie – reporters have to look surface smart, they might find themselves talking to a Senator before the day is out – and this was an experience in itself for the perpetually casual actor who tended to live in sneakers and jeans. He was assigned to a journalist, Fred Barbas, who was then on the trail of political corruption in Maryland. Hoffman eavesdropped on his phone calls. As he told Rolling Stone: 'I could hear people lying, that wonderful thing of how they lie . . . it got to the point where I was starting to drive him crazy. I was saying: "Did you ask him this, and did you ask him *this*?" And suddenly I realized I was in it.'

Not only that, when shooting began Hoffman would telephone Bernstein to corroborate facts and fill in the details of what really happened. The two men became friendly, spending Passover together with Bernstein's family. It was a strange and wary friendship. Hoffman rationalised it like this: 'I can't alienate him because I'm doing him and want to be able to hang around him. He can't alienate me because I'm doing him on the screen and I'll make him look like an asshole.' The actor won the writer's respect. His persistent 'phone calls to go over details so exasperated Bernstein that he conceded: 'You're finally learning; you're acting like a journalist.'

Inevitably this temporary marriage between the fantasy world of films and the journalistic world of facts went through some unharmonious periods. As Redford said: 'The ambivalence of the Post drove me nuts'. It also gave him a renewed objectivity about the project: 'I felt it was important to fall out of love with the Post, too.' Hoffman was more volatile. 'Screw it,' he told Redford, 'Let's fictionalize it. Everybody will know what paper we're really representing. What's the difference?'

Fact prevailed over fiction. Indeed so eager were they to make the film look authentic that Warner Brothers spent $450,000 to build an identikit Washington Post newsroom in their Burbank Studios. The publicity handout insisted that they even imported real Washington Post rubbish for the waste paper baskets. But films don't succeed on the basis of set dressing; they depend on people. Hoffman had insisted on director approval when he signed for the part and after Redford had failed to snare John Schlesinger, he agreed on Alan Pakula who had made *Klute*. 'If our project was to succeed we'd need the same kind of tension. Bob liked him because he felt he wouldn't jump on a liberal bandwagon. Redford saw the film as a detective story, not as a polemic against Nixon.'

The two actors got on well together although Hoffman was amused to note that while he could mingle happily with the crowds during location shooting in Washington, Redford had to remain in his caravan because of the commotion his appearance tended to arouse. Redford, in turn, was generous in his praise for his less worshipped colleague: 'One of the joys of the movie was working with Dustin; he has one of the most wonderful acting minds I've ever worked with. Working with him was like working with a stream of pure electricity. He's so intense and fluid you can't help but react. But he does tend to overdo it a little.'

Hoffman found Redford 'fun to play against. Fast and daring. If you stubbed your toe or dropped a pencil, he picked up on it right away and made it part of the scene. As actors we're very different, though. Bob jumps in, gets wet, jumps out again. He edits himself as he goes. I have a tendency to dive in and lie on the bottom for a while. I figure the part will surface when it's ready.'

There was no guarantee the film would be a hit. No political film since *Mr Smith Goes To Washington* had been one. Redford's previous film, *The Candidate*, had been one of his least successful. But from the moment – April 1976 to be precise – Frank Rich's review appeared in the New York Post it was roses, roses all the way. He wrote: 'But though *All The President's Men* is about the power of our press, it is just as much about the often unrealized power of our movies; the film is a rare and classic example of what Hollywood can do when it's willing to bank on good taste, shrewd intelligence, and deep personal conviction. Though not perfect *All The President's Men* is an absolutely breathless entertainment, and it successfully carries the weight of history on its shoulders.'

In one of those, not always common, instances where critical acclaim and public attendance are bestowed on the same film, it opened in 604 movie houses across America and made seven million dollars in its first seven days, more than *Godfather* did in the same period. Its ultimate box office rentals of $30,000,000 made it one of the most popular intelligent films in Variety's list of 'All-Time Champs.'

One man had reservations, despite the near-unanimity of the critics about the excellence of the film. He told People magazine: 'I'm not as ecstatic as the critics are about *All The President's Men*. It could have been a lot better. They cut some of the best scenes. I told Bob he was drying the picture out. I said he should add a scene where Woodward and Bernstein were really having it out, but he didn't. I would have fought more but

---

Marathon Man (1976)
Babe Levy in training round Central Park.

by the time I saw the film it was too late to make the radical changes I wanted. In my opinion the film is a little too smooth. I would have left a few hairs on the lens.'

Hoffman was right as far as the true facts were concerned. The relationship between the WASP Woodward, the son of a judge, and the less couth street-wise Jewish Bernstein had moments of competition bordering on confrontation. But undoubtedly the public warmed more to a 'buddy' relationship between Redford and Hoffman on the screen, just as they had appreciated the Redford-Newman duo in *Butch Cassidy and the Sundance Kid*. There had even been a danger that the star coupling of Redford and Hoffman might be an impediment to the attempted reality of the story but, as Frank Rich noted, 'the stars who play the roles accomplish the considerable task of bringing themselves down to life size.'

Hoffman's discontent did not just extend to the film. It extended to the critics as well. It was gutsy of him to attack them and honourable to do so when he had been praised by them as opposed to biting back at adverse reviews. 'All these critical superlatives are embarrassing. I'd rather have a critic dump on me than praise me. When a critic says a movie is great, he's just building up the importance of his job. Critics do to movies what plant lovers do to plants. They water them until they die. It's called assassination by adoration. Why we take these people seriously, I can't imagine? If you were looking for a baby to adopt, would you adopt the child of Pauline Kael and John Simon?'

The assassination committed by Miss Kael on his next film owed more to ridicule than adoration. John Schlesinger, who directed it, can hardly have thanked Hoffman for his attack on the critics, especially when Miss Kael deemed *Marathon Man* his 'worst film ever.' It was an excessive and hardly justified over-reaction to an inventive thriller by William Goldman which Hoffman performed as compellingly as ever and which

---

Previous page: *Marathon Man* (1976)
Babe asserts himself.

united his acting talents with an English actor whose desire to demonstrate his versatility was just as great as his: Laurence Olivier.

Olivier played Szell, a Nazi dentist, who ventures out of hiding in South America to retrieve a fortune in diamonds he has stowed in a Manhattan safe deposit box. Hoffman, although by now thirty-seven is a student whose brother Doc, (Roy Scheider) is killed by Szell when trying to relieve him of the diamonds. Hoffman gets involved and Olivier thinks he has some information (which he does not) and in a scene, memorable only to those who did not avert their eyes from the screen, tortures Hoffman by drilling into the nerves of his teeth.

Goldman's book had been deservedly popular with a tense plot that was never predictable and in the central character, Babe, he postulated what would happen if an essentially cerebral man, who drove himself to the threshold of pain in his training runs, was forced to go beyond that threshold in order to survive. If the film was a lesser piece, it was because the imperative for action overrode the necessary build-up in the Hoffman character.

It remained a cracking good tale – in essence a Nazi hunting down a Jew – but it evoked an inexplicably hostile response in some quarters. Not only Miss Kael who acknowledged 'Hoffman acts young, has never looked so fit, and there isn't a bum note in his performance' before going on to excoriate Schlesinger for what she considered his failure to 'get a grip on how scenes should play,'; Variety dismissed it as 'tedious, dull, violent nonsense.' Richard Corliss in Movies thought it 'kitsch of a pretty high order' but acknowledged Hoffman's talent: 'Hoffman is the star as character actor. Here he plays a Woody Allen nebbish but with a survivor's intelligence and, way down deep, a certain ferrety courage. Hoffman can be daring as a film actor . . . like Olivier's, Hoffman's performances are crammed with bits of business – a stage tendency, which can backfire under the camera's gaze – but he's such a smart, meticulous actor that his choices almost always seem right.'

Hoffman may not have got any pleasure out of either the admonitions or admiration of the critics but he did relish the experience of working with Schlesinger again after *Midnight*

Cowboy – it was the main reason he did the film – and he had fun with Laurence Olivier. 'He's a charming clown. I'd say the role that's closest to him as a person is Archie Rice in *The Entertainer*. He's a great human with great energy.'

Olivier himself found it hard to comprehend Hoffman's agonising approach to film acting. 'Why doesn't the boy just act?' the noble lord is reported to have said, 'Why must he go through all of this Sturm und Drang?' And Schlesinger found Hoffman less easy to direct than he had been in *Midnight Cowboy*. 'He's very difficult to satisfy and goes on insisting on takes way beyond the necessity for them. Something drives him on and on to perfection, and he is often not the best judge of when he's reached it. No actor is.'

Hoffman's track record would indicate that maybe he was a better judge of his own methods and performance than either of the two Englishmen but undoubtedly his quest for perfection had begun to sour his enjoyment of film making and his relations with others. His next two movies were to make an upsetting professional nadir in his screen life.

Chapter Six

The problems began with First Artists. This had been formed in 1969 by Paul Newman, Steve McQueen, Sidney Poitier and Barbra Streisand. The aim, like Fairbanks' United Artists before them, was to give the actors total creative control over their films. To get this they sacrificed their fees but took a percentage of profits.

Hoffman joined them in 1972 as his own desire for creative control was becoming more and more important to him, and he agreed to make two films for them.

Hoffman initially wanted to make a film with Ingmar Bergman but had to drop out because his wife was pregnant and he needed to be with her since they were doing the Lamaze method of natural childbirth. Later he blamed the failure of the film to materialize on First Artists who had run a check on the Swedish director and found that none of his films had grossed more than $5 million and therefore considered him a bad financial risk. The ground rules for a First Artists film were that it would be in colour, would not exceed two hours ten minutes, and not cost more than $3 million to make (although Hoffman's two films by mutual agreement cost more.) He was, at first, excited by it: 'In that framework you could do literally anything you wanted to. It was very exciting to, in a sense, be a painter and not just a colour on the palette.'

His anticipation at getting to look at scripts that would never normally reach him, since he did not have an agent, turned to disenchantment when he found that the scripts he *did* get from them were ones he had seen two years before. So he found a book on his own, *No Beast So Fierce*, written by Edward Lewis when he was a prisoner in jail. He had doubts about the project but claimed the president of First Artists, Phil Feldman, pressurised him into making the film because he had put so much development money into it.

Hoffman started out by directing *Straight Time* himself but found the task of directing and acting too exhausting, especially as he did not have a completed screenplay to work from. He still retains the intention to direct one day but acknowledges: 'I hope I don't act when I do direct. I'm in awe of the few who have done it successfully.' So he enrolled his old friend Ulu Grosbard, whose assistant he had been on *A View From The Bridge*, to take over. It was not a successful choice. As Time Magazine in the ubiquitous voice of Frank Rich noted: 'Ulu Grosbard is but a journeyman film maker. He substitutes slow pacing and dour photography for style.' Hoffman played a recidivist called Max Dembo who, after six years in jail, does everything possible to get back in. Although critics like Penelope Gilliatt in the New Yorker chose to go out on a limb in praise of the film – 'Ulu Grosbard has drawn a near-perfect performance of a very imperfect human being from Dustin Hoffman' they were out of tune not only with the audience who stayed away in sufficient droves to deny the star his percentage but also the star himself. First Artists accused Hoffman of 'publicily denigrating the film via press releases, various and sundry interviews with journalists and other public comment . . . making derogatory statements concerning the picture.' Hoffman denied the allegations but admitted to his anger in being denied the right to re-edit the film, having only the chance to recut the first twenty minutes before it was finished by First Artists. Moreover, what he believed to be a hiatus in filming in order to assemble a rough-cut and see what further material was necessary, turned out to be the end of shooting. These incidents promoted a major court case against First Artists and the termination of his friendship with Ulu Grosbard. The two men did not speak to each other again.

Rumours abounded that Hoffman's marriage was in trouble. They were assiduously denied but his subsequent divorce indicated that they were not without foundation. Certainly when I met him in Harrogate in Yorkshire in the spring of 1978, he was prepared to accept the adulation of the girls from the local school with the flirtatious charm of a bachelor. 'What are you up to?' I enquired. 'I'm fulfilling my contract with First Artists and then I'm going to get the fuck out of here,' he replied. It was probably the unhappiest time of his professional life. He had returned to England to play the part of an American journalist, Wally Stanton, in the film *Agatha* – a fictionalised account by Kathleen Tynan of the eleven days in 1926 when

Agatha Christie, the detective novelist, upset by discovering her husband's affair with his secretary, disappeared to the Old Swan Hotel in Harrogate. We stayed in the same hotel and, indeed, I talked to a chambermaid who remembered Miss Christie being there. But any attempt to make a documentary report on the film, which I had been commissioned by Warner Brothers to do, was frustrated by the most bitter and frenzied location I have ever encountered on a movie.

'Dustin won't have anything to do with publicity,' said the publicist, Chris Nixon, 'he's too busy rewriting the script.' He was, and such was his paranoia that when I had a drink with the star one evening – he remembered the more harmonious experience of *Straw Dogs* – he asked me in conspiratorial terms: 'What's this guy Nixon like? Who's side is he on?' Hoffman had made the director, Michael Apted's task almost impossible, by revising Mrs Tynan's script with two new writers, Arthur Hopcraft and his friend, Murray Schisgal, as they were shooting. In his own defence Hoffman said: 'I literally got on my knees and begged them not to start the film. Once you go on that floor to make a movie, it's crazy time. It's painting a picture on railroad tracks with the train getting closer. *Agatha* was every actor's nightmare. The script was literally being rewritten every day. It was a rainbow of green, yellow, pink revision pages.'

The only cool character on the set was the Italian cameraman, Vittorio Storaro, who, unconcerned with the details of the script, took a commanding interest in laying down elegant tracks for many of the shots – which ensured glamorous rushes but an editor's nightmare. Vanessa Redgrave who played Agatha was concerned with the script but found time to sell her Workers' Revolutionary Paper to the extras in the lunch hour. 'What do you think of Vanessa?' I asked Hoffman. 'I look up to her,' he replied. And then, losing none of his old twinkle confided, 'she gives me a stiff (pause) neck.'

The essential problem with the venture was that the part of

On the following page: *Kramer vs Kramer* (1979)
Ted Kramer plays Mother and Father to his son Billy
(Justin Henry).

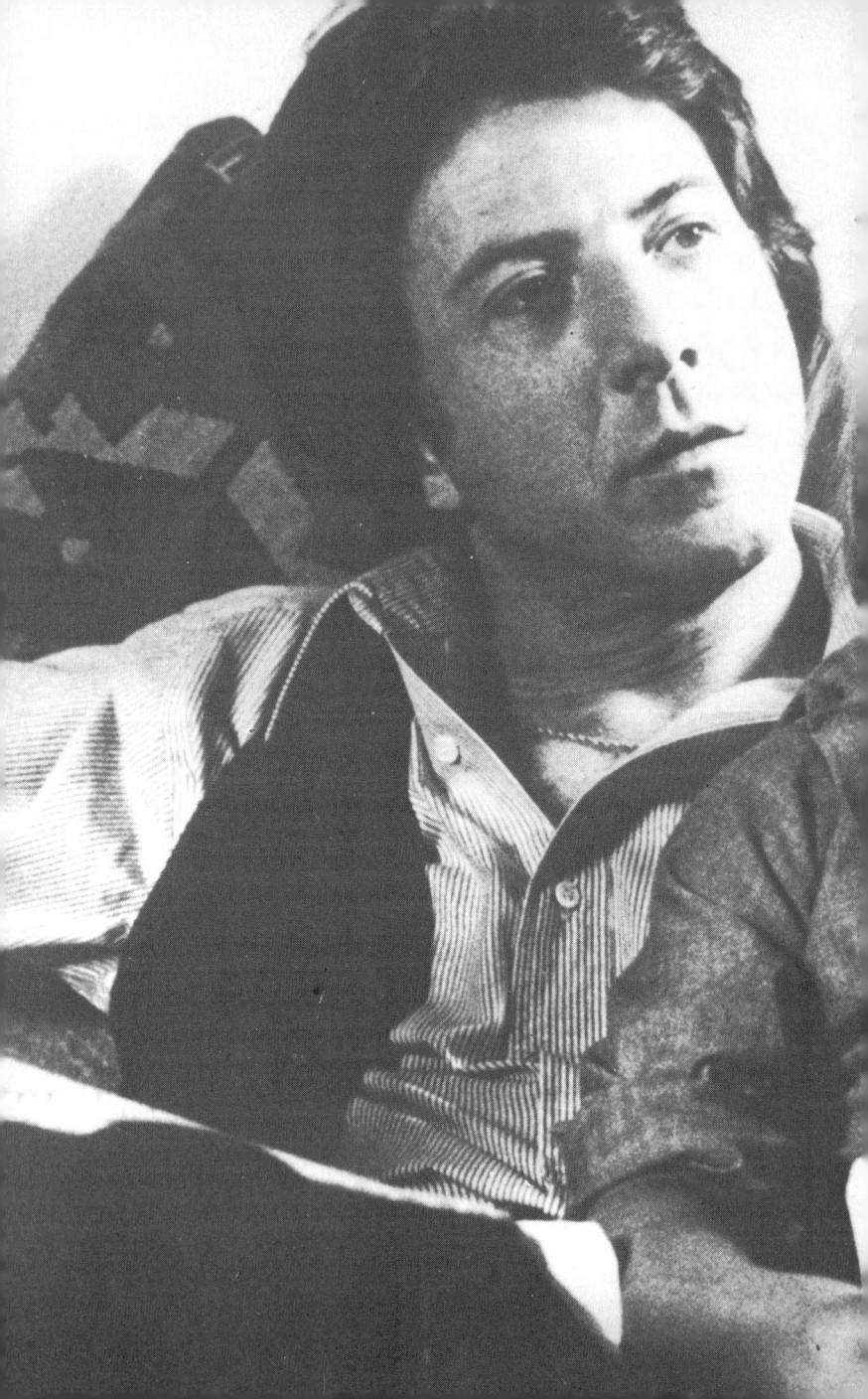

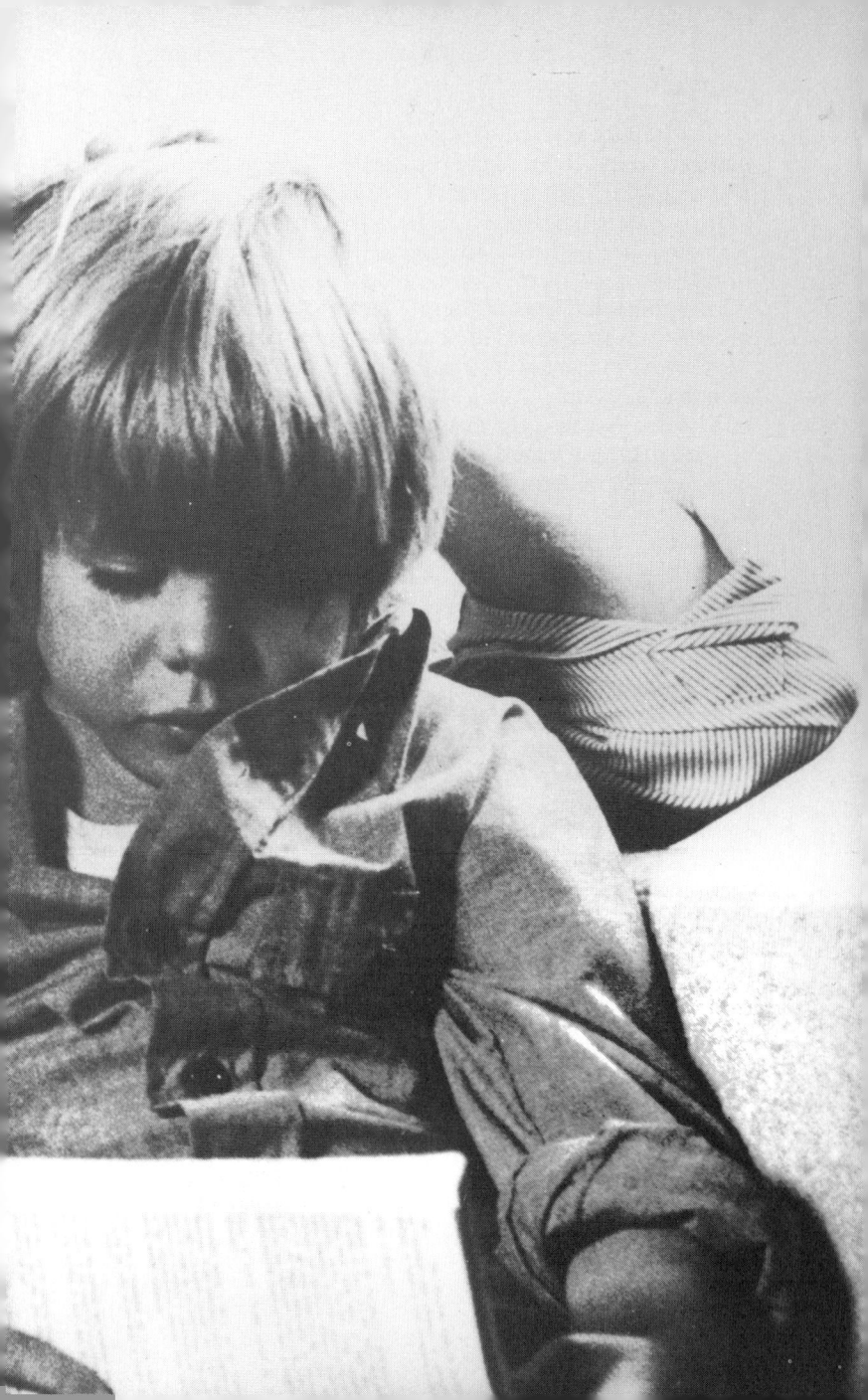

Wally Stanton was only a small cameo but because of Hoffman's contract with First Artists it had to be bolstered into a co-starring role. Even with the rewrites Hoffman was not satisfied: 'The scene that explains my character is missing. In that scene I was asked why I was so affected. The character is a failed novelist whose own failure causes him to be obsessed with Agatha. But that's not in the movie. First Artists gave me a letter saying that *Agatha* was to be finished in three days. I begged to be allowed to use my own money to shoot the final scene. I was refused.'

There was cause for complaint on both sides. First Artists alleged that Hoffman decided to do the picture 'in bad faith and with improper motives out of a desire to dispose of his commitments to First Artists with the least possible inconvenience to him and in the shortest time possible in order to move on to ventures which would be more lucrative and personally rewarding to him.' Hoffman had expressed as much, albeit more economically, to me and when he filed his $65 million lawsuit against First Artists, $4 million of this sum was to recompense him for lost earnings on the two films. He can have done the release of *Agatha* little good by attempting to take out an injunction in July 1978 to halt the film's distribution. It was rejected in the Los Angeles Superior Court by Judge David A. Thomas who, being asked, amazingly, to rule on creative rather than legal issues, pronounced: 'I find that there is greater harm which might be suffered by all the parties in permitting the editing to be done by Hoffman than in not permitting him to do it presently.' Hoffman used the time that might have gainfully being occupied in shaping the film by going to law school.

Considering the turmoil behind the scenes, the reviews for *Agatha* were not too bad. 'A complete surprise and a considerable pleasure' wrote David Denby in New York Magazine. 'Pleasantly endurable and aimless' said Canby in the New York Times, finding Hoffman 'comically inventive.' But in a detailed analysis of Hoffman's technique, Pauline Kael took him to task for his scene-stealing: 'he's even less relaxed now and more stage-actorish; you feel that in *Agatha* he has an image of the character in his mind and he's impersonating it.

Sometimes he has images of so many characters that he's impersonating a whole gallery of people; at other times, there's nobody there.' The public may not have rationalised it to this extent but after *Alfredo, Alfredo*, it proved Hoffman's least popular film.

Christmas of 1978 would have been a low point in Hoffman's life – he was suing his manager, his company and Warner Borthers and in turn his wife was suing him for divorce – were it not for the fact that he had just completed shooting a film that was to revivify his career beyond recognition: *Kramer vs Kramer*.

Avery Corman's novel, which was much more hostile to the wife who abandoned her son than the screenplay turned out to be, had been acquired by the producer Stanley R. Jaffe. To begin with Jaffe wanted Francois Truffaut to direct the film but when he became unavailable Robert Benton co-author of *Bonnie and Clyde* and director of *The Late Show* took over. It was, in hindsight, an advantage to have a director who was less of an author because when Benton began to work on the script he incorporated the character of Dustin Hoffman himself in the part of Ted Kramer, the advertising executive who finds himself bringing up his son on his own. They spent months together in a hotel room taping Hoffman's thoughts on the part. Hoffman told me that Benton even went home and wrote the way he talked.'He says that I say "terrific" all the time and in fact it's the last line of the film. She says in the elevator: "How do I look?" and I look at her and I say "terrific". He's one of the few directors that is aware of a very important concept: that a script has no integrity. It is there to be altered constantly, before you shoot, while you're shooting and even after you've shot because you can do a lot of work looping. You can actually rewrite dialogue on people's backs.'

Hoffman also drew on himself for the character, but only aspects of himself. He maintained: 'I've never played anything that was as disguised as this in the sense that it seems to be me but the people that know me know that it is not.' He drew on aspects of his father, Harry, and even his producer, Stanley Jaffe. It is his tradition to approach a part with a role-model in mind – his brother Ronald provided the point of departure for *The Graduate* and the superintendant of his old apartment building formed the basis of Ratso in *Midnight Cowboy*.

It was more than the coincidence of art imitating life that caused Hoffman to embark on *Kramer* while he was moving out of his family home and into an apartment of his own on Central Park West. His daughter and step-daughter stayed with their mother but came to visit him on the set, Karina even has a small part in the film. At the time he decided: 'you can't have career and a family' but at a dinner he had with his wife before their separation Anne asked him if he had noticed a particular birthmark on his daughter. He hadn't, 'but that stuck with me, it bothered me. I remember looking at Anne and saying "I bet you know every mark on those kids – every single mark" '. It is not without significance that, at the beginning of *Kramer vs Kramer*, Ted does not even know what grade his son is in at school.

As ever Hoffman did not find it difficult to resist the company of comely women on the set; on location days he often appeared to be surrounded by them. 'You notice I don't have any yes-men around me,' he joked, 'just no-women.' Professionally he involved himself intensely in a search for someone to play his son, Billy. Justin Henry got the part largely because he had a good relationship with his own father, portfolio manager for J.C. Penney, but more importantly because he had not acted before. Hoffman was anxious to be as honest with the child as possible. He told me that when Justin was confused 'he acted like children acting on TV. I told him that if he didn't find me funny in a scene "then don't laugh". He knew that his parents were separating and that he was going to live with Daddy. He came in every day not knowing what was going to happen. But it was a sandbox which we got into every day and played house.'

Eventually the games came to an end. 'The last day in the park I told him the truth, that I loved him. But that it's the case when you're making movies that you get these close relationships and then it's over. Before we knew it we were all crying – me, the cameraman and Justin, but the moment he started to cry we started to roll and that's in the film.'

Originally the producers wanted to give the part of Joanna Kramer to Kate Jackson. 'They thought they could get a multi-million dollar TV sale if she was in the package since she was in

Charlie's Angels,' said Dustin, 'so if they were thinking of trying to cover their costs by selling it to TV before filming started, they cannot have been too optimistic.' Fortunately, and memorably, the part went to Meryl Streep. She took the role very seriously and when I suggested to her that, as in Corman's book, the wife had behaved selfishly, she was vehement in her defence. 'You're crazy; I don't believe that. I think she was nuts a little bit, I think she was neurotic and very weak. So what should she do, take him in a back-pack across the country? She didn't know where she was going. I think she was suicidal. You don't bring your kids with you on a suicide mission.'

Her passionate involvement with the wife's dilemma encouraged Benton to ask her to write her own testimony for the courtroom battle over custody of the child. Miss Streep rose to the occasion. When asked why she is seeking custody she began very simply: 'Because he's my child and because I love him. I know I left my son. I know that's a terrible thing to do. Believe me I have to live with that every day of my life . . .'

The scene gave Miss Streep additional satisfaction, as she told me. 'Benton said: "Let's shoot it all". Dustin was furious. I could see the steam coming out of his ears. He hadn't been able to read it first to know what I was going to say. It really was a fun day.'

Without the need for contractual assurances, Benton involved Hoffman in the editing of the film just as closely as he had regarded him as a partner in its preparation and shooting. There was no early indication they were on to a hit. Indeed Hoffman related 'I did hear some reports from Columbia executives who were somewhat throttled because the film was, to them, no way in the spirit of the book. It didn't have a winner or a loser, a hero or a villain. They felt that commercially the public wants to identify with someone and collectively wants to hate someone else. Where it's ambiguous they feel it's non-commercial, it's arty.'

The shifting sands of studio executives in Hollywood are testimony to the fact that their reading of the public taste is often less than perfect. *Kramer* opened to widespread attention, four stars from Kathleen Carroll in the New York Daily News and critical raves elsewhere, more than sixty million dollars in box-office rentals making it Hoffman's most popular film to date, with Oscars for Robert Benton, Meryl Streep and, for the first time, Dustin Hoffman. It was a hard act to follow.

The last time I met Hoffman was in his room at the Inn on the Park in London. He was a changed man from the tense and often bitter character I had last seen in Harrogate. In part his relaxation was due to the fact that he was in town to promote the assured hit, *Kramer vs Kramer*, a very different way of life from the fraught uncertainty of the movie set. But after *Kramer* and his separation from Anne he had returned to Los Angeles and formed a new relationship with his parents: his father, Harry, had become his favourite tennis partner. They were with him in London, his father cheerfully relaying messages to his mother, who was downstairs having a massage, regarding where they would all eat that night and what plays Dustin had suggested they should go to. Hoffman was also with his new wife, Lisa Gottsegen. He had known her since whe was a child, as her grandparents lived next door to his parents in Los Angeles. His brother Ron had once dated her mother. In 1965 she had been ill in bed and Hoffman had come to her room to cheer her up. When he began to study law to understand his complex legal battles he accompanied her to San Fernando Valley College where she was also a law student. In 1980, six days after his divorce from Anne, he married her.

I reminded Hoffman that when we first met on *Straw Dogs* he had said he always wanted to 'come up different', yet with *Kramer* he was playing a more conventional role, was this the shape of parts to come? His eyes twinkled. 'I've spent the last six months working on something which I've never done before,' he told me. 'I'm very depressed about it and it excites me because I am not sure that I can pull it off. I did a screen test that succeeded in some aspects of the character, with other aspects I just fell on my face. I will go and spend three or four months working on it again. I was shocked at those parts of it that worked; I wasn't prepared that I could be different in that particular way.'

The character was called Shirley. As his friend, the writer Murray Schisgal said 'Dustin always felt he had a "Shirley" inside him'. They had worked on the idea after Hoffman had said to him: 'What if I were a woman? What would my life be like and how would I be different?' Later Shirley was to be immortalised as *Tootsie*.

Inspired, doubtless, by Dr Renée Richards, they tried to create a man who disguised himself as a woman to win tennis tournaments. Then they acquired a screenplay by Don McGuire about an actor who disguised himself as a woman in order to get parts. Before the film was finally released it passed through the hands of so many other writers that three large cardboard boxes were needed to take the twenty scripts to the Writers Guild to arbitrate on who should get the final writing credit (it ended up with Schisgal and Larry Gelbart.)

Hoffman knew the key to the film's success would be his own credibility as a woman. It took him more than a year to be satisfied. In the early screen tests he acknowledged that he looked like 'a female prison warder.' He tried out 17 different sorts of 34c bras, discounting the nightclub trick of putting birdseed in them to make them swing in favour of the more conventional silicone. His neck – too big for his body as a man – was a problem so they decided to let Tootsie, or Dorothy Michaels as she was to become in the film, play a hospital adminstrator with high necked clothing. The voice was a problem. He went to New York's Columbia University and they put an oscilloscope of a woman's voice on his throat, so that he could try to get his voice up to match the lines. He wanted her to be French because he had a high French falsetto but his director, Sydney Pollack, objected. One day, in the shower, he attempted a Southern accent. He tried it out on Lisa and she confirmed that for the first time he had begun to sound believable. He noted that the Southern accent lifts up at the end of sentences whereas normal male intonation begins to drop. He engaged Polly Holliday whom he had directed in Schisgal's *All Over Town* to talk Dixie with him. They did a scene from *A Streetcar Named Desire* with Hoffman as Blanche in front of Meryl Streep in his apartment. She approved.

It was now time to test her in costume in the real world. He tried her out on people in the street. No problems. He got his daughter, Jenna, to introduce him to her teacher as 'Aunt Dorothy from Arkansas'. The teacher knew Hoffman well but thought she was talking to a woman. 'That teacher treated me differently from before,' he observed. 'There is a kind of sisterhood among women I never got before. Women are wary with men.' Men, he also found out, are wary of women, especially strange middle-aged women. Dorothy went up to Jon Voight in the Russian Tea Rooms in New York. 'He just looked through me, he just wasn't interested. That happened a lot with men looking over my shoulder to find a prettier woman.'

He had wanted Dorothy to be as attractive as possible and was taken aback when a woman reporter, knowing Dorothy was Dustin, asked why she was not more attractive. He shrugged and conceded 'that's it.' With others who were not let into the secret his eyes were opened to a sadder truth. 'When men meet a not particularly attractive women, they relate to you in a way I've never been related to before in my life. I was constantly being rejected in a sort of unspoken way by every man I met. When women met me I suddenly realised there was no barrier. I was a member of this oppressed group that are called women. We wanted to show that being thought of as a woman could alter you as a man. I have the natural chauvinism I was raised with; I could never sit next to a woman and not think sexually about her.'

Jacob, his and Lisa's son, was eight weeks old when they started shooting *Tootsie*. 'He thinks going to work means me putting on a dress,' recalled Hoffman. 'Luckily we can afford therapy for him later.' For the internal character of Tootsie he drew heavily on his mother, Lilian. 'She's the heart of Tootsie. Dorothy has her strength, her vulnerability, her vitality and her sexual humour.' The passion with which he introduced these elements into the part was redoubled by an inner pain. Just before they began to shoot *Tootsie*, his mother died of a heart attack.

In the early scenes of the film Hoffman plays Michael Dorsey, a difficult-to-employ actor, and in this characterisation he drew more intimately than ever before on an actor who had suffered the degradations of trying to find work in New York in the sixties: himself.

'You're just the wrong height.'
'I can be taller.'

'We're looking for someone somewhat shorter.'
'I can play somewhat shorter.'
Or again.
'We're looking for someone different.'
'I can be someone different.'
'You don't understand. We're looking for someone else.'

These exchanges between a casting director and a vulnerable, desperate actor were familiar enough to Hoffman. More personal still was Dorsey's crankiness. He loses out on a tomato commercial because he 'overthinks' the role of the tomato. 'You have one of the worst reputations in town,' his agent tells him. 'No-one will work with you . . . you're too much trouble. Get some therapy.'

In an unintentional case of art imitating life, the agent was played by Sydney Pollack who was also attempting to direct the film. He had reputedly furious rows with Hoffman on the set, so much so that the New York gossip columns referred to the production as the 'troubled Tootsie.' These heated discussions meant that they sometimes only managed to take one shot a day and this, coupled with problems and delays in Hoffman's make-up, meant that this relatively simple picture took a hundred days to shoot – it could have been done in thirty – and cost a nightmarish $20 million, the same amount as they spent making *Gandhi*.

Pollack had a more than competent track record as a director. He had made five films with Robert Redford, most notably *The Way We Were* and, more recently, directed Paul Newman in the accomplished *Absence of Malice*. No star, not even Miss Streisand, prepared him for the intractable Hoffman. 'Dustin feels that his job as an actor with any integrity is to dig his heels in and fight as hard as he can for what he believes in. I don't have any quarrel with that,' conceded Pollack, 'I do have a quarrel with some of his other assumptions. For whatever reason, I think Dustin feels that directors and actors are biological enemies, the way the mongoose and the cobra are enemies. He sees every picture as what he calls a "silent war". And he's fought with most of his directors. I think if he would give a director half a chance and not assume that the director is trying to kill him, he would see that most directors want what he wants, which is the best possible picture.'

Their arguments revolved round matters of taste. Hoffman wanted to make the comedy more outrageous with some anatomical bathroom jokes. Pollack resisted these and, in this instance, his counsel prevailed. They would probably have been out of place. Pauline Kael in her review of the film pinpointed the much more subtle nuances that made the concept work. 'This isn't a simple female impersonation, on the order of *Charley's Aunt*. Michael finds himself when he's Dorothy – not because he has any secret desire to be a woman but because when he's Dorothy he's acting. He's such a dedicated, fanatical actor that he comes fully alive only when he's playing a role and you can see it in his intense, glittering eyes. There are always several things going on in Hoffman's face. He lets us see that Michael's mind is working all the time, and that he's making an actor's choices. Michael is thinking out Dorothy while he's playing her – he's thinking out what a woman would do. When he's giving a performance as Dorothy, he feels a freedom that he doesn't have when he's just Michael.'

The fact that the film's outrageous cost – including a reputed $4.5 million to Hoffman – and fractious history had become public knowledge made it a possible Aunt Sally for the reviewers. But Miss Kael, often one of his most implacable critics, was absolute in her enthusiasm for it. 'When Hoffman delivers the kind of performance he gives here, the talk in the media about his being overpaid is beside the point. This movie is inconceivable without him.' Andrew Sarris in the Village Voice confessed: 'For months I had been dreading the moment of Dustin Hoffman's manifestation in drag. All the sub-rosa production stories spelt disaster. How could a stormy petrel of a perfectionist like Hoffman achieve the lightness of touch for such a delicate imposture?' His verdict: 'I am not sure after only one viewing that *Tootsie* is an instant classic, but it clicks in a way that I never anticipated.'

The confetti of adulation scattered down on Hoffman from America's leading critics as even he had never experienced it before. '*Tootsie* returns the original meaning to the term situation comedy', (The New York Times), 'miraculous' (Daily News) 'it is not just the best comedy of the year; it is popular art on the way to becoming cultural artifact.' (Time). Unfortunately for all concerned, the Oscar ceremony of 1983 belonged to *Gandhi* with only Jessica Lange getting an award for Best Supporting Actress. Hoffman was beaten by the indisputibly inspired performance by Ben Kingsley and even if he had been nominated in the Best Actress category – and there were rumours that he might be – his old friend Meryl Streep had given the performance of a lifetime in *Sophie's Choice*.

The public however voted differently from the industry and they voted with their dollars. By the end of the year *Gandhi* had taken a respectable $24 million in box-office rentals; *Tootsie* had taken $94,571,613, making it the eighth most successful film ever made, more popular even than *Superman*. Hoffman had a percentage of the profits ensuring a substantial legacy with which Jacob could pay his therapist. He had been there before – but never to such an extent – and knew the dangers of having a hit of these proportions. 'Success can really cripple you. We live in a culture based on success. But life isn't for that.'

Meryl Streep probably gave me the best pen-portrait of Hoffman. 'He's the most wonderful combination of generous and selfish I've ever met all wrapped up in one man. He really wants to be the greatest actor who ever lived. But he knows you're only as good as the repartee is with the other actor, you bring each other out, so he's torn all the time – he wants you to be good, but he doesn't.'

Having mastered the problem of playing a female lead there seems no reason why Hoffman should not play both roles in a love story. He must have thought about it since he said: 'if I could do the make-up in ten minutes, I'd love to take parts from Glenda Jackson.'

He is 46 now, seemingly at peace with his wife and his children, but relentlessly pursued by his own quest for perfection in his acting. 'I like to challenge the mystery of why one runner wins by a tenth of a second? What is that transcending, primal thing that enables you to push yourself beyond, beyond – further than what is possible? That is what I try for, somehow, in my work.'

In the future, we, the audiences, are likely to be the beneficiaries of his efforts.'

The Films of Dustin Hoffman

Marathon Man (1976)
Babe escapes the ordeal in his bathroom into a friendless city.

The Films of Dustin Hoffman

1967

The Tiger Makes Out (Columbia Pictures/Elan)
Running Time: 94 mins, *Producer:* George Justin, *Director:* Arthur Hiller, *Script:* Murray Schisgal (from his play *The Tiger*), *Cast:* Eli Wallach, Anne Jackson, Bob Dishy, David Burns, Charles Nelson Reilly, Dustin Hoffman.

1967

The Graduate (UA/Embassy Pictures)
Running Time: 105 mins, *Director:* Lawrence Turman (Oscar Nomination), *Director:* Mike Nichols (Oscar), *Script:* Calder Willingham and Buck Henry, *Cast:* Anne Bancroft (Oscar Nomination), Dustin Hoffman (Oscar Nomination), Katharine Ross (Oscar Nomination), William Daniels., Elizabeth Wilson, Buck Henry.

1969

Midnight Cowboy (United Artists)
Running Time: 113 mins, *Producer:* Jerome Hellman (Oscar), *Director:* John Schlesinger (Oscar), *Script:* Waldo Salt (Oscar), from James Leo Herlighy's novel, *Cast:* Dustin Hoffman (Oscar Nomination), Jon Voight (Oscar Nomination), Sylvia Miles (Oscar Nomination), John McGiver, Brenda Vaccaro.

The Films of Dustin Hoffman

1969

John and Mary (Twenthieth Century Fox/Debrod)
Running Time: 92 mins, *Producer:* Ben Kadish, *Director:* Peter Yates, *Script:* John Mortimer, from Mervyn Jones novel, *Cast:* Dustin Hoffman, Mia Farrow, Michael Tolan, Olympia Duhahis, Cleavon Little, Tyne Daly.

1969

Madigan's Millions (AIP)
Running Time: 75 mins, *Producer:* Sidney Pink, *Director:* Stanley Prager, *Screenplay:* James Henaghan, *Cast:* Dustin Hoffman, Elsa Martinelli, Ceasar Romero.

1970

Little Big Man (Cinema Center)
Running Time: 147 mins, *Producer:* Stuart Millar, *Director:* Arthur Penn, *Script:* Calder Willingham, from Thomas Berger's novel, *Cast:* Dustin Hoffman, Faye Dunaway, Martin Balsam, Chief Dan George, Jeff Corey, Richard Mulligan.

The Films of Dustin Hoffman

1971

Straw Dogs (Talent Associates/Amerbroco)
Running Time: 118 mins, *Producer:* Daniel Melnick, *Director:* Sam Peckinpah, *Script:* David Zelag Goodman from 'The Siege of Trenchers Farm' by Gordon Williams, *Cast:* Dustin Hoffman, Susan George, Colin Welland, T.P. McKenna, Sally Thompsett, David Warner, Ken Hutchinson, Ken Norton.

1971

Who Is Harry Kellerman and Why is he saying those terrible things about me? (Cinema Center)
Running Time: 108 mins, *Producer:* Herb Gardner, *Director:* Ulu Grosbard, *Script:* Herb Gardner, *Cast:* Dustin Hoffman, Barbara Harris (Oscar Nomination), David Burns, Jack Warden, Betty Walker, Dom Deluise.

1973

Alfredo, Alfredo (Paramount)
Running Time: 97 mins, *Producer:* Pietro Germi, *Director:* Pietro Germi, *Script:* Ieo Benvenuti, *Cast:* Dustin Hoffman, Stefania Sandrelli, Danika LaLoggia, Saro Urzi, Carla Gravina, Daniele Patella, Clara Colosino.

The Films of Dustin Hoffman

1973

Papillon (Papillon Partnership/Corona/General Production Co)
Running Time: 150 mins, *Producer:* Robert Dorfmann, *Director:* Franklin J. Schaffner, *Script:* Dalton Trumbo and Lorenzo Semple Jr, from Henri Charrière's novel, *Cast:* Steve McQueen, Dustin Hoffman, George Coulouris, Victor Jory, Anthony Zerbe, Don Gordon.

1974

Lenny (UA)
Running Time: 111 mins, *Producer:* Marvin Worth (Oscar Nomination), *Director:* Bob Fosse (Oscar Nomination), *Script:* Julian Barry (Oscar Nomination), *Cast:* Dustin Hoffman (Oscar Nomination), Valerie Perrine (Oscar Nomination), Rashel Novikoff, Jan Miner, Stanley Beck, Gary Morton.

1974

All The President's Men (Warner Bros/Wildwood)
Running Time: 138 mins, *Producer:* Walter Coblenz (Oscar Nomination), *Director:* Alan J Pakula (Oscar Nomination), *Script:* William Goldman (Oscar), from Carl Bernstein and Bob Woodward's book. *Cast:* Robert Redford, Dustin Hoffman, Jason Robards (Oscar), Jane Alexander (Oscar Nomination), Jack Warden, Martin Balsam, Hal Holbrook.

The Films of Dustin Hoffman

1976

Marathon Man (Paramount)
Running Time: 126 mins, *Producer:* Robert Evans, *Director:* John Schlesinger, *Script:* William Goldman from his novel, *Cast:* Dustin Hoffman, Laurence Olivier (Oscar Nomination), Roy Scheider, William Devane, Marthe Keller, Fritz Weaver.

1978

Straight Time (Warner Bros/First Artists/Sweetwall)
Runnting Time: 114 mins, *Producers:*Stanley Beck, Tim Zinnemann, *Director:* Ulu Grosbard, *Script:* Alvin Sargent, Edward Bunker, Jeffrey Boam, from Edward Bunker's novel 'No Beast So Fierce', *Cast:* Dustin Hoffman, Theresa Russell, Harry Dean Stanton, Gary Busey.

1978

Agatha (Warner Bros/First Artists/Sweetwall/Casablanca)
Running Time: 98 mins, *Producers:* Jarvis Astaire, Gavrick Losey, *Director:* Michael Apted, *Script:* Kathleen Tynan and Arthur Hopcraft, *Cast:* Dustin Hoffman, Vanessa Redgrave, Timothy Dalton, Helen Morse, Celia Gregory, Tony Britton, Timothy West.

———The Films of Dustin Hoffman———

1979

Kramer vs. Kramer (Columbia/Stanley Jaffe)
Running Time: 105 mins, *Producer:* Stanley Jaffe (Oscar), *Director:* Robert Benton (Oscar), *Script:* Robert Benton (Oscar), *Cast:* Dustin Hoffman (Oscar), Meryl Streep (Oscar), Jane Alexander, Justin Henry.

1982

Tootsie (Columbia/Mirage/Punch)
Running Time: 116 mins, *Producer:* Sydney Pollack (Oscar Nomination), *Director:* Sydney Pollack (Oscar Nomination), *Script:* Larry Gelbart and Murray Schisgal, from Don McGuire's story. *Cast:* Dustin Hoffman (Oscar Nominated), Jessica Lange (Oscar), Teri Garr, Dabney Coleman, Charles Durning, Sydney Pollack.

Tootsie (1982)

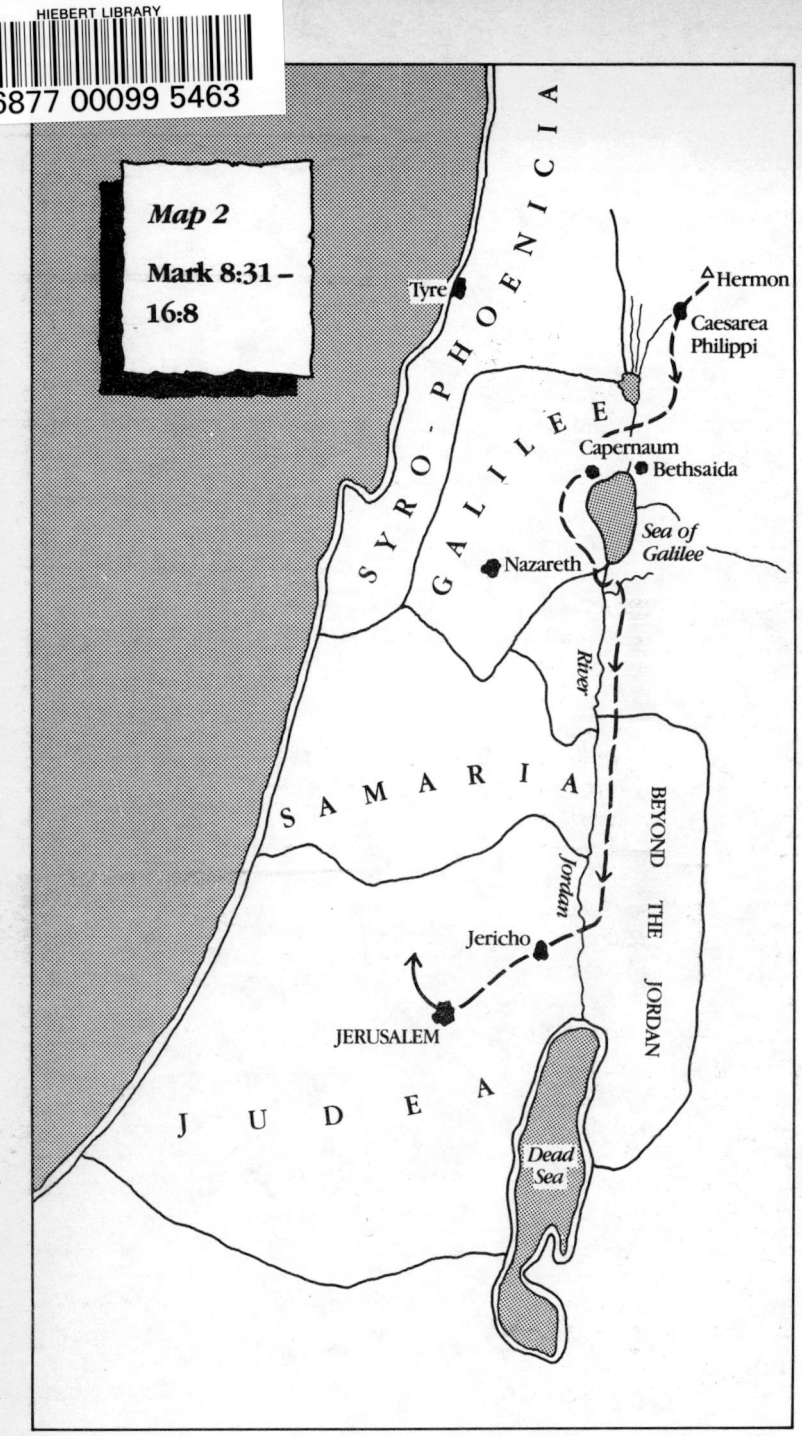

'Journeying toward Jerusalem' (*Mark 8:31 – 16:8*)

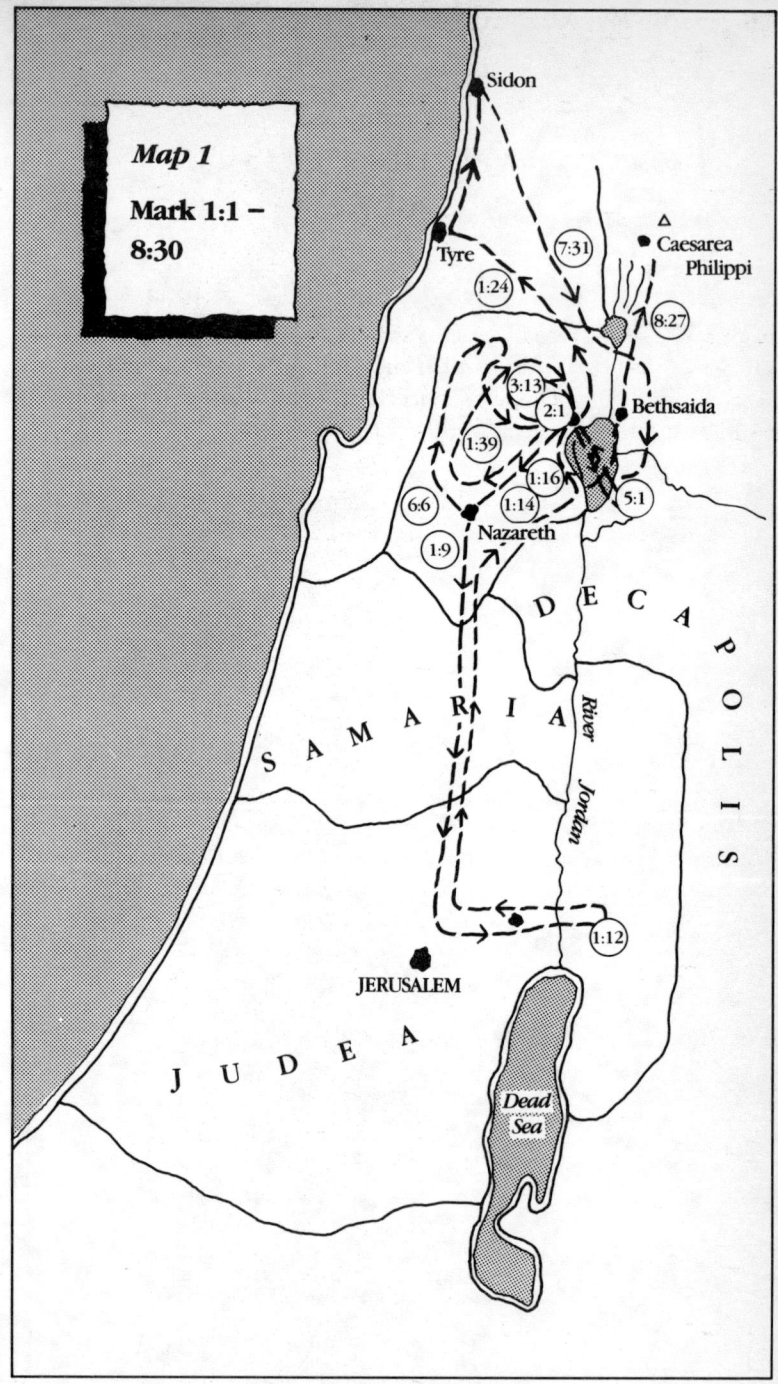

'Through towns and villages teaching' (*Mark 1:1 – 8:30*)

APPENDIX 2
MAPS

The purpose of the two maps is to show at a glance how Jesus travels a lot, in various directions, in the first half of Mark's gospel; but in the second half of the gospel, once Jesus is sure of Peter's faith, he makes straight for Jerusalem.

APPENDIX 1
THE WEEK OF RE-CREATION

In this diagram one can see at a glance how Mark has taken the traditional Jewish week, reflecting the week of creation in Genesis, and moved it all forward by one day, as the week of re-creation. Because of the Resurrection, Sunday is now the Holy Day, and God is creating again after the sabbath rest.

	Genesis 1:1 – 2:4		Mark 11:11 – 16:8	
1	evening morning	(1:5)		
2	evening morning	(1:8)	it was already late on the following day	11:11 11:12
3	evening morning	(1:13)	when evening came in the morning	11:19 11:20
4	evening morning	(1:19)	watches of the night it was now two days before the Passover	13:35ff. 14:1
5	evening morning	(1:23)	(Simon's supper) on the first day of Unleavened Bread	14:3 14:12
6	evening morning	(1:31)	when it was evening as soon as it was morning	14:17 15:1
7	(sabbath) (sabbath)	(2:2)	when evening had come (sabbath)	15:42 (15:42)
8(1)			(Saturday evening) when the sun had risen	(15:47 – 16.1) 16:2

speaking of 'those who [1] have ... been enlightened, who [2] have tasted the heavenly gift, and [3] have become partakers of the Holy Spirit, and [4] have tasted the goodness of the word of God and the powers of the age to come' (Hebrews 6:4f.).

Chapter 16

These are mysteries, and we may well reflect on the gospel as a whole to see if it tells us even more than the individual parts.

The first half of the gospel was about faith, the second half has been about love. The first five chapters of Mark follow the themes of baptism; the sixth to eighth chapters are mainly about bread, food, recognition. We seemed to see the first half of the mysteries of Christian initiation in the first half of the gospel of Mark: baptism; Eucharist as bread.

The second half of the gospel divided similarly into two: the journey to Jerusalem, and the events of Holy Week. We seemed to see in the journey to Jerusalem either the sacrament of confirmation or rather the basic Christian 'response' theme, in which Jesus succeeded where Peter did not. The power of transfiguration or transformation into someone who can do the impossible (confess the divinity of Jesus and our own adoption by God in the face of suffering and persecution) belongs to God alone; but once it has arrived on earth it increases and multiplies. Others will do what Jesus did, but after him.

The Holy Week theme is all dependent on the blood of Jesus. The blood of Jesus is the key to the re-creation or making divine of all things merely human.

So the four quarters of the gospel run along the themes of: baptism (1:2 – 5:43); Eucharist as bread (6:1 – 8:30); confirmation, or the power to love in spite of opposition (8:31 – 10:52); Eucharist as blood (11:1 – 16:8).

We also reflected that perhaps the first half of the gospel is linked with the transfer of the synagogue service in a modified form into the first half of the Christian Eucharist; and the second half of Mark's gospel seems linked with the transfer from the temple sacrifices to the second half of the Christian Eucharist, the commemoration of the Lord's Supper.

The Letter to the Hebrews also seems to point to a fourfold pattern in the initiation of Christians in the very early Church, young man does remind me that in Greek, St Mark's language, "young man" is almost the same as "new man". He seems to picture how we shall all be when the resurrection is fulfilled in heaven: young, new, at your right hand, and dressed in white robes. Help me to throw away my old cloak like Bartimaeus, or to leave it behind like the boy in Gethsemane, and to put on the garment of the risen Jesus instead. The sun is risen, so let me live like someone in the sunshine, not like one for whom the dawn has not yet come, or for whom the sun has already set.'

Verse 6

'Without having seen Jesus I love him. I believe he suffered the crucifixion rather than lose me or the likes of me from his flock. And this voice that is speaking and telling me Jesus is risen, I know it is your voice, eternal owner of all the sheep, my Father. Jesus died and tore the curtain that hid from my eyes the place where you live. The temple where you live, Father, is now revealed as being my own body. As I look out through my eyes, you and you alone see exactly what I see. You and you alone share my every thought, my every feeling. Jesus died that I might find you, and now we are together and no one can separate us.'

Verse 7

'So when we go with the disciples and Peter to where Jesus is leading us, we do not go alone. Jesus leads, and you, Father, have come to greet us and forgive us while we were still a long way from home. Jesus refused wine before his crucifixion because he had promised not to drink it until he drank it new in the kingdom: now he is preparing his banquet and there will be wine in plenty when you and I, Father, and the rest of your flock come to where he is. Then at last I shall see Jesus face to face, he will turn round and lead us no further, for we shall have reached our home.'

Verse 8

'If the final silence of Mark is a silence of joy, then I pray for all Christians the joy that comes of knowing the sun is risen and will never set. And if there are clouds, one day the Son of man will come to us upon the clouds.'

Chapter 16
SUGGESTIONS FOR PRAYER

Verse 1

'Father in heaven, if ever I should become unsure of the reality and power of Jesus, let me never become indifferent. Let me always at least mourn for him, and wish I could find him alive again.'

Verse 2

'But Jesus is risen. He is like the sun in my life. His message of peace and forgiveness for sinners is backed up by you, Father. You acknowledge our Jesus as your own Son. The sun has already risen. Perhaps I cannot see the sun always for the clouds in the way, but I know he is there. My very life, my very warmth of heart depends on him. And this sun will never set again, either now or in eternity. This is a new sun, in a new heaven. Praise to you, Father, for raising him from the dead and showing him to the chosen witnesses.'

Verses 3 and 4

One may wonder whether Peter (the Rock, the Stone) had anything to do with this stone's being remembered and included in the resurrection memories. A stone that stands in the way of God's will is bound to be moved out of the road without more ado. Jesus was the stone rejected, but now he is become the cornerstone, and the other stone which seemed to seal the victory of evil over good has been swept aside.

'Father, give me the warm-heartedness of these women, to go straight for what my heart says is the right thing to do, and worry about obstacles afterwards. You and I will be alive and well when all that stood in our way has long since been dropped into the sea.'

Verse 5

'Heavenly Father, I know that this description of a young man dressed in a white robe is a biblical way of saying that you spoke to the two Marys and Salome directly, so that they could never afterwards doubt the truth of what they had heard. But the gospel is sudden, but it does well depict the awesome mystery that has arrived, a mystery which will never have an ending.

There is another way in which thinking about Peter helps to make rounded sense of Mark's ending. Mary Magdalene, Mary the mother of James and Salome are told in their direct message from God: 'But go, tell his disciples and Peter that he is going before you to Galilee; there you will see him, as he told you.' This leaves us at the end of the whole gospel with Jesus the Shepherd going ahead, leading the way, back to the green pastures on the hillsides by the running water, where he will again feed us at no cost until everyone is satisfied. Him we cannot see as yet, but there we shall see him, as he told us; in the meantime it is up to the disciples to gather themselves with Peter (a shepherd they *can* see) and go the way he has told them. We know that the context of the message of the young man has to do with the Shepherd, because it is a direct reference to what Jesus said to the eleven on their way to Gethsemane (see Mark 14:26ff.). Peter and the other witnesses to the resurrection cannot promise their converts or would-be converts a direct vision of Jesus in glory, not yet. To some it may be given, but the gospel is written for all, even the least.

We may also take it that now Jesus is risen, Peter will have the strength to die for him, just as Peter promised, too rashly and too soon, on the same walk to Gethsemane.

At the end of this chapter I have added two Appendices. Appendix 1 gives a diagram to show what I have called Mark's week of re-creation. He alone of the four evangelists makes a complete Holy Week of it. Matthew drops one of Mark's days; Luke is completely indefinite. John does indeed put the entry into Jerusalem on Mark's day, but does not follow the passage of the early days of the week; nor does he actually state how many days the arrest and trial of Jesus took.

Appendix 2 gives a couple of maps to illustrate the dramatic difference between the first and the second half of Mark's gospel, as regards the journeying of Jesus. To me the pattern seems to illustrate how Jesus fulfils the prophecy of the Servant. For a long time he is the sharp sword hidden in the shadow of God's hand, the arrow sharpened and ready in the quiver; then suddenly the right moment of action arrives and he goes straight to the target.

Chapter 16

scattered, the passover lamb slaughtered, Jerusalem doomed, the King of the Judeans crucified, the body of Jesus broken and the blood all shed, the sun darkened. . . . What could be the point of such a catalogue unless the apostles are now preaching with rock-like confidence the tree of life, the living temple, the little ones with free access to God, the flock reunited, the Lamb risen, the new Jerusalem, the King of kings, the body and blood of Christ as the fruit of the tree, the eternal sun risen, never to set again?

All the main elements of the resurrection story are there in Mark: that Jesus of Nazareth died, for our sins, in accordance with the scriptures (witnesses are named); that he was buried (witnesses are named); that he rose, on the third day, as he himself had foretold through his knowledge of the scriptures; that there was a divine message for all the disciples and in particular for Peter; that there were witnesses to the empty tomb; that the main witnesses throughout were women. The message that Jesus of Nazareth 'is risen, he is not here' is stated in biblical language to be a message direct from God, allowing for no possible doubt — even though the women themselves had not seen the risen Jesus at that moment.

Why then does Mark leave the gospel there, without detailing how this witness or that witness saw Jesus risen? If we think of this gospel as Peter's gospel before it was ever Mark's, then a number of reasons can be found. Peter in preaching the Good News from Pentecost onwards never ceased to preach Jesus risen and seen to be risen. But Peter was usually preaching as one who had seen the risen Lord to those who had not: 'without having seen him, you love him', as it says in Peter's First Letter. The gospel of Mark leaves the story of Peter at the last moment before he saw Jesus for himself. Peter on that morning had to take the word of three women, that his Lord was risen. In order to convert people, Peter preached what he had seen; in order to console people and in order to initiate them into the Christian mysteries, he remembered instead how once he too had to take the resurrection on trust.

'Without having seen him you love him; though you do not now see him you believe in him and rejoice with unutterable and exalted joy' (1 Peter 1:8). One could go on to say that the ending of St Mark's gospel expresses just such a joy, a joy that rendered the women speechless and awestruck. The last sentence of the deadly thing, it will not hurt them; they will lay their hands on the sick, and they will recover.'

¹⁹So then the Lord Jesus, after he had spoken to them, was taken up into heaven, and sat down at the right hand of God. ²⁰And they went forth and preached everywhere, while the Lord worked with them and confirmed the message by the signs that attended it. Amen.

[Note: *Other ancient authorities add after verse 8 this shorter alternative ending.*]
But they reported briefly to Peter and those with him all that they had been told. And after this, Jesus himself sent out by means of them, from east to west, the sacred and imperishable proclamation of eternal salvation.

* * *

The ending of Mark's gospel is a matter of some dispute. I take the line, well supported by many gospel commentators, that Mark meant to end it where it ends, at our Chapter 16, verse 8. Verses 9–20 were added early on by another hand: they are canonical and inspired, but not written by Mark. Likewise the other short alternative ending given in our text is not by Mark. What seems to have troubled those who added on extra verses is that unlike the other evangelists St Mark does not give us an appearance of Jesus himself, but only the divinely inspired message of the young man, that Jesus is risen.

The witness to the resurrection in Mark's gospel does not depend simply on that message. There are built in to the text of the gospel dozens of indications that the gospel was written in the light of Jesus' resurrection. For instance, Peter and James and John were told to tell no one what they had seen on the mountain, until the Son of man should have risen from the dead. Well, now the story is out, so Peter and James and John must be satisfied that Jesus is risen. Again, there is the fact that Jesus is identified so closely in Mark's gospel with the prophesied Servant of Yahweh: without the glory at the end of the Servant's story, Jesus could not have qualified as being the Servant. And — to me most telling of all — what would be the point in Mark's telling us of so many things falling to pieces, unless it is to contrast them with the re-created forms of the same? The fig tree withered, the temple to be destroyed, the Holy of Holies exposed, the flock

CHAPTER 16

---
*

AND when the sabbath was past, Mary Magdalene, and Mary the mother of James, and Salome, bought spices, so that they might go and anoint him. ²And very early on the first day of the week they went to the tomb when the sun had risen. ³And they were saying to one another, 'Who will roll away the stone for us from the door of the tomb?' ⁴And looking up, they saw that the stone was rolled back; for it was very large. ⁵And entering the tomb, they saw a young man sitting on the right side, dressed in a white robe; and they were amazed. ⁶And he said to them, 'Do not be amazed; you seek Jesus of Nazareth, who was crucified. He has risen, he is not here; see the place where they laid him. ⁷But go, tell his disciples and Peter that he is going before you to Galilee; there you will see him, as he told you.' ⁸And they went out and fled from the tomb; for trembling and astonishment had come upon them; and they said nothing to any one, for they were afraid.

* * *

[Note: *Other texts and versions add as 16:9–20 the following passage.*]
⁹Now when he rose early on the first day of the week, he appeared first to Mary Magdalene, from whom he had cast out seven demons. ¹⁰She went and told those who had been with him, as they mourned and wept. ¹¹But when they heard that he was alive and had been seen by her, they would not believe it.

¹²After this he appeared in another form to two of them, as they were walking into the country. ¹³And they went back and told the rest, but they did not believe them.

¹⁴Afterwards he appeared to the eleven themselves as they sat at table; and he upbraided them for their unbelief and hardness of heart, because they had not believed those who saw him after he had risen. ¹⁵And he said to them, 'Go into all the world and preach the gospel to the whole creation. ¹⁶He who believes and is baptized will be saved; but he who does not believe will be condemned. ¹⁷And these signs will accompany those who believe: in my name they will cast out demons; they will speak in new tongues; they will pick up serpents, and if they drink any

am a child of God. Not only that, I am descended by faith from a long line of kings, starting with King David.'

And since all the second half of Mark's gospel has been pointing to the blood of Christ in the Eucharist, as the first half of the gospel was pointing to the bread, so do I say of the wine in the Eucharist, 'Truly this is the Son of God, this is the blood of the divine one. His body too is good, is divine, but the divinity was hidden till he shed his blood in a love beyond the power of a mere human being.' 'By this divine wine, feed and strengthen the power that is in me to do the impossible, to love as God alone loves.'

Mark lists the witnesses to Jesus' death and the burial of his body. Within three days that temple will be rebuilt.

Chapter 15

Verses 33–38

When Mark was writing his gospel, already he and Peter and thousands of others had received not only faith in Jesus but the power to love Jesus under trial and persecution, the power which was beyond them at the time of Jesus' crucifixion. So we are not going beyond our rights in praying about *being on the cross with Jesus* as well as watching his death from below. In faith, and with the first gift of the Holy Spirit, we adore him on the cross. With love, and with the second gift of the Holy Spirit, we join any sufferings of our own to his, for him to use as his own. No matter how low in heart we sink, we are still in his company when we say to his Father and ours, 'My God, my God, why have you forsaken me?' What Peter at first failed to do, what the centurion will do as a pure gift of God, this is open to anyone now Jesus has opened the door.

'No wonder, Jesus, that you died with a cry of triumph on your lips. Just when human nature would judge all was lost for ever, you knew in dying that all was gained for ever. By your death you tore down the last of the barriers that human beings had erected to keep God's little ones from coming to him and his mercy. Gate after gate, guard after guard, permission after permission, and even then only carefully selected people could approach the throne of God on behalf of the rest outside. But now by your death any little child, any poor sinner can come straight to God. How can I, how can we ever thank you enough?! As we use the right of approach to God which you have won for us, may we never forget we do so through you, the Son of God who alone could have torn that curtain in two.'

Verses 39–47

The intention of Mark's gospel clearly is that we the readers should echo the brave statement of the centurion. We say, to God and to anyone else who may be listening, 'Truly this man Jesus was the Son of God'. In the light of the resurrection which is to come in the gospel we add, 'Truly this man Jesus is and always will be the Son of God'. In addition, we prepare to say to anyone who might challenge us, 'And Jesus is my brother; so that I too remember always that I am a son (a daughter) of the same Father. Make me always sensitive to his will, able to find it in my heart and ready to do it. May I, may all of us in our world, be creative and not destructive. Where destruction has happened, give us hands that heal and mend. Show us by what mystery you employ your death to cure the whole world for ever, that we may work along with the mystery.'

Verses 16–21

When Jesus spoke up for who he was at his trial, there was 'the kingdom of God come with power', since only the power of God can recognize and acknowledge the Son of man before men. Since Jesus is who he says he is, the Son of man coming in glory, then to him an everlasting kingdom is given. 'Help me, Jesus, to recognize your human and divine royalty beneath all this mockery and wanton cruelty. No wonder people are frightened, and are unwilling to let the power of God enter their lives! When horrible things happen to me, I do not change, I hope I do not become less lovable; so why should I be afraid of you in your distress? Use, if you will, the times when I have to help you carry your cross whether I like it or not, to teach me to love the one whose cross I help to carry.'

Verses 22–32

Jesus is taken outside the city walls and killed, like the beloved son in his own parable who was taken outside the vineyard. The word of God, the seed of God's word, if it finds no room in one place, finds its way to another place and flourishes there. If Jerusalem will not be the bride, then 'outside the city' will become the bride, the whole wide pagan world; and from the new Jerusalem the old Jerusalem is not excluded. The Syrophoenician woman had great faith; the centurion will show divine love completely beyond his own powers. 'Jesus, I do not wish to turn you away simply because you died a terrible death. Open my heart to welcome your word. As the old Irish prayer has it, "Some fruit from the tree of thy passion fall on us tonight".'

Chapter 15
SUGGESTIONS FOR PRAYER

Verses 1–5

In this chapter, along with so many other things being re-created as the week of re-creation goes by, now the kingdom is being remade as the Kingdom of God. First of all we may believe in Jesus as our King and offer him homage and thanks. We want our homage to be sincere and the very opposite of the mockery the soldiers gave him; we want to thank him our King for giving his life for us his people, the shepherd for laying down his life for us his sheep, for acting like our servant though he is Lord of us all. I admit that I am no better than the least of his people, yet he died rather than have me excluded from his Kingdom.

Secondly we pray for the second gift of this gospel, not faith now but love. I do not want to feel comfortable with an easy life while Jesus my elder brother the King suffers indignity. 'May I always admit, Jesus, that I am a child of God, sharing your divine blood; may I always admit that Mary is my mother in faith as she is your mother, making me royal in origin as well as divine. May I accept life's trials and indignities peacefully, sharing all my troubles with you, Jesus. You have no body now on earth but ours: I give mine to you, for you to go in me the way you went in your own earthly life. I do not ask for extra sorrows unless you give me extra strength, but you may certainly use any sorrows of mine as your own.'

This would be a good place to read over prayerfully the fourth Servant Song (Isaiah 52:13 – 53:12). We might remember that Peter does not appear in this Chapter 15 of St Mark, but Peter after the resurrection is fascinated by the Servant Songs of Isaiah and other prophecies of the suffering Christ, as we can see from the First Letter of Peter and the things Peter says in Acts.

Verses 6–15

'Jesus, you are the Son of your Father, of your "Abba"; you are always sensitive to his will as your only reason for acting, and you are the Author of Life, the one through whom all things were created and in whom all things are restored. Grant that I may are the Christ'. Jesus on trial proclaims the whole of the gospel, 'Yes, I am the Christ, the Son of the Blessed'. Peter could not find the strength to make the second response, about the Son of God. It was left to a pagan, a Roman officer, to speak out the divinity of Jesus in the face of a hostile crowd, just as it had been another 'nobody', a blind beggar, who first called Jesus 'Son of David' and kept on doing so when the crowd told him to be quiet. This saying of the centurion is not simply an act of faith: as I have tried to show through these pages, the centurion's words are an act of love. He expresses faith, yes, but in the face of a hostile crowd; he believes and speaks out when it would be a lot more comfortable to keep quiet. We will never know just what was in the centurion's mind: perhaps he contrasted the serenity of Jesus with the malice and envy of his persecutors. Picking up words from them, in his admiration he could say, 'If one side of this deadly dispute is true and the other is false, I prefer to side with this man on the cross: truly, he died with a cry of triumph and I believe he was what he said he was'. So he speaks his mind plainly, and does not care who hears him. The gift of love is given to him freely. He is as it were the first-fruits of Jesus' death; and he is a man in charge of a hundred others.

Since here in the crucifixion we have most undoubtedly the body and blood of Christ, we may note that it was when the (divine) blood of Jesus was all shed that the centurion was inspired to proclaim the divinity of the whole person. If a man sheds from his body all his blood as an act of divine love, then divine he is; and not just his blood but his body as well is now revealed as divine. The new temple will last forever, always fruitful.

Certainly, in the shedding of Christ's blood we are in the realm of love everlasting. As St Ignatius of Antioch put it: 'Take a fresh grip on your faith (the very flesh of the Lord) and your love (the life blood of Jesus Christ)'. And in another place: 'I am glad for the bread of God, even the flesh of Jesus Christ, who is the seed of David; and for my drink I crave that blood of his which is love imperishable'. Ignatius's other saying, 'Faith is the beginning, and love is the end', sums up the two halves of Mark's gospel very neatly.

Chapter 15

from up north, since they could be so easily stirred up against Jesus by the chief priests.

The soldiers led Jesus out to crucify him, to the place called Golgotha, outside the city walls. He refused the wine mixed with myrrh, which was a kind of anaesthetic: he must have wanted to know what he was doing and saying right to the end. He found himself in the kind of company he had chosen for preference over the past few years, with a robber on each side of him. Now Jesus was at last 'the fruit' on the tree, his body and his flowing blood there on the cross, being offered back to the owner of the vineyard. Unlike his disciples, he had completely resisted 'the birds of the air, the rocky ground, the thorns and thistles' and is fruitful 'for many', that is, for all humanity. Jesus has given back all the fruit to the owner: there is nothing left for himself. 'He cannot save himself.' The temple of his body will be completely destroyed before it is rebuilt. Peter and the others will be fruitful in their turn, but only as a result of what Jesus is suffering here; they could not be fruitful on their own. In this chapter of Mark, for the first time Peter is nowhere mentioned, nowhere to be found. Many of the women are there as witnesses, close by or far off, but none of the men till after Jesus' death.

When Jesus quoting a psalm says, 'My God, my God, why have you forsaken me?' he addresses God for the one and only time not as 'Father'. Usually, as we know from the other gospels, he changed 'God' or 'Yahweh' to 'Father' even when he was quoting from a psalm. We can surely take this as a sign that at this moment, at the ninth hour, Jesus was totally emptied of self, and felt himself totally empty. All that the bystanders did about it was to offer him a sponge full of vinegar: sour grapes. Nevertheless, the loud cry that Jesus gave before dying was a cry of triumph. The curtain of the temple, shrouding off the Holy of Holies and the mercy seat within, was torn in two. Now through Jesus anyone may have access to God himself and his mercy. From now on the tent of meeting between God and his children will be the body and blood of Christ.

The centurion saw how Jesus died and said, 'Truly this man was the Son of God'. Here we have one of the key sentences of Mark's gospel, the gospel of Jesus Christ the Son of God. Peter half way through the gospel provided the response of faith, 'You

'As soon as it was morning . . .' Mark is still counting off each evening and morning of the week of re-creation. Now on this morning Jesus is handed over to Pilate; Pilate asks him, 'You are the King of the Judeans?' Jesus replies, 'You have said so'. First, I do not think enough note has been taken of the fact that the people in question are the Judeans, not the rest of the Jewish people. Jesus has come on purpose to the capital of David's old kingdom, which happens to be in Judea. Secondly, in agreeing that he is King of the Judeans, Jesus is admitting to his human origins as descendant of David through his, Jesus', own mother Mary. Before the chief priests, elders and scribes Jesus has acknowledged God as his own Father: now here before Pilate, in effect he acknowledges Mary as his mother. Apart from these two claims, about his Father and his mother, he says nothing at his trial, according to Mark. He is silent as a sheep before its shearers. Mark's gospel would lead us to believe that Jesus' power to speak up in these circumstances was at least partly a result of his prayer in the garden: 'the flesh is weak', and Jesus had flesh, so Jesus had to pray.

Thirdly, about the King, we might notice how sudden is the appearance of this theme: five or six times between now and his death Jesus is called King of the Judeans, once (by the chief priests and the scribes) the King of Israel, and in addition he has a crown, a purple cloak and mock homage done to him. Up to now the most he has been called in this line is Son of David, and that only by one man. The last of the main great strands of prophecy about the Christ is falling into place: Mark has shown us Jesus as Shepherd, Jesus as Son of man, Jesus as Servant; now while the other prophecies become ever more true, Jesus appears as King. Not Herod's sort of king, not the sort of king Pilate represents, but the king who is truly shepherd and servant of his people, even to the extent of laying down his life for them.

Mark has already given us the clues to work out for ourselves the meaning of the word Barabbas. 'Bar', he told us earlier, means 'Son of', and 'Abba' means 'Father'. So Barabbas is the son of his father, whoever his father may be, and a rebel and a murderer. Jesus, by direct contrast, is the Son of God his Father, and obedient, and the one who brings back to life. The crowd here are presumably Judeans rather than supporters of Jesus

Chapter 15

myrrh; but he did not take it. ²⁴And they crucified him, and divided his garments among them, casting lots for them, to decide what each should take. ²⁵And it was the third hour, when they crucified him. ²⁶And the inscription of the charge against him read, 'The King of the Jews.' ²⁷And with him they crucified two robbers, one on his right and one on his left. ²⁹And those who passed by derided him, wagging their heads, and saying, 'Aha! You who would destroy the temple and build it in three days, ³⁰save yourself, and come down from the cross!' ³¹So also the chief priests mocked him to one another with the scribes, saying, 'He saved others; he cannot save himself. ³²Let the Christ, the King of Israel, come down now from the cross, that we may see and believe.' Those who were crucified with him also reviled him. [Note: *Other ancient authorities insert verse 28*: And the scripture was fulfilled which says, 'He was reckoned with the transgressors'.]

³³And when the sixth hour had come, there was darkness over the whole earth until the ninth hour. ³⁴And at the ninth hour Jesus cried with a loud voice, 'Eloi, Eloi, lama sabachthani?' which means, 'My God, my God, why hast thou forsaken me?' ³⁵And some of the bystanders hearing it said, 'Behold, he is calling Elijah.' ³⁶And one ran and, filling a sponge full of vinegar, put it on a reed and gave it to him to drink, saying, 'Wait, let us see whether Elijah will come to take him down.' ³⁷And Jesus uttered a loud cry, and breathed his last. ³⁸And the curtain of the temple was torn in two, from top to bottom. ³⁹And when the centurion, who stood facing him, saw that he thus cried out and breathed his last, he said, 'Truly this man was the Son of God!'

⁴⁰There were also women looking on from afar, among whom were Mary Magdalene, and Mary the mother of James the younger and of Joses, and Salome, ⁴¹who, when he was in Galilee, followed him, and ministered to him; and also many other women who came up with him to Jerusalem.

⁴²And when evening had come, since it was the day of Preparation, that is, the day before the sabbath, ⁴³Joseph of Arimathea, a respected member of the council, who was also himself looking for the kingdom of God, took courage and went to Pilate, and asked for the body of Jesus. ⁴⁴And Pilate wondered if he were already dead; and summoning the centurion, he asked him whether he was already dead. ⁴⁵And when he learned from the centurion that he was dead, he granted the body to Joseph. ⁴⁶And he bought a linen shroud, and taking him down, wrapped him in the linen shroud, and laid him in a tomb which had been hewn out of the rock; and he rolled a stone against the door of the tomb. ⁴⁷Mary Magdalene and Mary the mother of Joses saw where he was laid.

CHAPTER 15

*

AND as soon as it was morning the chief priests, with the elders and scribes, and the whole council held a consultation; and they bound Jesus and led him away and delivered him to Pilate. ²And Pilate asked him, 'Are you the King of the Jews?' And he answered him, 'You have said so.' ³And the chief priests accused him of many things. ⁴And Pilate again asked him, 'Have you no answer to make? See how many charges they bring against you.' ⁵But Jesus made no further answer, so that Pilate wondered.

⁶Now at the feast he used to release for them one prisoner for whom they asked. ⁷And among the rebels in prison, who had committed murder in the insurrection, there was a man called Barabbas. ⁸And the crowd came up and began to ask Pilate to do as he was wont to do for them. ⁹And he answered them, 'Do you want me to release for you the King of the Jews?' ¹⁰For he perceived that it was out of envy that the chief priests had delivered him up. ¹¹But the chief priests stirred up the crowd to have him release for them Barabbas instead. ¹²And Pilate again said to them, 'Then what shall I do with the man whom you call the King of the Jews?' ¹³And they cried out again, 'Crucify him.' ¹⁴And Pilate said to them, 'Why, what evil has he done?' But they shouted all the more, 'Crucify him.' ¹⁵So Pilate, wishing to satisfy the crowd, released for them Barabbas; and having scourged Jesus, he delivered him to be crucified.

¹⁶And the soldiers led him away inside the palace (that is, the praetorium); and they called together the whole battalion. ¹⁷And they clothed him in a purple cloak, and plaiting a crown of thorns they put it on him. ¹⁸And they began to salute him, 'Hail, King of the Jews!' ¹⁹And they struck his head with a reed, and spat upon him, and they knelt down in homage to him. ²⁰And when they had mocked him, they stripped him of the purple cloak, and put his own clothes on him. And they led him out to crucify him.

²¹And they compelled a passer-by, Simon of Cyrene, who was coming in from the country, the father of Alexander and Rufus, to carry his cross. ²²And they brought him to the place called Golgotha (which means the place of a skull). ²³And they offered him wine mingled with

anything to fear from his own weakness. As the Letter of James puts it: 'Your faith is put to the test to make you perfect and thence fully developed' (see James 1:3f.). We pray that we too may have our moments of shame turned into pure gold.

Verses 53–64

Peter enters into temptation, led by his love for Jesus but not aware enough of his own weakness. 'Lead us not into temptation.' Meanwhile Jesus is on trial. What he actually said about the temple was, according to John's gospel, 'Destroy this temple, and in three days I will raise it up', and he spoke of the temple of his body. 'Made with hands' means also 'from the earth', and 'not made with hands' means 'from heaven'. The blood of Jesus was 'not made with hands' at any time, within the context of Mark's gospel, since his Father is God. But the body, and all things created, are to be re-created. I pray for the re-creation of myself and of all people through Christ the Son of the Blessed.

Jesus has the power of his transfiguration, and he has prayed earnestly and long in preparation for this moment. So his blood speaks out in him for who he is: the Christ, the Son of the Blessed. The Holy Spirit speaks in him, as Jesus promised would happen. At the same time he takes under his wing all his adopted brothers and sisters, no matter how unworthy they seem. Jesus dies for me. I pray never to forget.

Verse 65

Readers might like to turn here to the third of the Servant Songs, in Isaiah 50:4–9, and compare it prayerfully with the scenes at the trial of Jesus.

Verses 66–72

Peter, on the other hand, is warming himself at the fire. He must have been very mortified to have failed to answer the challenge of a maid. The whole gospel of Mark seems to express Peter's delight at being one of those who were with Jesus, yet here he is denying it. The 'dumb and deaf spirit', of the kind that can only be cast out by prayer, had taken hold of him. And the wonder of it is, that once Peter the Rock has broken down like this at the fire, there remains a truly precious stone or metal which can never after be corrupted. Having done what he did, and then being forgiven by Jesus in the resurrection, he knew there were no bounds to his Master's forgiveness. He no longer had

Chapter 14

I pray besides that I may not boast of my loyalty, nor of anything else, lest I create even more sadness for myself when I fall to temptation. The energy spent in boasting would be better spent on watchfulness.

Verses 32–42

Jesus takes his companions to the Mount of Olives, to a place called Gethsemane ('the olive press'). Here, if you will, Jesus too was crushed. We can take comfort in seeing the only-begotten Son of God filled with dread and distress, because God certainly loved him. So when we the adopted children feel in our turn distress and trouble, we need never think God does not love us any more. Jesus was not being punished, nor was he being picked on. No more are we being punished or picked on, either. This we believe.

The three, Peter and James and John, who were with him on the mountain and at the raising of Jairus's daughter, are near enough to hear the perfect prayer that Peter should have prayed if only he knew how at the time: 'Abba, Father . . .' There are four prayers that belong to the second half of the gospel of Mark, prayers that Peter should have prayed, to bring his strength to full power: 'I believe; help my unbelief'; 'Jesus, Son of David, have pity on me'; 'Master, let me see again'; and now, 'Abba, Father, all things are possible to you; remove this cup from me; yet not what I will, but what you will'. I pray these prayers now, and save them as well for all moments of dread, of fear, of temptation.

Verses 43–50

The kiss of Judas reminds us that one who knows another intimately is in the best position to hurt or betray the other. We pray for the strength to love God and our neighbour loyally and for ever — a power which is beyond our own strength.

Verses 51 and 52

We pray to be reclothed in a new garment and live our lives in a new and different way, based on our experience of God's endless forgiveness.

We thank Jesus always for sharing his divine life with us as he took on our human body and human life. A wonderful exchange!

Verses 17–21

Evening came, the Thursday evening by our reckoning. We all shift uneasily in our places as Jesus says that one of our number will betray him. The better we know ourselves, the better we know our own weakness. We pray that our betrayals may be like Peter's rather than like Judas's. Some people in their prayers are moved to plead for pity for Judas himself.

Verses 22–25

The Christian Eucharist has two distinct halves: the liturgy of the word and the liturgy of the action. God's word comes to us, that we are his children; and in return we act lovingly towards him along with his Son. We have seen the beginnings of the liturgy of the word in the first half of the gospel of Mark as Jesus was edged out of the synagogues; now we have the replacement of the covenant, the replacement of the temple sacrifices by the one passover lamb who is Christ. We feel the immense debt we owe to the Jewish tradition, and we feel a great sorrow that the origins of Christianity were in division, not in peace. As Catholics, we are glad that now we may drink the cup again. The bread of the Eucharist gives strength to our awareness of being loved by God our Father along with his Son now so close to us. The cup of the precious blood gives strength to our desire to love God in return for his love, in the way in which we love our brothers and sisters. This covenant is new, because no one has ever dared to call God 'Abba' ('Daddy') before; and God's love in *this* covenant is unconditional. We contemplate these wonderful truths, and others that come to us through our presence at the Eucharist.

Verses 26–31

I pray in sympathy with Jesus my shepherd, who had to be stricken and to lose us all before he could gather us again to himself. As I grow older and as I move from one place to another in my life, I am aware that I too have to leave behind many that I have loved and cared for. I trust that along with Jesus I also one day will see my little flock gathered to me again.

Chapter 14

Peter does not give away that the bystanders recognized him by his Galilean accent. Here, finally, was the fire at which the pure gold was refined from Peter the Rock.

SUGGESTIONS FOR PRAYER

Verses 1 and 2

As we come close to the passion of Jesus, we pray to him as to our passover lamb, in endless gratitude that his blood meant our freedom from slavery. We have moved not simply from being no people to being the people of God, but we have become each of us children of God, brothers and sisters of Jesus himself.

Verses 3–11

This story encourages us to believe that time, money, energy, emotional effort spent upon Jesus are never wasted, and never go unnoticed by him. This is particularly so if we have, so to speak, broken the jar as well as given the ointment: that is, if we have taken a step for him that cannot be recalled. Even without vows or promises for the future, we can all resign the past into his hands. We renew our dedication to him, and refuse to regret it. My story, too, will one day be retold and treasured, in the kingdom of God — this too I believe.

Verses 12–16

This is another story, like the fetching of the colt for Jesus' entry into Jerusalem, which is easy to pray for those who can imagine themselves into the scene. I imagine myself as one of the two going as instructed to prepare the guest room for the passover supper. Scholars argue about whether this was the actual passover supper, on the correct evening, but clearly St Mark sees it as Jesus' passover supper, at which Jesus himself took the place of the passover lamb. To prepare my heart I could reread the original story in Chapter 12 of Exodus.

Some of the early Fathers of the Church see the water which is mixed with the wine at the Eucharist as symbolizing human life. The bread stands for the human body (made with hands); the water, human life; the wine, divine life (not made with hands).

demon had taken him over for the time being. Mark makes sure we know Jesus calls his Father 'Abba', the word used by children as well as by adults. Earlier Mark has shown us Jesus telling the disciples God is 'your Father' — 'your Father will forgive you'. Scholars tell us Jesus would have used the word 'Abba' there, too. When Jesus tells the three companions to pray 'that you may not enter into temptation', he means they should make that the subject of their prayer on this occasion, not simply pray about whatever comes into their heads.

When the crowd came with swords and clubs, 'one of those who stood by drew his sword, and struck the slave of the high priest and cut off his ear'. This neither says nor denies that Peter was the one who drew his sword. Peter was presumably embarrassed later, at having done this.

The young man who fled naked may be Mark himself, but the symbolism behind the story says that the old garment must be left behind, so that the young man may sit at the right hand on Easter Sunday, dressed in a white robe (washed white in the blood of the Lamb, as Christians would say).

On trial Jesus is asked the two questions at the heart of Mark's gospel: Are you the Christ? and Are you the Son of the Blessed? Jesus has the power; Jesus has prayed, so he can answer. Presumably if the temple authorities were expecting the Christ to come some day, then some day someone would answer 'Yes' to those questions, and be right to do so, without blasphemy. The reason why Jesus was held to be blaspheming must have been that his version of the Christ did not tally with what was expected: he had what the authorities considered to be the wrong attitudes to God, to morality, to sinners, to the sick, and so on.

Jesus, in acknowledging God as his Father, was here like a tree giving back the fruit asked for by the owner of the vineyard. Jesus admitted even in the face of extreme hostility that he was God's own Son. Immediately he begins to get the treatment reserved for the Servant, spittle and blows.

In Mark's gospel, Peter is twice said to be 'warming himself'. John's gospel says the same, but adds that it was cold — cold where John was, away from the fire. Luke was not there, but he muses on the story and tells how the light from the fire showed up Peter for who he was. Peter who was given the keys is the one who denied Jesus to a maid in the gateway. In Mark's gospel

Chapter 14

incidentally it was normal in that time and place to mix in water when drinking wine.

Before the Eucharist, Jesus talks about his betrayer. The work of the betrayer is inevitable if the scriptures are to be fulfilled. It is not so much the Son of man who has to go in this way according to the scriptures, as the Servant and the Shepherd; but Jesus has identified the three figures in himself, so the Son of man must go — much to the shock of the Twelve and the other disciples. Jesus then says what must surely be the hardest saying in the gospels: 'It would have been better for that man if he had never been born'. We need to remember that Christian churches have never said that anyone is in hell, not even Judas. We are not told when Judas left the supper.

Then, the Eucharist. First, Jesus took bread, and blessed, and broke it, and gave it to them, and said, 'Take; this is my body'. As with the first half of the gospel, all is love for the Twelve, there are no overtones of death. But then he took a cup, and when he had given thanks he gave it to them, and they all drank of it. And he said to them, 'This is my blood of the (new) covenant, which is poured out for many'. There by the meaning of the words the body is in one place, the blood in another, shed from the body. In mystery, the passover lamb has been sacrificed, as it will be in physical reality the next day. As the synagogue worship was replaced for Jesus' followers on the hillsides and seashores in the early days, so now the temple sacrifice is being made new, along with the temple itself, as part of this week of re-creation. All will be complete on the Sunday morning, when Jesus will drink the wine new in the kingdom of God.

They go, without Judas, to the Mount of Olives. The flock of the Shepherd will be scattered, but the flock too will be re-created once this week is over, gathered together and following Jesus again. Like the fig tree, like the temple, like the sacrifice of the lamb, like Jerusalem herself, the Shepherd and the flock will have to lose their life in order to find it again in the kingdom of God. Peter makes his boast of never denying Jesus, not even 'if I must die with you'.

At Gethsemane, Jesus prays. In spite of his distress, he prays for three hours. On his trial, he will be able to speak up for who he is. Peter does not pray, and will be as if a dumb and deaf

The first verse of this chapter announces the Wednesday: it introduces for a Christian reader the idea of Jesus as the passover lamb. Also, within the context of Mark's gospel on its own, the verse hints that here will be the pure teaching of Jesus, as opposed to the leaven of the Pharisees and the leaven of Herod which we saw in the first half of the gospel. Here will be pure sacrifice, and true kingship. The way Mark has arranged the story of this day seems to mean that the chief priests had decided to wait till after the feast to arrest Jesus; but then Judas's reaction to the anointing at Bethany was to go and offer to betray Jesus, so the arrest was brought forward.

Simon's meal at which Jesus was anointed may be read as being a supper, thus marking the evening of Wednesday in Holy Week. In our version of the gospel text, with Peter as the speaker, Peter excludes himself from the number of those who complained about waste of money. If we were to do the same with Matthew's gospel and make Peter the speaker there also, we would have Peter including himself among the complainers. This is just one of many places where the 'trick' of making Peter the speaker works for Mark's gospel, but not for the other gospels. As for the value of the ointment, if a denarius was a day's wages for a labourer, then as I write (1988) the ointment would have been worth something like £6,000. One may suspect that Jesus was not only being anointed for burial, but anointed king as well, since Mark only proclaims the kingship of Jesus openly in his passion and death.

Judas was one of the Twelve. Mark reminds us five times in all that Judas was one of the Twelve, and twice besides calls him 'the betrayer'. This seems to me to come from one who was himself one of the Twelve: a natural way for Peter to speak, but less natural for Mark. The chief priests promised to give Judas money. By implication of the evangelist, the blood of Christ is worth more than £6,000, worth more than any money. It is precious or priceless (see 1 Peter 1:19).

Next, the first day of Unleavened Bread, when they sacrificed the passover lamb — Thursday morning has come. Our version of the story of the preparation of the upper room agrees with that of Luke's gospel in that both make Peter one of the two who went ahead to prepare. A man with a jar of water leads the way:

Chapter 14

seized him. ⁴⁷But one of those who stood by drew his sword, and struck the slave of the high priest and cut off his ear. ⁴⁸And Jesus said to them, 'Have you come out as against a robber, with swords and clubs to capture me? ⁴⁹Day after day I was with you in the temple teaching, and you did not seize me. But let the scriptures be fulfilled.' ⁵⁰*And we all forsook him, and fled.*

⁵¹And a young man followed him, with nothing but a linen cloth about his body; and they seized him, ⁵²but he left the linen cloth and ran away naked.

⁵³And they led Jesus to the high priest; and all the chief priests and the elders and the scribes were assembled. ⁵⁴*And I had followed him at a distance, right into the courtyard of the high priest; and I was sitting with the guards, and warming myself at the fire.* ⁵⁵Now the chief priests and the whole council sought testimony against Jesus to put him to death; but they found none. ⁵⁶For many bore false witness against him, and their witness did not agree. ⁵⁷And some stood up and bore false witness against him, saying, ⁵⁸'We heard him say, "I will destroy this temple that is made with hands, and in three days I will build another, not made with hands."' ⁵⁹Yet not even so did their testimony agree. ⁶⁰And the high priest stood up in the midst, and asked Jesus, 'Have you no answer to make? What is it that these men testify against you?' ⁶¹But he was silent and made no answer. Again the high priest asked him, 'Are you the Christ, the Son of the Blessed?' ⁶²And Jesus said, 'I am; and you will see the Son of man sitting at the right hand of Power, and coming with the clouds of heaven.' ⁶³And the high priest tore his mantle, and said, 'Why do we still need witnesses? ⁶⁴You have heard his blasphemy. What is your decision?' And they all condemned him as deserving death. ⁶⁵And some began to spit on him, and to cover his face, and to strike him, saying to him, 'Prophesy!' And the guards received him with blows.

⁶⁶*And as I was below in the courtyard, one of the maids of the high priest came;* ⁶⁷*and seeing me warming myself, she looked at me, and said, 'You also were with the Nazarene, Jesus.'* ⁶⁸*But I denied it, saying, 'I neither know nor understand what you mean.' And I went out into the gateway.* ⁶⁹*And the maid saw me, and began again to say to the bystanders, 'This man is one of them.'* ⁷⁰*But again I denied it. And after a little while again the bystanders said to me, 'Certainly you are one of them; for you are a Galilean.'* ⁷¹*But I began to invoke a curse on myself and to swear, 'I do not know this man of whom you speak.'* ⁷²*And immediately the cock crowed a second time. And I remembered how Jesus had said to me, 'Before the cock crows twice, you will deny me three times.' And I broke down and wept.*

*   *   *

one who is dipping bread in the same dish with me. ²¹For the Son of man goes as it is written of him, but woe to that man by whom the Son of man is betrayed! It would have been better for that man if he had not been born.'

²²And as we were eating, he took bread, and blessed, and broke it, and gave it to us, and said, 'Take; this is my body.' ²³And he took a cup, and when he had given thanks he gave it to us, and we all drank of it. ²⁴And he said to us, 'This is my blood of the covenant, which is poured out for many. ²⁵Truly, I say to you, I shall not drink again of the fruit of the vine until that day when I drink it new in the kingdom of God.' [Note: In verse 24, other ancient authorities insert *'new'* before *'covenant'*.]

²⁶And when we had sung a hymn, we went out to the Mount of Olives. ²⁷And Jesus said to us, 'You will all fall away; for it is written, "I will strike the shepherd, and the sheep will be scattered." ²⁸But after I am raised up, I will go before you to Galilee.' ²⁹I said to him, 'Even though they all fall away, I will not.' ³⁰And Jesus said to me, 'Truly, I say to you, this very night, before the cock crows twice, you will deny me three times.' ³¹But I said vehemently, 'If I must die with you, I will not deny you.' And we all said the same.

³²And we went to a place which was called Gethsemane; and he said to us, 'Sit here, while I pray.' ³³And he took with him me and James and John, and began to be greatly distressed and troubled. ³⁴And he said to us, 'My soul is very sorrowful, even to death; remain here, and watch.' ³⁵And going a little farther, he fell on the ground and prayed that, if it were possible, the hour might pass from him. ³⁶And he said, 'Abba, Father, all things are possible to thee; remove this cup from me; yet not what I will, but what thou wilt.' ³⁷And he came and found us sleeping, and he said to me, 'Simon, are you asleep? Could you not watch one hour? ³⁸Watch and pray that you may not enter into temptation; the spirit indeed is willing, but the flesh is weak.' ³⁹And again he went away and prayed, saying the same words. ⁴⁰And again he came and found us sleeping, for our eyes were very heavy; and we did not know what to answer him. ⁴¹And he came the third time, and said to us, 'Are you still sleeping and taking your rest? It is enough; the hour has come; the Son of man is betrayed into the hands of sinners. ⁴²Rise, let us be going; see, my betrayer is at hand.'

⁴³And immediately, while he was still speaking, Judas came, one of the twelve, and with him a crowd with swords and clubs, from the chief priests and the scribes and the elders. ⁴⁴Now the betrayer had given them a sign, saying, 'The one I shall kiss is the man; seize him and lead him away safely.' ⁴⁵And when he came, he went up to him at once, and said, 'Master!' And he kissed him. ⁴⁶And they laid hands on him and

CHAPTER 14
---- * ----

IT was now two days before the Passover and the feast of Unleavened Bread. And the chief priests and the scribes were seeking how to arrest him by stealth, and kill him; ²for they said, 'Not during the feast, lest there be a tumult of the people.'

³And while he was at Bethany in the house of Simon the leper, as he sat at table, a woman came with an alabaster jar of ointment of pure nard, very costly, and she broke the jar and poured it over his head. ⁴But there were some who said to themselves indignantly, 'Why was the ointment thus wasted? ⁵For this ointment might have been sold for more than three hundred denarii, and given to the poor.' And they reproached her. ⁶But Jesus said, 'Let her alone; why do you trouble her? She has done a beautiful thing to me. ⁷For you always have the poor with you, and whenever you will, you can do good to them; but you will not always have me. ⁸She has done what she could; she has anointed my body beforehand for burying. ⁹And truly, I say to you, wherever the gospel is preached in the whole world, what she has done will be told in memory of her.'

¹⁰Then Judas Iscariot, who was one of the twelve, went to the chief priests in order to betray him to them. ¹¹And when they heard it they were glad, and promised to give him money. And he sought an opportunity to betray him.

¹²*And on the first day of Unleavened Bread, when they sacrificed the passover lamb, we said to him, 'Where will you have us go and prepare for you to eat the passover?'* ¹³*And he sent two of us, and said to us, 'Go into the city, and a man carrying a jar of water will meet you; follow him,* ¹⁴*and wherever he enters, say to the householder, "The Teacher says, Where is my guest room, where I am to eat the passover with my disciples?"* ¹⁵*And he will show you a large upper room furnished and ready; there prepare for us.'* ¹⁶*And we set out and went to the city, and found it as he had told us; and we prepared the passover.*

¹⁷*And when it was evening he came with the twelve.* ¹⁸*And as we were at table eating, Jesus said, 'Truly, I say to you, one of you will betray me, one who is eating with me.'* ¹⁹*We began to be sorrowful, and to say to him one after another, 'Is it I?'* ²⁰*He said to us, 'It is one of the twelve,*

faced by an ordeal too big for me. If I have not prayed, let me not stumble into situations I cannot cope with, but give me the humility to stand back and let somebody stronger do it instead. I ask this through Christ my saviour. Amen.' 'Lord Jesus, if ever I do let you down, may I remember how Peter let you down, as you knew he would; yet you still loved him. By his trial you turned him into a precious stone, one of the elect no longer able to be deceived. Please do the same for me, now that I recognize myself as the least of your servants.'

Chapter 13

Verses 20–23

The elect, it seems, cannot be led astray for long. 'We thank you, God our Father, for ensuring that there will always be those among us, shepherds and other leaders, who have the gift of knowing your voice without fear of deceit. By them the sheep, the followers, will be kept in the right paths; because of the elect the sorrows will be less for the rest of humanity. Help us always to recognize your chosen leaders.'

Verses 24–27

In these seven days of re-creation which we know as Holy Week, not only is the fig tree re-created in the cross with the body and blood of Christ, not only is the temple re-created, not only is there a new Jerusalem, but there is to be a new heaven and a new earth as well, and a new sun and a new moon and new stars. As children whose father on the side of Mary is Abraham, we will ourselves be numerous as the stars, a number that none but God can count, each with our own new name. We marvel at this, and thank our heavenly Father. We notice that in a sense it has already come to pass, since the heavens were darkened for the three hours Jesus was on the cross.

Verses 28–31

'Jesus, you the king came to your own city, you the bridegroom came to your own bride. She rejected you and cast you out. In a mysterious way her very rejection of you made the whole world into your bride, not excluding Jerusalem herself. The word of God is always fruitful.'

'I am aware that you are always close to my gates, the gates of my senses. Since your death on the cross has brought you to the whole world including me, may I welcome you wholeheartedly into the "city" that is me. With every sign of summer that I see in my world, may I be ready and waiting for you to appear.'

Verses 32–37

The warnings to 'Take heed and watch' are best accepted with Peter in mind. 'Father, please give me the wisdom to pray when

Verses 4–8

In this gospel of Mark ever since Peter's words of faith Jesus has been, in one way or another, warning Peter and the others against over-confidence. Now explicitly he warns them (and all of us) to be careful. Even someone who has faith and has once 'seen' and 'heard' can be deceived later on, as Peter would be deceived in following Jesus into the courtyard of the high priest. We pray for the gift of discernment, the gift of recognizing the voice of Jesus from other voices when the world turns against us or things go badly wrong.

Verses 9–13

Jesus warns us that strife and persecution do not mean that we are on the wrong track. When other people turn against us for doing what we knew was the right thing for us to do, we may take comfort from Jesus' words. Persecution may take quite simple forms: teachers find their religion lessons provoke opposition, parents find their children want to give up coming to church, people in many walks of life find they are picked on for trying to be honest. 'Holy Spirit, my answers to those who challenge my faith may be halting or even nothing but silence — do you please speak through my poor words, speak through my very silence! May I not reproach myself afterwards for having said the wrong thing, since it was you who spoke for me. I offer my discomfort, as Jesus offered his pain, for the very people who are causing it. Make us all one. And when I am incapable of praying properly, do you Holy Spirit speak for me there as well, in my silence, even in my boredom which is in truth nothing but homesickness.'

Verses 14–19

The temple would be desecrated before it was destroyed. 'Lord Jesus, when you re-create us as temples of your everlasting presence, remove from our memory, if it seems good to you, any pain and horror and desecration that there may have been in our lives here on earth. May we never have to undergo more than we can stand. Grant this in your pity.'

Chapter 13

8:38, 'of him will the Son of man also be ashamed, when he comes in the glory of his Father with the holy angels'; and 11:25, 'so that your Father also who is in heaven may forgive you your trespasses'.

The last short parable again has echoes of Peter and his immediate future. Peter is, in Christian tradition, the doorkeeper, the keeper of the keys. Peter in the Acts of the Apostles and in the First Letter constantly uses the theme of Jesus as Servant and ourselves as servants too. Peter did not watch or pray. He slept and was surprised by events. He was boasting in the evening of the day, sleeping at midnight, betraying his Master at cockcrow, and weeping bitter tears in the morning. What is more, the final sentence of this chapter is Jesus' answer to a question put on the lips of Peter by St Luke. In Luke's gospel Peter listens to the parable about the servants and asks, 'Lord, are you telling this parable for us or for all?' (Luke 12:41). Here in Mark's gospel is Jesus' answer: 'What I say to you I say to all: Watch'. (In a similar way, St Matthew in his gospel singles out Peter as the one who asked Jesus for an explanation of the parable about clean foods, the explanation which appears in Chapter 7 of Mark, as we have seen above.) Thus ends the Tuesday of Mark's week of re-creation, according to our Western way of counting the days.

SUGGESTIONS FOR PRAYER

Verses 1–3

Looking at these words from our standpoint after the resurrection of Jesus, we thank him for giving us an entirely new concept of what 'wonderful' and 'precious' mean. We are being re-created into imperishable beings like himself, no longer afraid of the end of the world nor of the end of any created thing. We pray as Christians to be interlocked closely like stones in the wall of a strong building. We are grateful for the support of those who came before us and helped to bring us up into adulthood; we enjoy the company of those on either side of us; and we pray for the strength to uphold those who in their turn depend on us. We treasure the presence of Christ binding us together. We adore him for giving his precious blood to make us into precious, everlasting stones in his temple.

The next chapter will bear out, in the case of Jesus, how the Holy Spirit speaks for the one on trial: all that Jesus will say is that he is the Christ, the Son of God, and the king of David's line. Peter on the other hand, still without the Spirit, can only deny his Master.

'The desolating sacrilege' is understood to mean the placing by the Romans of a statue of the emperor in the Holy of Holies of the temple — a deliberate sacrilege the like of which had happened once before in Jewish history. This and the next few verses clearly refer to the destruction of Jerusalem, and not to 'the end of the world'. For instance, it would not much matter whether the season was summer or winter, if this were the end of the world; but to someone trying to escape armies invading Jerusalem, the season could matter a lot. Incidentally, when Jesus in Chapter 11 spoke about faith being able to move 'this mountain', the mountain in question was Mount Zion, on which Jerusalem is built. Someone who believes in God as Father will still be alive when this temple, city and mountain are all gone.

We may think of verses 20–27 as being 'about the end of the world', but there is probably more profit if we think of them as referring to our own death, when as far as we are concerned the sun, moon and stars of this universe will go out. The Son of man will gather the elect. The book of Revelation, not always the most comforting of documents, seems to imply in its Chapter 7 that the elect are not an exclusive few who will get safely to heaven, but simply the nucleus of a countless number of every nation, race and tongue gathered round them. I like to think that the elect are the shepherds, and the countless flock are all around them.

We should, as instructed, learn the lesson from the fig tree. It has already put forth its leaves in Chapter 11 above, so summer is already near in Chapter 11, and he, the Son of man, is already near, at the very gates of Jerusalem. Peter, of all people, should have caught the message, since he was the one so observant of the fig tree. 'This generation will not pass away', indeed it would only be thirty-six hours before Peter would learn his own frailty.

'. . . but only the Father.' The title of Father has far more significance in the gospel of Mark than the few times it is used would seem to indicate. In fact, the gospel does not make sense *unless* God is Father of Jesus and thence Father of us. See above

Chapter 13

Everything else will perish, except what is begotten by God.

The chapter falls into logical sections. First, Jesus *begins* to preach about 'Take heed' to his closest followers. The same message has never been explicit till now. Then, Jesus says the temple will come down, and the two sets of brothers ask him 'When?' (verses 1–4). Jesus gives some signs — but they are not the end, only the beginning (5–8). There will be persecutions, right up to the end (9–13). The end is foretold, first of Jerusalem (14–19) then of all created things (20–22). All of that was '*before*hand' (23). *After*, comes the Son of man (24–27). We are warned: he is already near (28–31) — but no one knows how near — so Watch! (32–37).

It always seems to me to be appropriate that in a gospel connected by tradition with Peter, there should be mention of the wonderful stones of the temple, destined to come down one by one. Peter (the Stone or the Rock) then appears time and again in Acts and in the First Letter of Peter, talking about stones and precious stones and things imperishable and the precious blood and the imperishable seed, and the temple of living stones that was then, in the days of the resurrection and the Spirit, being built up stone by stone. We have already said that for St Mark this fourth quarter of the gospel is the week of re-creation. Here is the temple to be re-created. When the body of Christ would shed its blood in a love that could only be divine, then his body too would be revealed as divine. There would be the new temple.

Peter and James and John and Andrew reappear as a separate grouping as they question Jesus here. Andrew is no longer paired with his brother Peter because Peter and James and John now have a more permanent place as chosen witnesses together.

The wars and rumours of wars, the earthquakes and famines are sadly still with us, as they were with us when Jesus spoke, and before and after the destruction of Jerusalem. The persecutions probably get special mention in Mark's gospel because it was first published in its present form in Rome during a time of persecution. Christians there needed the encouragement of knowing Jesus had foretold what they were going through, but that ultimately there was nothing to be over-alarmed about. Once they had taken on an allegiance which was wider than family and wider than the Roman Empire, they were sure to get into trouble with family or with the civil law.

being would be saved; but for the sake of the elect, whom he chose, he shortened the days. ²¹And then if anyone says to you, "Look, here is the Christ!" or "Look, there he is!" do not believe it. ²²False Christs and false prophets will arise and show signs and wonders, to lead astray, if possible, the elect. ²³But take heed; I have told you all things beforehand.

²⁴'But in those days, after that tribulation, the sun will be darkened, and the moon will not give its light, ²⁵and the stars will be falling from heaven, and the powers in the heavens will be shaken. ²⁶And then they will see the Son of man coming in clouds with great power and glory. ²⁷And then he will send out the angels, and gather his elect from the four winds, from the ends of the earth to the ends of heaven.

²⁸'From the fig tree learn its lesson: as soon as its branch becomes tender and puts forth its leaves, you know that summer is near. ²⁹So also, when you see these things taking place, you know that he is near, at the very gates. ³⁰Truly, I say to you, this generation will not pass away before all these things take place. ³¹Heaven and earth will pass away, but my words will not pass away.

³²'But of that day or that hour no one knows, not even the angels in heaven, nor the Son, but only the Father. ³³Take heed, watch and pray; for you do not know when the time will come. ³⁴It is like a man going on a journey, when he leaves home and puts his servants in charge, each with his work, and commands the doorkeeper to be on the watch. ³⁵Watch therefore — for you do not know when the master of the house will come, in the evening, or at midnight, or at cockcrow, or in the morning — ³⁶lest he come suddenly and find you asleep. ³⁷And what I say to you I say to all: Watch.'

* * *

This chapter is another collection of sayings of Jesus loosely bound together. There are memory links in the form of recurring words running through the sayings, links such as *temple, stones, take heed, lead astray, in my name, the beginning, the end, in those days, deliver up, the hour, pass away, the elect, watch*. The subject matter has to do with the approaching end of all merely created things, whether it be the destruction of the temple or the end of the world. But as told by St Mark the chapter in its context also has to do with the imminent failure of Peter and James and John to watch and pray with Jesus in the garden some twenty-four hours later. Their flesh, like all flesh, was weak. They did not as yet share fully the divine, imperishable blood of Jesus.

CHAPTER 13
———— ✻ ————

^{1}AND as he came out of the temple, one of us said to him, 'Look, Teacher, what wonderful stones and what wonderful buildings!' ^{2}And Jesus said to him, 'Do you see these great buildings? There will not be left here one stone upon another, that will not be thrown down.'

^{3}And as he sat on the Mount of Olives opposite the temple, I and James and John and Andrew asked him privately, ^{4}'Tell us, when will this be, and what will be the sign when these things are all to be accomplished?' ^{5}And Jesus began to say to us, 'Take heed that no one leads you astray. ^{6}Many will come in my name, saying, "I am he!" and they will lead many astray. ^{7}And when you hear of wars and rumours of wars, do not be alarmed; this must take place, but the end is not yet. ^{8}For nation will rise against nation, and kingdom against kingdom; there will be earthquakes in various places, there will be famines; this is but the beginning of the sufferings.

^{9}"But take heed to yourselves; for they will deliver you up to councils; and you will be beaten in synagogues; and you will stand before governors and kings for my sake, to bear testimony before them. ^{10}And the gospel must first be preached to all nations. ^{11}And when they bring you to trial and deliver you up, do not be anxious beforehand what you are to say; but say whatever is given you in that hour, for it is not you who speak, but the Holy Spirit. ^{12}And brother will deliver up brother to death, and the father his child, and the children will rise against parents and have them put to death; ^{13}and you will be hated by all for my name's sake. But he who endures to the end will be saved.

^{14}"But when you see the desolating sacrilege set up where it ought not to be (let the reader understand), then let those who are in Judea flee to the mountains; ^{15}let him who is on the housetop not go down, nor enter his house, to take anything away; ^{16}and let him who is in the field not turn back to take his mantle. ^{17}And alas for those who are with child and for those who give suck in those days! ^{18}Pray that it may not happen in winter. ^{19}For in those days there will be such tribulation as has not been from the beginning of the creation which God created until now, and never will be. ^{20}And if the Lord had not shortened the days, no human when we preach to others that they are children of God our King. Before the world may we always be seen to be servants of God and servants of the poor and the underprivileged, even though in our hearts we know we are your royal brothers and sisters.'

Verses 41–44

'"Dearest Jesus, teach me to be generous . . .; to give, and not to count the cost . . ." Teach me to be as generous as this poor widow in giving thanks to your Father.'

Chapter 12

Verses 28–34

We pray to be able to keep these two great commandments, in the light of the New Covenant rather than of the Old. We pray to be able to keep them in the correct order of priority, letting God love us before we attempt to reflect his love back to him. Faith is the beginning, the end is love.

Similarly, we always receive the bread of the Eucharist before we receive the chalice, and the order is correct. 'With the body of Christ may we receive all the unconditional love of God our Father as he welcomes us to his table; when we receive the wine, the blood of Christ, from the chalice may we attempt to give back to God through our neighbour the love he has given us, and to give it cost what it may.' In the first of these commandments we need the Holy Spirit coming from God to us with love. For the second of these two commandments we need the Holy Spirit going from Christ-in-us back to our Father by way of our neighbour in need. 'Open our ears to listen to your words of love, even though the whole world turn against us. Open our mouths and our hearts to give the Good News to all others, even if they seem to reject it.'

Verses 35–37

Some of the eucharistic prayers of the early Church refer to the wine as 'the holy vine of David'. In our receiving of the Eucharist, Jesus shares with us not only his divinity — which puts all of us in one sense higher than David was — but also his royalty, which he inherited from David through his mother Mary. We thank Jesus for letting us share with him his inheritance of the kingdom of his ancestor David, and the new Jerusalem and the new temple of living stones, all imperishable now because of his being the Son of God.

Verses 38–40

Jesus would never want us to fall back into the old trap, and to start putting our own imagined importance before the real needs of the poor, the widows and the orphans. 'Jesus, help us to do as you did and keep our own royal and divine status a secret even expect some of the same rejection in my own life. To support other living stones above and around me, I need the purification of learning how God loves me even when I seem rejected. Otherwise, how can I comfort others and support them in their times of rejection?

Verses 12–17

All through our lives we are in process of being taken over by the divine blood of Jesus, namely by our divine adoption as children of God. 'By the mystery of this water and wine, may we come to share in the divinity of Christ, who humbled himself to share in our humanity.' Our likeness to God our Father is there in us from the beginning, but we pray that this likeness to our Father may become ever clearer to ourselves and then ever clearer to our neighbours, who may then find the same likeness in themselves. We pray to judge everything that happens to us in the light of our being children of God. 'Father, when we fail, you are still well pleased with us, so our weakness does not matter by comparison. Father, when like Peter we aim too high before we are ready, you are still well pleased with us, so even our pride does not matter in the end. Your fatherly love reaches to the depth of our depression and to the height of our foolishness.'

Verses 18–27

In human terms, marriage is often connected in people's minds with immortality, but immortality of a certain kind. A man may die content, believing he has started off or continued a dynasty. 'I may die, but my descendants will still be walking the earth.' A woman may feel fulfilled once she has brought a child into the world, even if and when she comes to die herself. The resurrection Jesus speaks of is infinitely more satisfying, in that he says we ourselves shall be alive to see the fruits that God has produced through us and to enjoy them for ever. The vineyard story is a love story, and we do not leave a marriage behind when we die: we go to a wedding feast. 'Lord Jesus, teach us to trust in the power of God, and to understand the scriptures.'

Chapter 12
SUGGESTIONS FOR PRAYER

Verses 1–9

On a personal level, I may think of the vineyard as representing all that I have, and the stewards as representing myself. What is the fruit God is asking of me? First of all, to acknowledge him as the source of all that I have, all that I am, my Father. Then, not to keep the fruit to myself, but to share with others God's love for me as his child. I pray to remember always that my very existence is God's gift, and that his love for me as a child of his is completely beyond my deserts; and I pray for the power to share with others his love for me. Power will be needed, because in our weakness we easily conclude that God has turned against us when fortune turns against us. We pray and reflect on the beloved son in Jesus' story, who was no less beloved by his father even when he was killed and cast out of the vineyard.

In the celebration of the Eucharist, as we offer to God, the owner of this vineyard, the wine, the fruit of the vine, the blood of Christ, we pray to unite with the will of Christ our own desire to please the Father, no matter what it may cost.

In the story the owner of the vineyard does not ask back the whole vineyard, but only some of the fruit of the vines within the boundary hedge. 'You, dear Father, do not ask us for whole burnt offerings. You do not ask the destruction of our vineyard, nor even for all the fruit. You give me gifts, and you ask that some of the gifts be used for your sake in loving others. You do not ask for the whole gift back. It may seem to me that my death will be the end and destruction of all gifts, but this vineyard accepted on your terms is everlasting; the tree of life will always be there for me. This I believe through Jesus your beloved Son. Amen.'

Verses 10 and 11

The apostles, and particularly Peter in the time after the Resurrection, used this passage about 'the stone rejected' to show how it was necessary for the Christ to suffer and so to enter his glory. If I am to be a living stone in the new temple, then I can

Jacob', to show his enemies that they already proclaim the resurrection without realizing it.

Then Jesus was asked by a scribe, which commandment was the first of all. It is worth noting that Jesus begins his answer with the quotation, *'Hear, O Israel'*. Then he goes on to complete the answer, within the confines of the Old Testament, since that was what the scribe asked for. The commands to love God and to love one's neighbour take on further meaning in the context of this chapter and of the gospel of Mark as a whole. To love God above all, in Mark's gospel, comes to mean letting God love me, letting him adopt me as his own son or daughter, thus hearing and listening to the Good News, since this is what God wants above all. To love my neighbour as myself then comes to mean to love everyone else as a child of God such as I am myself; and the first step towards such a love is to proclaim the Good News to my neighbour. Jesus kept both these commandments, *hearing* what his Father said at the baptism, *acknowledging* his divine blood and indeed *showing* his divine blood to the whole world, in an open invitation to his neighbour to come and share his inheritance. Such a gift to God is better than all whole burnt offerings and sacrifices. After this in Mark's gospel there are no more questions put to Jesus in public until his trial.

The five conflict stories are over, but the word 'scribe' acts as a memory link with the question that follows, asked by Jesus himself, about the teaching of the scribes. Jesus points out, in slightly veiled terms, that the other side of his descent is from King David. But because his own blood is divine, he is above David even though David was the royal founder of the fortunes of Jerusalem and the temple.

Another teaching about the scribes follows, about their diverting money and diverting the glory from God to themselves. The prophets through the centuries had insisted on the need for anyone who called himself religious to have a care for widows, not to exploit them.

'Widow' then becomes a memory link to the famous and wonderful story of Jesus and the widow who gave up to God her two copper coins, all she had. If anyone loved God with all her heart, she did.

Chapter 12

steal heaven. We notice that Jesus is most like the figure called 'a beloved son' in the story. Although a son, Jesus is to be treated just like the servants: wounded in the head, treated shamefully, beaten and killed. Within the limits of Mark's gospel, Peter and James and John would have been the first to catch the reference to Jesus himself, since they alone had heard him called 'beloved son' on the mountain.

The reference to Psalm 118 about 'the stone which the builders rejected' would seem to be particularly remembered by St Peter, whose own new name meant Rock or Stone. This gospel of Mark is traditionally linked with Peter; the present series of conflict stories is probably taken over by Matthew and Luke from Mark; Peter will quote this passage when he in turn is arrested by the temple authorities; and it appears lastly in the First Letter of Peter, so that every mention of it in the New Testament has some link with Peter. The old temple will soon come down, but a living temple will be built instead, with Jesus for its cornerstone.

The trap laid for Jesus over Caesar's taxes, and his answer, acquire a further meaning when looked at in the context Mark gives to the story. We noted early on, when Levi the tax collector first followed Jesus, that an apostle may be likened to a collector of people, on whom the image of God is deeply stamped, into God's treasury. The fruit which Jesus, Son of God, gives back to God the owner of the vineyard will prove as the gospel unfolds to be his owning up to his sonship under trial even when it will cost him his own life-blood. Jesus acknowledged his own likeness to his Father, and thus insisted he belonged nowhere else but in God's treasury.

The argument about resurrection also takes on further meaning, given that the story is told in its present context. The fig tree and the temple could not last for ever, but the tree of life and the temple of living stones will last for ever. At the heart of the mystery is the blood of Jesus: he is Son of God, so that his blood alone of all things in this world is immortal, imperishable. In the resurrection there is no more need of procreation, all are brothers or sisters of Jesus. And the longings for immortal love in our hearts will be stilled, fulfilled. There is something both majestic and very simple in the way Jesus brings together two familiar phrases, 'God of the living' and 'the God of Abraham, Isaac and

⁴¹And he sat down opposite the treasury, and watched the multitude putting money into the treasury. Many rich people put in large sums. ⁴²And a poor widow came, and put in two copper coins, which make a penny. ⁴³*And he called us to him, and said to us, 'Truly, I say to you, this poor widow has put in more than all those who are contributing to the treasury.* ⁴⁴For they all contributed out of their abundance; but she out of her poverty has put in everything she had, her whole living.'

*   *   *

The whole of this chapter is included by St Mark in the day we would call Tuesday of Holy Week. The day started at verse 20 of Chapter 11 and will continue till the end of Chapter 13. This present chapter consists mainly of four more stories of conflict between Jesus and the Jerusalem religious authorities: the parable about the vineyard, then questions about taxes to Caesar, about marriage and resurrection, and about the greatest commandment. Mark has now shown us Jesus teaching in the temple on the Monday and on the Tuesday, and can thus be consistent within his gospel when he will later give us Jesus' words at his arrest: 'Day after day I was with you in the temple teaching, and you did not seize me.' Presumably in fact these stories of conflict refer to incidents which happened over a much longer period than two days.

Jesus 'began to speak to them in parables'. Again, Mark is consistent in writing thus, because so far Jesus has never spoken to the chief priests and the scribes of the temple and the elders in parables. The parable of the vineyard as it stands is more like an allegory than a parable, since every feature seems to have its own meaning: the owner of the vineyard is God, 'the vineyard of the Lord is the house of Israel', the tenants are the religious authorities, the servants are the prophets, the one beloved son is Jesus, and crucifixions took place outside the city walls. The temple authorities were diverting not simply the money of the people, but the people's concerns away from a care for God's wishes into anxieties and purposes created by men. The temple authorities had apparently forgotten they could not lay claim to the kingdom of heaven by right of conquest; Jesus said the kingdom could only be reached in God's way, namely by inheritance or by gift. We cannot buy heaven, and neither can we

Chapter 12

and they asked him a question, saying, ¹⁹'Teacher, Moses wrote for us that if a man's brother dies and leaves a wife, but leaves no child, the man must take the wife, and raise up children for his brother. ²⁰There were seven brothers; the first took a wife, and when he died left no children; ²¹and the second took her, and died, leaving no children; and the third likewise; ²²and the seven left no children. Last of all the woman also died. ²³In the resurrection whose wife will she be? For the seven had her as wife.'

²⁴Jesus said to them, 'Is not this why you are wrong, that you know neither the scriptures nor the power of God? ²⁵For when they rise from the dead, they neither marry nor are given in marriage, but are like angels in heaven. ²⁶And as for the dead being raised, have you not read in the book of Moses, in the passage about the bush, how God said to him, "I am the God of Abraham, and the God of Isaac, and the God of Jacob"? ²⁷He is not God of the dead, but of the living; you are quite wrong.'

²⁸And one of the scribes came up and heard them disputing with one another, and seeing that he answered them well, asked him, 'Which commandment is the first of all?' ²⁹Jesus answered, 'The first is, "Hear, O Israel: The Lord our God, the Lord is one; ³⁰and you shall love the Lord your God with all your heart, and with all your soul, and with all your mind, and with all your strength." ³¹The second is this, "You shall love your neighbour as yourself." There is no other commandment greater than these.' ³²And the scribe said to him, 'You are right, Teacher; you have truly said that he is one, and there is no other but he; ³³and to love him with all the heart, and with all the understanding, and with all the strength, and to love one's neighbour as oneself, is much more than all whole burnt offerings and sacrifices.' ³⁴And when Jesus saw that he answered wisely, he said to him, 'You are not far from the kingdom of God.' And after that no one dared to ask him any question.

³⁵And as Jesus taught in the temple, he said, 'How can the scribes say that the Christ is the son of David? ³⁶David himself, inspired by the Holy Spirit, declared,

> "The Lord said to my Lord,
> Sit at my right hand,
>   till I put thy enemies under thy feet."

³⁷David himself calls him Lord; so how is he his son?' And the great throng heard him gladly.

³⁸And in his teaching he said, 'Beware of the scribes, who like to go about in long robes, and to have salutations in the market places ³⁹and the best seats in the synagogues and the places of honour at feasts, ⁴⁰who devour widows' houses and for a pretence make long prayers. They will receive the greater condemnation.'

CHAPTER 12

———— �֎ ————

AND he began to speak to them in parables. 'A man planted a vineyard, and set a hedge around it, and dug a pit for the wine press, and built a tower, and let it out to tenants, and went into another country. ²When the time came, he sent a servant to the tenants, to get from them some of the fruit of the vineyard. ³And they took him and beat him, and sent him away empty-handed. ⁴Again he sent to them another servant, and they wounded him in the head, and treated him shamefully. ⁵And he sent another, and him they killed; and so with many others, some they beat and some they killed. ⁶He had still one other, a beloved son; finally he sent him to them, saying, "They will respect my son." ⁷But those tenants said to one another, "This is the heir; come, let us kill him, and the inheritance will be ours." ⁸And they took him and killed him, and cast him out of the vineyard. ⁹What will the owner of the vineyard do? He will come and destroy the tenants, and give the vineyard to others. ¹⁰Have you not read this scripture:

"The very stone which the builders rejected
has become the head of the corner;
¹¹this was the Lord's doing,
and it is marvellous in our eyes"?'

¹²And they tried to arrest him, but feared the multitude, for they perceived that he had told the parable against them; so they left him and went away.

¹³And they sent to him some of the Pharisees and some of the Herodians, to entrap him in his talk. ¹⁴And they came and said to him, 'Teacher, we know that you are true, and care for no man; for you do not regard the position of men, but truly teach the way of God. Is it lawful to pay taxes to Caesar, or not? ¹⁵Should we pay them, or should we not?' But knowing their hypocrisy, he said to them, 'Why put me to the test? Bring me a coin, and let me look at it.' ¹⁶And they brought one. And he said to them, 'Whose likeness and inscription is this?' They said to him, 'Caesar's.' ¹⁷Jesus said to them, 'Render to Caesar the things that are Caesar's, and to God the things that are God's.' And they were amazed at him.

¹⁸And Sadducees came to him, who say that there is no resurrection;

Chapter 11

I have them already. Perhaps from your eternal point of view, you can see I have them already, whereas I from my time-bound point of view cannot see the truth of it yet.'

A powerful exercise is to go back over my life, remembering anyone who ever hurt or harmed me, and to forgive them. I acquit them, I no longer expect them to pay for my forgiveness, as my Father has not made me pay for his forgiveness. If I find it hard to *feel* forgiving, then at least I can try to pray blessings on them. Perhaps I should pray too for those I may have hurt or harmed in my life.

Verses 27–33

The ultimate reality that comes 'from heaven' is the blood of Christ, his divine Sonship which then embraces us all. The baptism of John, calling on people to recognize their need for forgiveness, ploughed and watered the ground so that the seed of God could enter in. The temple authorities had as yet seen no need for forgiveness in themselves, so they could not recognize what came from heaven. We pray that our own hearts may be opened and may by the power of God stay open till they become fruitful.

[*For a diagram of Mark's 'week of re-creation', see Appendix 1 on p. 133.*]

thorns and thistles, and rocky ground, but will eventually receive power from the risen Jesus to be fruitful in their turn. We offer our own failures as disciples, that the power of the Son of man may finally triumph in us. We pray that these seven days of the re-creation may see our own hearts re-created as well.

Verses 15–19

Mark does not say Jesus was angry: he had a task to perform and he performed it, that was all. He drove out the traders from the temple, overturned the tables with the money-changers' money on, and overturned the seats of the pigeon-sellers. Mark does not say he overturned the cages of the pigeons.

We pray in enormous gratitude to God and to Jesus whom he sent, because we do not have to pay for heaven, we do not have to earn eternal life by good works, for heaven is our inheritance; we share now the divine blood of Christ our brother. As the first letter of Peter tells us, 'You were ransomed . . . not with perishable things such as silver or gold, but with the precious (i.e. priceless) blood of Christ'. As if we could have paid for heaven! In our gratitude, please God we shall do great things for him and for the cause of Christ, but God is our Father and he is not measuring or weighing our worthiness or unworthiness.

We ask to be made sensitive to other people. We want never to *use* God as a means to anything; we want never to use one another as short-cuts to anyone else or to anything else.

Verses 20–25

'Father, when I am anxious I make mountains out of molehills. Take my biggest problems in life, be they real or only imagined, and drop them in the sea. I have your love secure, so nothing else matters, nothing else has any real size. If my difficulties are slow to drop into the sea, let me remember that your love for me will outlive the highest mountain.'

'I know your forgiveness is mine, even before I ask for it. Grant me your forgiveness, Father. Other gifts which I have asked for many times and seemed not to receive, I find it difficult to believe

Chapter 11

We note that there is a certain similarity between where those Hosannas come in the gospel of Mark and where they come in the Eucharist. In the first half of the gospel Jesus led the people out of the synagogues and gave them the Word himself, until Peter came to believe; in the second half of the gospel Jesus moves towards Jerusalem and there replaces the worship of the temple with his own sacrifice. Today, derived from the synagogue worship, we have the Liturgy of the Word at Mass; then comes the creed, the act of faith; then after a while we move, with Hosannas, into the commemoration of the Lord's Supper and his death and resurrection. 'Lord Jesus, give us to feel, each time we say or sing our "Hosanna in the highest!" that we are entering in mystery with you into the holy city.'

Verse 11

Jesus the bridegroom enters the city that could have been 'his bride'. We know she will reject him, and cast him out again to die. But his love is everlasting, and will survive — indeed, will come back stronger than ever. We pray to Jesus to deal in the same way with our own rejections of him: to forgive us, to seek us out even more lovingly, to work his wonders in other, unexpected people who will then turn round and capture our hearts for him again.

Verses 12–14

We see Jesus unable to find fruit on the fig tree that should be life-giving. We recall the image of the tree of life in the Book of Revelation, always fruitful at any season. And we know that the reality is Jesus on the cross, and the mystery of the fruit of the cross, his body and blood which he left us. We thank Jesus for this tree of life, which has never let us down and will never let us down. We thank God our Father, who is so to speak always at home, never out or away when we come looking for love or attention.

The 'seed' parables of Jesus, preached from boat to shore early in the gospel, all ended up with fruitfulness. The fig tree and the temple are fruitless; Jesus is fruitful; the disciples and Peter have struggled along through attacks from the birds of the air, through

John the Baptist. Those who came to John humbly admitting that they had sins and needed forgiving were ready for Jesus. Those who fell into the sin against the Holy Spirit and would not let God forgive them were still unwilling, here in the temple, to listen to Jesus. This is the unforgivable sin, but men and women need not stay in it. Jesus' death, willingly accepted by him, would be strong enough to turn the hearts even of those unwilling to be forgiven.

Just as there were five stories of conflict early in Mark's gospel, between Jesus and the local religious authorities, so now there are five stories of conflict with the religious authorities in Jerusalem. This argument about the baptism of John is the first of the five.

SUGGESTIONS FOR PRAYER

Verses 1–8

Some people find it easy and helpful to imagine themselves into a gospel scene. For those who do, this scene of the two disciples fetching the colt is an easy one to pray, since there are plenty of instructions and there is plenty to do. My version of the text makes Peter to be one of the two disciples: whoever prays the passage may imagine himself or herself as the other disciple.

Somebody once said to me, 'That colt could have as an epitaph, "*He was put upon*". Not a bad epitaph!' Yet how we all shy away from being put upon, imposed upon.

Verses 9 and 10

We sense the excitement of the crowds. In Mark's gospel this triumphant entry into Jerusalem looks like a challenge to the authorities: Come on now, ask me if I am the Christ, and I will tell you. Jesus will answer the question, at his trial. The time has almost come. 'Jesus, teach us the true nature of your kingdom. As we echo each time at our Eucharist, "Blessed is he who comes in the name of the Lord! Hosanna in the highest!", may we allow you to be the kind of king you are, and not expect you to fit in with our own notion of how you should rule.'

Chapter 11

As in a mirror, we can see the fig tree that fails and the temple that will destroyed as reflections, of a tree with fruit for God at every season, and of an imperishable temple of living stones. The key to understanding the link between temple and tree is the blood of Jesus, which is divine: his body is thought of by Mark as human until it sheds the blood, but his blood, his descent from his Father, is always divine, precious, imperishable, always fruitful. Without too much effort, we may reflect that there was a fig tree in the Garden of Eden (see Genesis 3:7), that Peter three times talks about Jesus on the cross as 'hanging on a tree' like a fruit, that the tree of life in Revelation 22:2 bears fruit at all seasons. What is only human is bound to decay in time; what is divine is everlasting.

What seems to have been wrong with the temple was that it made people think God's love was up for sale and could be bought with human coins. For Jesus, on the other hand, God's love is free, God adopts us freely as his children if we will only let him. Our good actions are no more than a way of saying 'Thank you', not a way of buying love or favours from God. So Jesus clears all signs of trade out of the temple. Nor will he allow anyone to carry anything through the temple, making of the temple of God a short-cut to save themselves the trouble of carrying things all the way round the outside. We may never make God a short-cut to some lesser purpose of our own. God is personal. No person may be made a means, a short-cut, to anything or anyone else. Every person is a temple.

The little discourse on faith is very powerful. Faith removes mountains, makes molehills out of mountains. For if God is my Father, living for ever and loving for ever, then mountains in my way do not really matter: they will all be removed sooner or later, since I will live longer than the mountain. Again (as with the epileptic boy and elsewhere in Mark's gospel) we see the destructive aspect of water shown to whatever opposes God or God's children. Some translations render the next verse (verse 24): 'If you ask for something in prayer, believe that you have it already, and it will be yours'. So, for example, we believe we are forgiven already, therefore we ask for it, and it will be ours. Then comes 'Forgive, and you will be forgiven', a theme given much more prominence in the gospels of Matthew and Luke.

Finally in this chapter we see again the crucial role played by death and resurrection of Jesus? It must be because the original story of the week of creation: evening — morning; evening — morning (see Genesis 1:1 – 2:4) is being contrasted by Mark with the week of re-creation, when God re-created the world in seven days, and made the first day of the week (Sunday) into the new holy day. God has, so to speak, finished his sabbath (Saturday) rest and started creating again.

I find the account of the two disciples being sent into the village to fetch the colt very satisfying in the version where Peter tells the tale of himself as one of the two. One thing this version clarified for me: it is only the two who fetched the colt who spread their two cloaks over the colt's back for Jesus. Everybody else spread theirs on the road, or else cut leafy branches to lay before him.

Jesus seems to have chosen to enter the city in this manner, as an only slightly veiled admission of the fact that he was the Christ. The crowd certainly took up the hint, possibly for the wrong reasons, still not knowing what kind of Messiah to expect. Yet these were the people who came in to the city with him, perhaps supporters of his from Galilee who would know him a lot better than the people of Jerusalem knew him. Those crying 'Hosanna' may not have been the same as those who soon would cry 'Crucify him'. The cry of Bartimaeus, 'Jesus, Son of David', is taken up in a different form by the crowd spreading the leafy branches along the road: 'Blessed is the kingdom of our father David that is coming'.

What follows in this chapter links closely the temple and the fig tree. The two themes are sandwiched together: temple, fig tree, temple, fig tree, temple. On Sunday evening Jesus looks around the temple; on Monday morning he finds leaves but no fruit on the fig tree, then he goes on to cleanse the temple of money-changers and trade, till the evening comes; on Tuesday morning Peter notices the fig tree has withered, then Jesus goes on into the temple and is challenged about his authority to cleanse the temple. If we compare the fig tree and the temple: the fig tree had healthy-looking leaves, but no fruit, since it was not the season for fruit — sooner or later it must die as all creatures must die; the temple looks splendid but is not producing fruit for God, and he who will be called the Son of God has come out of season, looking for fruit from the temple, but has found none — the temple too must come to an end sooner or later.

Chapter 11

²⁰And as we passed by in the morning, we saw the fig tree withered away to the roots. ²¹And I remembered and said to him, 'Master, look! The fig tree which you cursed has withered.' ²²And Jesus answered us, 'Have faith in God. ²³Truly, I say to you, whoever says to this mountain. "Be taken up and cast into the sea," and does not doubt in his heart, but believes that what he says will come to pass, it will be done for him. ²⁴Therefore I tell you, whatever you ask in prayer, believe that you receive it, and you will. ²⁵And whenever you stand praying, forgive, if you have anything against any one; so that your Father also who is in heaven may forgive you your trespasses.'

[Note: *Other ancient authorities add verse 26*: 'But if you do not forgive, neither will your Father who is in heaven forgive your trespasses.']

²⁷And we came again to Jerusalem. And as he was walking in the temple, the chief priests and the scribes and the elders came to him, ²⁸and they said to him, 'By what authority are you doing these things, or who gave you this authority to do them?' ²⁹Jesus said to them, 'I will ask you a question; answer me, and I will tell you by what authority I do these things. ³⁰Was the baptism of John from heaven or from men? Answer me.' ³¹And they argued with one another, 'If we say, "From heaven," he will say, "Why then did you not believe him?" ³²But shall we say, "From men"?' — they were afraid of the people, for all held that John was a real prophet. ³³So they answered Jesus, 'We do not know.' And Jesus said to them, 'Neither will I tell you by what authority I do these things.'

*   *   *

We have now reached the final quarter of Mark's gospel. The first quarter ended with the raising of Jairus's daughter; the first half of the gospel was completed by Peter's act of faith; the third quarter was the journey of Jesus to Jerusalem, and now the final part will all take place in or near Jerusalem. The formal pattern underlying this last quarter of the gospel seems to be what we would call Holy Week. Whether St Mark is following an early Christian custom, or whether the custom comes from St Mark, nobody seems to be sure. If we follow St Mark's timings in the days that follow, we can say that he tells us Jesus entered Jerusalem riding on a colt on what we would call a Sunday evening (since it was already late when he reached the temple), and that he was found to be risen on the following Sunday morning. Why can such a pattern be strong enough to underlie the passion,

CHAPTER 11
*

AND when we drew near to Jerusalem, to Bethphage and Bethany, at the Mount of Olives, he sent two of us, ²and said to us, 'Go into the village opposite you, and immediately as you enter it you will find a colt tied, on which no one has ever sat; untie it and bring it. ³If any one says to you, "Why are you doing this?" say, "The Lord has need of it and will send it back here immediately."' ⁴And we went away, and found a colt tied at the door out in the open street; and we untied it. ⁵And those who stood there said to us, 'What are you doing, untying the colt?' ⁶And we told them what Jesus had said; and they let us go. ⁷And we brought the colt to Jesus, and threw our garments on it; and he sat upon it. ⁸And many spread their garments on the road, and others spread leafy branches which they had cut from the fields. ⁹And those who went before and those who followed cried out, 'Hosanna! Blessed is he who comes in the name of the Lord! ¹⁰Blessed is the kingdom of our father David that is coming! Hosanna in the highest!'

¹¹And he entered Jerusalem, and went into the temple; and when he had looked round at everything, as it was already late, he went out to Bethany with the twelve.

¹²*On the following day, when we came from Bethany, he was hungry.* ¹³And seeing in the distance a fig tree in leaf, he went to see if he could find anything on it. When he came to it, he found nothing but leaves, for it was not the season for figs. ¹⁴And he said to it, 'May no one ever eat fruit from you again.' *And we heard it.*

¹⁵*And we came to Jerusalem.* And he entered the temple and began to drive out those who sold and those who bought in the temple, and he overturned the tables of the money-changers and the seats of those who sold pigeons; ¹⁶and he would not allow anyone to carry anything through the temple. ¹⁷And he taught, and said to them, 'Is it not written, "My house shall be called a house of prayer for all the nations"? But you have made it a den of robbers.' ¹⁸And the chief priests and the scribes heard it and sought a way to destroy him; for they feared him, because all the multitude was astonished at his teaching. ¹⁹*And when evening came we went out of the city.*

Chapter 10

Jesus has followed one road from his transfiguration down to Capernaum, then across the Jordan, then to Jericho in Judea. Now his way will take him into Jerusalem, Son of David into David's city, then along the way of the cross, until in his risen self he again goes ahead of his disciples.

but will ask for the status of 'servant' instead. St Paul tells us that Jesus emptied himself of the divine status and took the form of a servant or slave. We pray for the *power* to do the same: we all have divine status as sons and daughters of God, but we wish not to trade on that divine status but to be accepted *as if* we were 'only servants'. We pray above all for the aspect of the servant by which he does not open his mouth or complain when his master seems to be harsh. In other words, 'God, give me the power to love you and trust you even when everything goes wrong, through Jesus our good Teacher. Amen.' Furthermore, it takes more than a little faith to get up from my place at the table to go and find others who have got lost on their way home, and to do this at the risk of finding my place taken on my return.

The shape of the gospel story seems to indicate that Jesus did not expect everyone to reach the same degree of service. After all, there will always be far more sheep than shepherds. Jesus still had compassion on the crowds, when he concentrated more and more on his disciples.

Verses 46–52

The most obvious way of praying the story of Bartimaeus is to pretend to be Bartimaeus and take his place. I imagine myself by the roadside with my cloak out in front of me to catch the coins thrown to me. I hear the noise of the crowd, and ask who it is. Then in my heart I cry out insistently, 'Jesus, Son of David, have pity on me', again and again. If feelings within me tell me to be quiet, I cry out all the more, 'Son of David, have pity on me'. I hear Jesus' disciples coming to me and saying, 'Take heart; rise, he is calling you'. I throw aside my mantle (I won't need that again) and come to Jesus. He asks me as he earlier asked James and John, 'What do you want me to do for you?' I ask him for whatever I need most, but I always include, 'Master, let me see again'. 'I used to be able to see God as my loving Father, but now I seem to have lost my vision — too many things have gone wrong for me and mine. Master, let me see again.' As and when my sight comes back to me, like Bartimaeus I use it to follow Jesus on the Way. Before Christians were ever called Christians they were called Followers of the Way.

Chapter 10

reunite us in the end. We notice that Jesus does not ask or expect anyone to leave wife or husband for his sake; and in the 'hundredfold' list he does not promise a hundredfold of fathers. We have only one Father according to the Good News, and he is in heaven. St Mark alone promises the hundredfold 'now in this time', not just in heaven. We pray for ourselves, that the seed of faith in us may grow tall and strong, not tangled up by thorns and thistles.

Verses 32–36

Twice in this chapter, Jesus says to someone, 'What do you want me to do for you?' Before we pray about the answers given by James and John or by Bartimaeus, we would do well to frame our own answer: what do I reply to Jesus when he asks me that wonderful question?

Verse 37

Jesus answers our prayers surely, but not always in ways we expect. Each of us in the Eucharist 'sits next' to Jesus: we do not need to get anyone else to ask him things for us; he is right beside us. Indeed, whenever we sit and pray, he 'sits at our right hand or at our left'.

Verses 38–40

If the character of the sacrament of baptism is that it gives us our own place at the table, and the bread of the children, then the character of the sacrament of confirmation is that it gives us the right to serve at the table, and a share in the chalice.

Verses 41–45

God himself has been our Servant from before the world; Jesus the Servant mirrors his Father. Service is not, surely, a temporary thing which will end in heaven, since love serves and cannot help serving, except when it is being served by another. But the irksomeness of serving will have an end, and the pain and the tragedy will have an end. So we may allow that for us mortals 'to serve' can and will often be a painful word. Thus the prodigal son in St Luke's gospel reckons he is no longer fit to be called 'son',

Verses 13–16

We pray warmly for the little children we know, and for those who care for them and teach them. Children stay small such a short time: we pray for all those we have known and loved since they were little. We pray to be warm, patient and friendly with all the children we meet; we give them respect as knowing many things about the kingdom of God which we have forgotten.

Verses 17–22

'"No one is good but God alone." But you are our good Teacher, Jesus, Son of God, divine wisdom! In these chapters you confidently adjust and go beyond the commandments Moses taught. You looked at this rich man and loved him. I believe that you loved him just as much, if not more, when he could not match up to your invitation. Look upon me, also, with love when I live up to your ideals, but look upon me with even more love and sympathy when I turn away sorrowful because I cannot cope with what you ask of me.'

Verses 23–27

Again we must ask for *power* to make it possible to do the impossible: that those of us with riches (and we all have some, not necessarily in money but in gifts and talents) may be able to give them up if asked to by God. This means either actual poverty which some are called to, or the kind of poverty we are all called to, which means not being unduly attached to what we have; to be the opposite of a miser; to be generous. No point in talking about it: this is a grace we can only pray for.

Verses 28–31

Every Christian is called to the freedom of heart just mentioned above: to prefer God's will to anything — house, brothers, sisters, mother, father, children, lands — if it came to a clear choice between God's will and any of them. Some Christians over all the centuries have felt themselves called to a more radical separation from all these, even before circumstances demanded they leave behind house or brothers or the rest. We pray to prefer the will of God to anything or anyone on the list, confident that Jesus will an object-lesson to Peter and the others about how to follow Jesus to the cross and to glory. Bartimaeus is blind, and he knows it; Peter thought he could see. Bartimaeus is a beggar; Peter thinks he already has all he needs . . . and so on. The blind man asks to see *again*, according to some other good translations; like Peter he once was able to see, but lost his vision. As we have been repeating, it is one thing to see God's love when all goes well, and quite another thing to believe in God's love when absolutely everything goes wrong. The latter belief is not faith so much as love, and love is a power we do not possess of ourselves, we must ask for it repeatedly — as does blind Bartimaeus, shouting, 'Jesus, Son of David, have pity on me', louder than ever when told to be quiet.

God's word is two-fold. First comes the Good News: 'You are my beloved Son; with you I am well pleased'. Then comes the invitation: 'This is my beloved Son; listen to him'. Bartimaeus, knowing himself for what he was, a blind beggar, shows the rest of us what we really are, and how to follow Jesus on the way to Jerusalem, the cross and glory. The response to the Good News is faith; the response to the invitation is love. 'Faith is the beginning, love is the end.'

The first five chapters of Mark contain mainly stories related to baptism; from Chapter 6 until Peter's confession of faith come stories related in one way or another to bread, recognition, faith. Three misunderstandings ended in Peter's faith. Then comes the journey to Jerusalem, three misunderstandings ending when Jesus opens the eyes of a blind beggar who once could see. The beggar, begging now from no one but Jesus, follows his Master on the way of the cross. The power to love is coming to the weak.

SUGGESTIONS FOR PRAYER

Verses 2–12

Those who are married will want to pray for the power to be faithful to one another; those who are not married will want to pray for the gift of faithfulness for the married couples they know. To be faithful until death is not something we possess by our own strength; we have to ask for it. We pray too for those about to be married, that the two may be joined together by God.

stumbling block to the children instead of as a rock of support. By rights, according to what Jesus said, they should be dropped into the sea with a great millstone round their necks. We may take heart from the fact that they eventually turned around and were forgiven for their blindness.

The story of the rich man is placed by St Mark at the point where Jesus is setting out again on his journey. Once the exchange is over, and Jesus has discussed the matter of riches with his disciples, he is on the move once more towards Jerusalem. Jesus makes his third solemn prediction of the passion, in more detail than ever before. James and John reply with a request which shows how little they understand, and this gives Jesus his cue for the third discourse on the nature of true greatness. The discourse, too, is clearer than ever before. 'The Son of man came not to be served but to serve, and to give his life as a ransom for many (i.e. for all).' There can be no doubt that, for St Mark, Jesus knows he is to die, innocent for the guilty; that he goes to his death willingly because it is the will of his Father that he should do the things which will enrage his murderers; that he sees his coming death as foretold in the scriptures, and particularly in the Servant songs of Isaiah; that thus he will enter glory. As Servant, he will carry God's message to all those to whom he has been sent, including the sick, the sinners, the children. If his enemies hate him for this, so be it. Jesus is the beloved Son, but he empties himself and acts as if he were only a servant.

If the theme following the first prophecy of the passion had echoes of the birds of the air (Satan) trying to snatch up the tiny seed of faith, and the theme following the second prophecy had echoes of the thorns and thistles of the same parable, here following the third prophecy the theme seems to echo the 'rocky ground' element of the parable. James and John are enthusiastic, but shallow. They want the top places, but very soon they will run away from danger like the rest. When Jesus asked them, 'What do you want me to do for you?', they showed complete misunderstanding of Jesus' mission. Their request in reply to Jesus is contrasted by St Mark with the perfect reply of Bartimaeus the blind beggar whose story comes next.

There is not a *series* of incidents after the third and last discourse on true greatness, just the one incident; but the story of Bartimaeus is one of the richest in the gospel. This blind beggar is

Chapter 10

Nazareth, he began to cry out and say, 'Jesus, Son of David, have mercy on me!' ⁴⁸And many rebuked him, telling him to be silent; but he cried out all the more, 'Son of David, have mercy on me!' ⁴⁹And Jesus stopped and said, 'Call him.' *And we called the blind man, saying to him, 'Take heart; rise, he is calling you.'* ⁵⁰And throwing off his mantle he sprang up and came to Jesus. ⁵¹And Jesus said to him, 'What do you want me to do for you?' And the blind man said to him, 'Master, let me receive my sight.' ⁵²And Jesus said to him, 'Go your way; your faith has made you well.' And immediately he received his sight and followed him on the way.

* * *

Still moving steadily towards Jerusalem, Jesus leaves Capernaum and travels down the far side of the Jordan till he is across from Judea (see map 2, p. 136). We have heard and prayed about the second prophecy of the passion and the second discourse on the true meaning of greatness; now we come to the series of incidents related to that second discourse.

If the first prophecy of the passion, and what followed it, seemed to bear some relation to 'the birds of the air' snatching the little seed of faith from Peter and the others, this present series of incidents would seem to relate to the 'thorns and thistles' of the same parable, 'the cares of the world, and the delight in riches, and the desire for other things' which can 'enter in and choke the word'. Jesus has some forthright things to say about marriage, about divorce and adultery, and about little children who must be welcomed. To the rich man who wanted to be perfect, and to his own disciples afterwards, he spoke of riches and the power to be free in heart which comes of following him, Jesus. In this last exchange with the disciples, which took place in whichever house they were lodging in on the way, there is once again emphasis on the *power* of God, which is a theme linked with the Son of man and the transfiguration. Jesus has the power, but as yet even his disciples do not. Jesus looked upon the rich man and loved him; we can be confident that he still looked upon him and loved him when the man went away sorrowful.

To return to the little children: here we see an example of what Jesus already condemned in the previous chapter of Mark. Peter (the Rock, the Stone) and the other disciples are acting as a those who have riches to enter the kingdom of God!' ²⁴And we were amazed at his words. But Jesus said to us again, 'Children, how hard it is for those who trust in riches to enter the kingdom of God! ²⁵It is easier for a camel to go through the eye of a needle than for a rich man to enter the kingdom of God.' ²⁶And we were exceedingly astonished, and said to him, 'Then who can be saved?' ²⁷Jesus looked at us and said, 'With men it is impossible, but not with God; for all things are possible with God.' ²⁸I began to say to him, 'Lo, we have left everything and followed you.' ²⁹Jesus said, 'Truly, I say to you, there is no one who has left house or brothers or sisters or mother or father or children or lands, for my sake and for the gospel, ³⁰who will not receive a hundredfold now in this time, houses and brothers and sisters and mothers and children and lands, with persecutions, and in the age to come eternal life. ³¹But many that are first will be last, and the last first.'

³²And we were on the road, going up to Jerusalem, and Jesus was walking ahead of us; and we were amazed, and those who followed were afraid. And taking the twelve again, he began to tell us what was to happen to him, ³³saying, 'Behold, we are going up to Jerusalem; and the Son of man will be delivered to the chief priests and the scribes, and they will condemn him to death, and deliver him to the Gentiles; ³⁴and they will mock him, and spit upon him, and scourge him, and kill him; and after three days he will rise.'

³⁵And James and John, the sons of Zebedee, came forward to him, and said to him, 'Teacher, we want you to do for us whatever we ask of you.' ³⁶And he said to them, 'What do you want me to do for you?' ³⁷And they said to him, 'Grant us to sit, one at your right hand and one at your left, in your glory.' ³⁸But Jesus said to them, 'You do not know what you are asking. Are you able to drink the cup that I drink, or to be baptized with the baptism with which I am baptized?' ³⁹And they said to him, 'We are able.' And Jesus said to them, 'The cup that I drink you will drink, and with the baptism with which I am baptized, you will be baptized; ⁴⁰but to sit at my right hand or at my left is not mine to grant, but it is for those for whom it has been prepared.' ⁴¹And when the ten heard it, we began to be indignant at James and John. ⁴²And Jesus called us to him and said to us, 'You know that those who are supposed to rule over the Gentiles lord it over them, and their great men exercise authority over them. ⁴³But it shall not be so among you; but whoever would be great among you must be your servant, ⁴⁴and whoever would be first among you must be slave of all. ⁴⁵For the Son of man also came not to be served but to serve, and to give his life as a ransom for many.'

⁴⁶And we came to Jericho; and as he was leaving Jericho with us and a great multitude, Bartimaeus, a blind beggar, the son of Timaeus, was sitting by the roadside. ⁴⁷And when he heard that it was Jesus of

CHAPTER 10

AND he left there and went to the region of Judea and beyond the Jordan, and crowds gathered to him again; and again, as his custom was, he taught them. ²And Pharisees came up and in order to test him asked, 'Is it lawful for a man to divorce his wife?' ³He answered them, 'What did Moses command you?' ⁴They said, 'Moses allowed a man to write a certificate of divorce, and to put her away.' ⁵But Jesus said to them, 'For your hardness of heart he wrote you this commandment. ⁶But from the beginning of time, "God made them male and female." ⁷"For this reason a man shall leave his father and mother and be joined to his wife, ⁸and the two shall become one." So they are no longer two but one. ⁹What therefore God has joined together, let not man put asunder.'

¹⁰*And in the house we asked him again about this matter.* ¹¹*And he said to us, 'Whoever divorces his wife and marries another, commits adultery against her;* ¹²*and if she divorces her husband and marries another, she commits adultery.'*

¹³*And they were bringing children to him, that he might touch them; and we rebuked them.* ¹⁴*But when Jesus saw it he was indignant, and said to us, 'Let the children come to me, do not hinder them; for to such belongs the kingdom of God.* ¹⁵Truly, I say to you, whoever does not receive the kingdom of God like a child shall not enter it.' ¹⁶And he took them in his arms and blessed them, laying his hands upon them.

¹⁷And as he was setting out on his journey, a man ran up and knelt before him, and asked him, 'Good Teacher, what must I do to inherit eternal life?' ¹⁸And Jesus said to him, 'Why do you call me good? No one is good but God alone. ¹⁹You know the commandments: "Do not kill, Do not commit adultery, Do not steal, Do not bear false witness, Do not defraud, Honour your father and mother."' ²⁰And he said to him, 'Teacher, all these I have observed from my youth.' ²¹And Jesus looking upon him loved him, and said to him, 'You lack one thing; go, sell what you have, and give to the poor, and you will have treasure in heaven; and come, follow me.' ²²At that saying his countenance fell, and he went away sorrowful; for he had great possessions.

²³*And Jesus looked around and said to us, 'How hard it will be for*

laid himself open to such a fate, yet he came later to understand his weakness, turned around, and found both water and fire to be now on his side. We ask God's mercy for our own stubbornness in facing the wrong way in our own lives. We ask instead to be salted with fire.

Chapter 9

to lift up his light in the face of persecution. We pray to understand the two sides of our vocation: that we, like Jesus, will suffer *and so* enter glory.

Verses 14–29

There is a spirit which can still attack us even though we have been first enlightened as Peter was. Like epilepsy, it may not show itself at first, but under stress we may give way and deny Jesus publicly as Peter did. We may at that moment be deaf to all Jesus has taught us, and we may be dumb or talking nonsense instead of speaking the straight truth about what we believe. (My friend who suffers from epilepsy is painfully aware that some onlookers associate her attacks with mental illness — hence too the way the gospel refers to an *unclean* spirit in the epileptic boy.) Jesus knows and shows that the power to witness to the truth comes from prayer. The prayer to pray is, 'I believe; help my unbelief', over and over again.

Verses 30–50

The second prediction of the passion and resurrection is more obviously linked with the word 'servant'. At any time during this part of the gospel one may well wish to read prayerfully the prophecies in Isaiah concerning the Servant of God, prophecies which Jesus certainly looked to in understanding his role, and which St Mark certainly has in mind throughout the second half of the gospel. The texts are: (a) Isaiah 42:1–9; (b) 49:1–6; (c) 50:4–9 and (d) 52:13 – 53:12. So far, the first two of the four prophecies are the more relevant, and can be seen to fit Jesus' gentle way with people, his secrecy about his own identity, his desire to reach all peoples, and his readiness to listen to his Father so that he may know how to speak to the weary.

I remember that Jesus' vocation to be the Servant is also my vocation, since I am called to be 'another Christ'. These prophecies are written about me also, so I take them to heart. Accordingly, I listen to the discourse of Jesus on the subject of true greatness. I read it through slowly, asking for the power to do what Jesus wants. When we read of the millstone thrown into the sea, and of the unquenchable fire, we remember that Peter

God, through Jesus Christ the Son of God. Anyone can admit to being God's child when life is going smoothly. To acknowledge him as Father when everything goes wrong takes a power we do not possess from ourselves. Yet God does not call without giving us the power to answer the call, if we will but ask for it earnestly.

I picture the day of my confirmation, the day I was called to witness to my faith. I imagine myself at the scene of the transfiguration. I bring the two together and reflect that I too was transfigured on the day I was confirmed.

Jesus is the new Moses, the new lawgiver with a new covenant. We will gladly listen to the discourses of Jesus, knowing that the new covenant is one of love with no strings attached. God will not cease to love me even if I answer the call to love in return very poorly. Again I pray for my ears to be opened, this time to hear the second part of the word of God, about how I may love him in return for such great love.

The Holy Spirit moves in two directions: the same Spirit, but two directions. In the first half of the gospel, the Spirit comes from God to me with love. In the second half of the gospel, the Spirit wishes to move from me back to God, through the people I am called to love. I am but a mirror, and can only reflect what light or warmth is given to me. My lamp was lit in baptism for me alone; but now I am invited to hold it up to shine on others with warmth, even if I thereby feel cold or dark myself. I offer myself to the Spirit in the new direction he wishes to take. I know that in losing my life to him I shall only find it again, transfigured.

Verses 9–13

Jesus here as in many places in the second half of the gospel unites the prophecies of 'Son of man' and 'Servant'. The prophecy in Daniel is all about glory and clouds of heaven and angels and coming from heaven and everlasting dominion (power) — whereas the Servant in Isaiah must be gentle, must suffer, die and rise again. Peter and the disciples could accept the one, but not yet the other. Peter at least had received the Holy Spirit coming to enlighten him personally, but he had not yet received the power

Chapter 9
SUGGESTIONS FOR PRAYER

Verse 1

'The kingdom of God come with power.' In the context 'power' means the power to speak up for Jesus as the Christ, the Son of God, in the face of opposition or persecution. It also comes to mean the power to do as Jesus did, namely to speak up for ourselves as the sons or daughters of God in spite of opposition or disappointment coming from within or from outside of ourselves. We begin by praying for this power, which comes from God and not from ourselves.

Verse 2

Here as in several other places in the gospel Peter, James and John are picked out by Jesus as special witnesses. We are privileged to share what they saw and experienced. We prepare to look at the scene of the transfiguration either through Peter's eyes or as a fourth witness.

Verses 2–8

All Christians would see the initiation of newcomers to the faith as having two distinct aspects. One, God has adopted the newcomer as his own child, with an unconditional love for the child. Two, ever afterwards the newcomer is called and invited to love God in return, in loving his fellow human beings. Some denominations of Christians have for many centuries celebrated the first aspect in the sacrament of baptism, but the second aspect in the sacrament of confirmation. As a Catholic I now write about what is celebrated in confirmation, but the reality is and always has been present in the life of every Christian.

On the day I was confirmed, the Church celebrated my transfiguration. It was as if the Bishop, speaking in the name of the Father, had said over me what the voice of the Father said over Jesus: 'This is my beloved son; listen to him', or, 'This is my beloved daughter; listen to her'. On that day I was invited by my heavenly Father to speak out, and everyone else was to listen. What was I to say? Only the same as Jesus, namely to speak out in times of peace and in times of persecution that I am the child of and they were afraid to ask him. After that comes the second discourse by Jesus on the true meaning of greatness. Mark seems here as elsewhere to present a collection of various sayings of Jesus loosely linked to the main subject of true greatness. The sayings begin and end with the need for peace and not rivalry, and the other sayings in between are linked to one another by recurring words and phrases such as: greatest, first, last, servant, child, in my name, cause to stumble, sea, water, fire, salt. In Mark's gospel, all the way from the first prediction of the passion and resurrection to the entry into Jerusalem, the theme of Jesus as the promised Servant of Yahweh is never far away, the Servant who would move quietly but swiftly to his destiny, would suffer and die for all people and who would see a worldwide nation come into being as a result of his sacrifice.

In other unexpected ways this small discourse has links with the story which immediately preceded it. The boy with epilepsy was often cast into the fire and into the water. Water and fire are both used as symbols in Christian thinking, especially to denote the Holy Spirit: the water denotes the Holy Spirit coming as God's love to the Christian, the fire denotes the reflected love which thereupon comes from the Christian to love God in return and to spread God's love to others. The negative side of these symbols speaks of someone like the unready Peter, the Rock who causes little ones to stumble and sinks like a stone in water, the Rock who broke down at the fire. We have to pray, to pray humbly, to pray like a servant or a little child; we have to face the right way before the water and the fire become lifegiving and transforming.

On the way south from the region of Caesarea Philippi and the mountain, Jesus is now proceeding directly towards Jerusalem. If we wish to locate a house for the saying of Jesus about the need for prayer (verse 28f.), we could imagine it as being the house Peter originally came from in Bethsaida. The house where the second discourse on greatness took place could be pictured as Peter's house in Capernaum. Mark does not always use a house for Jesus' private words with his closest disciples: on the lake, as we saw, the location seems to have been the boat itself. As a storyteller, Mark is consistent with himself.

Chapter 9

The ailment of the child cured when Jesus came down the mountain is fairly obviously what we would call epilepsy. I myself know someone who suffers from epilepsy. She has had it from childhood, not from birth. She has to be extremely careful of water and fire, since she could so easily drown or burn herself when under an attack. She insists on people calling her attacks 'attacks' and not 'fits', since she senses that they come from some alien source: that is, she is not really herself when they occur. During an attack she is dumb and can foam at the mouth. She is usually thrown to the ground and contorted. For the length of the attack she is also deaf to anything anyone says to her. This is a temporary dumbness and deafness, sometimes brought on by emotional stress.

This story of Jesus has close links with the situation of Peter and the other disciples. At Caesarea Philippi Peter had his ears opened and his tongue loosened, and he learnt to hear and to speak. But what he was there able to do he will shortly be unable to do. Under the emotional stress of persecution, facing hostile comments and questions at the fire in the high priest's courtyard, he will be deaf to all Jesus has taught him and he will be dumb when asked if he is Jesus' disciple. This kind of 'unclean spirit', says Jesus of the epileptic boy, is only cast out by prayer. Peter will fail to pray when Jesus has warned him to pray, particularly in the garden of Gethsemane, so he is bound to break down under stress. The type of prayer Peter and the others should have prayed is given various forms in the gospel. Here the words are supplied by the father of the epileptic boy: 'I believe; help my unbelief', or, 'I believe; help the little faith that I have'. Peter did believe: we have only just heard his words of faith, 'You are the Christ'. But his seedling of faith is only small. The birds of the air could still come in *from outside* and snatch it from him. He needs to pray, for his faith to be strengthened to resist the attack that may come. Faith needs to grow into love.

Jesus, on the other hand, did listen to his Father; he did pray in the garden, and on trial he did echo the words of the Father, replying 'I am' to the question, 'Are you the Christ, the Son of the Blessed?' By ourselves, we cannot do such things, but with the power of God (for which we have to pray) we can.

Then comes the second prediction by Jesus of his own death and resurrection. The disciples did not understand the saying, is not quenched. ⁴⁹For every one will be salted with fire. ⁵⁰Salt is good; but if the salt has lost its saltness, how will you season it? Have salt in yourselves, and be at peace with one another.' [Note: *Verses 44 and 46, which are identical with verse 48, are omitted by the best ancient authorities.*]

* * *

Once Jesus turns his face firmly towards Jerusalem, St Mark adopts a formal pattern in his narrative. In all there are three main predictions by Jesus of his passion. Each is followed by a discourse from Jesus aimed at helping the shocked listeners to understand the true meaning of greatness. Then each discourse is followed by an incident or a series of incidents reflecting the current message of Jesus. In Chapter 8 we have seen and prayed over the first prediction of the passion, and the discourse that followed it. Now we come to the related incidents, namely what we call the transfiguration of Jesus and the cure of the epileptic boy.

In both incidents, but particularly in the transfiguration, the prophecies about the Son of man play a part. 'Power' is featured, and what is *possible* to God but not to human beings. 'Glory' of God is there in the cloud and in the brightness of Jesus' clothing. Jesus wears his own clothing, but its brightness comes from heaven, not from earth. Further, the voice of his Father from heaven tells Peter and the others to 'listen to him', echoing the other prophecy, about the prophet-like-Moses ('to him they will listen'). Around this time, we note, Jesus is first pictured as giving formal discourses as opposed to parables. In recognition of the fact that Jesus is the fulfilment of the law and the prophets, Moses and Elijah withdraw from the vision and only Jesus is left.

The story of the transfiguration holds a similar place in the second half of Mark's gospel to that held by the baptism of Jesus in the first half. There even seems to be a certain dialogue of faith and love going on between the Father and the human race, with Jesus in the centre. At the baptism the Father said to Jesus, 'You are my beloved Son; with you I am well pleased'. Peter at his confession of faith said to Jesus, 'You are the Christ'. In the transfiguration the Father said about Jesus, 'This is my beloved Son; listen to him'. At the crucifixion the centurion said, 'Truly, this man was the Son of God'.

Chapter 9

asked his father, 'How long has he had this?' And he said, 'From childhood. ²²And it has often cast him into the fire and into the water, to destroy him; but if you can do anything, have pity on us and help us.' ²³And Jesus said to him, 'If you can! All things are possible to him who believes.' ²⁴Immediately the father of the child cried out and said, 'I believe; help my unbelief!' ²⁵And when Jesus saw that a crowd came running together, he rebuked the unclean spirit, saying to it, 'You dumb and deaf spirit, I command you, come out of him, and never enter him again.' ²⁶And after crying out and convulsing him terribly, it came out, and the boy was like a corpse; so that most of them said, 'He is dead.' ²⁷But Jesus took him by the hand and lifted him up, and he arose. ²⁸And when he had entered the house, his disciples asked him privately, 'Why could we not cast it out?' ²⁹And he said to them, 'This kind cannot be driven out by anything but prayer.'

³⁰*We went on from there and passed through Galilee. And he would not have anyone know it;* ³¹*for he was teaching us, saying to us, 'The Son of man will be delivered into the hands of men, and they will kill him; and when he is killed, after three days he will rise.'* ³²*But we did not understand the saying, and we were afraid to ask him.*

³³*And we came to Capernaum; and when he was in the house he asked us, 'What were you discussing on the way?'* ³⁴*But we were silent; for on the way we had discussed with one another who was the greatest.* ³⁵*And he sat down and called the twelve; and he said to us, 'If any one would be first, he must be last of all and servant of all.'* ³⁶*And he took a child, and put him in the midst of us; and taking him in his arms, he said to us,* ³⁷*'Whoever receives one such child in my name receives me; and whoever receives me, receives not me but him who sent me.'*

³⁸John said to him, 'Teacher, we saw a man casting out demons in your name, and we forbade him, because he was not following us.' ³⁹But Jesus said, 'Do not forbid him; for no one who does a mighty work in my name will be able soon after to speak evil of me. ⁴⁰For he that is not against us is for us. ⁴¹For truly, I say to you, whoever gives you a cup of water to drink because you bear the name of Christ, will by no means lose his reward.

⁴²'Whoever causes one of these little ones who believe in me to sin, it would be better for him if a great millstone were hung round his neck and he were thrown into the sea. ⁴³And if your hand causes you to sin, cut it off; it is better for you to enter life maimed than with two hands to go to hell, to the unquenchable fire. ⁴⁵And if your foot causes you to sin, cut it off; it is better for you to enter life lame than with two feet to be thrown into hell. ⁴⁷And if your eye causes you to sin, pluck it out; it is better for you to enter the kingdom of God with one eye than with two eyes to be thrown into hell, ⁴⁸where their worm does not die, and the fire

CHAPTER 9

*

ᴀɴᴅ he said to them, 'Truly, I say to you, there are some standing here who will not taste death before they see the kingdom of God come with power.'
² And after six days Jesus took with him me and James and John, and led us up a high mountain apart by ourselves; and he was transfigured before us, ³ and his garments became glistening, intensely white, as no fuller on earth could bleach them. ⁴ And there appeared to us Elijah with Moses; and they were talking to Jesus. ⁵ And I said to Jesus, 'Master, it is well that we are here; let us make three booths, one for you and one for Moses and one for Elijah.' ⁶ For I did not know what to say, for we were exceedingly afraid. ⁷ And a cloud overshadowed us, and a voice came out of the cloud, 'This is my beloved Son; listen to him.' ⁸ And suddenly looking around we no longer saw anyone with us but Jesus only.

⁹ And as we were coming down the mountain, he charged us to tell no one what we had seen, until the Son of man should have risen from the dead. ¹⁰ So we kept the matter to ourselves, questioning what the rising from the dead meant. ¹¹ And we asked him, 'Why do the scribes say that first Elijah must come?' ¹² And he said to us, 'Elijah does come first to restore all things; and how is it written of the Son of man, that he should suffer many things and be treated with contempt? ¹³ But I tell you that Elijah has come, and they did to him whatever they pleased, as it is written of him.'

¹⁴ And when we came to the disciples, we saw a great crowd about them, and scribes arguing with them. ¹⁵ And immediately all the crowd, when they saw him, were greatly amazed, and ran up to him and greeted him. ¹⁶ And he asked them, 'What are you discussing with them?' ¹⁷ And one of the crowd answered him, 'Teacher, I brought my son to you, for he has a dumb spirit; ¹⁸ and wherever it seizes him, it dashes him down; and he foams and grinds his teeth and becomes rigid; and I asked your disciples to cast it out, and they were not able.' ¹⁹ And he answered them, 'O faithless generation, how long am I to be with you? How long am I to bear with you? Bring him to me.' ²⁰ And they brought the boy to him; and when the spirit saw him, immediately it convulsed the boy, and he fell on the ground and rolled about, foaming at the mouth. ²¹ And Jesus

Chapter 8

Verses 31–38

Like Peter, I find that the sudden introduction of talk about suffering and rejection and death and a cross gives me quite a jolt. The gospel story so far has been all comforting to any person of good will. I pray to be able to accept Jesus' words in trust: 'I am willing to trust, Jesus, that whatever you tell me to do will be for the best, will end in a resurrection. You rebuked Peter, just as you rebuke in me the desire to leave everything at the comfortable stage of faith without growing into love. Protect the little plant of faith that is in me, let the birds of the air not have it all: let me come to my senses as Peter did eventually. If ever I fail to speak up for you and your words in a hostile crowd, forgive me as you forgave Peter and let my shame be for my purifying.'

'Now that you speak no longer in parables but plainly and openly, let me ponder your words and try to obey them. I think there are far more sheep than shepherds in this world, as there were when you fed the five thousand, and I feel sure your more difficult words will only be taken to heart by the shepherds. I would wish to be called among the shepherds, to help in your work, though I know my salvation comes not from being a good shepherd but from trust, the trust of a lamb in you its chief shepherd, the trust which is the same thing as faith.'

just done in his words to the disciples. We pray in particular: 'Father, may we see *and understand* that Jesus is the Christ, the promised Saviour, as you said at his baptism. May I *with complete faith* hear you saying to me also, "You are my beloved child; with you I am well pleased". And may we *know* Jesus present with us in the bread of the Eucharist, his body, keeping us as one, sustaining our journey, shepherding us.'

Verse 30

These are mysteries, and we may well reflect on the first half of the gospel as a whole to see if it tells us even more than the individual parts.

So far we have been moving towards faith, and Jesus and Peter between them have shown us the way. 'Faith is the beginning', said Ignatius of Antioch, and the gospel so far has been about faith. From now on faith will grow into love: 'Love is the end, and where the two are together, there is God'. Ignatius also said, 'Faith is the body of Christ', and so far we have dealt only with bread and water, not yet with wine or blood.

If the first five chapters of Mark follow the themes of baptism, the sixth to eighth chapters have been mainly about bread, about food, and about recognition. We seem to see the first half of the mysteries of Christian initiation in the first half of the gospel of Mark: baptism; Eucharist as bread.

The first half of the gospel shows Jesus replacing the synagogue services; the second half will show him replacing the temple worship. The first half of the gospel shows the seed of God — the Good News that we are God's children — being sown, and finally its germination in Peter.

Peter's act of faith in Jesus is spoken before Jesus, and among friends. It will be a different matter when he tries to speak out among enemies: that requires something beyond faith, namely divine love, which as yet in the gospel of Mark only Jesus possesses.

*

Chapter 8

that Jesus gives us in the bread of the Eucharist may not taste very exciting most of the time, but it has sustained us and it will continue to sustain us on our way home. We thank Jesus for his compassion, and reflect upon our own life as a journey with Jesus through the desert to the promised land.

Verse 10

Mark seems to be saying that Jesus here leaves Gentile territory and comes to his own part of the world. If this is so, we may be glad and rejoice that we, of Gentile and pagan ancestry, have now been included in the chosen people of God, and fed; and like the small fish we too have been born in living water. This, by the way, is almost the last journey over water Mark tells us about. Water has been frequently present throughout the first half of the gospel.

Verses 11–21

We may pray about the 'one loaf' there in the boat with Jesus and the disciples. Jesus implies that when he is present, one loaf is enough, because the Providence of God is present. We might compare a family out for a long walk on holiday: the littlest child grows tired and weary, and starts to lag behind. What do the mother and father do? Leave the child behind on the hillside and take the rest of the family home before dark? No, of course not! In a good family no one is home until everyone is home. There is only one loaf, one family. Either mother or father, or an elder brother or sister, stays behind to keep pace with the poor little one, or even to carry the child if necessary. We can identify with the parents, with the child, with the elder brother or sister, and we see that 'one loaf' is right. We may use these reflections also at communion time.

Verses 22–29

We, like Peter and the others, have been through a stage of not seeing Jesus at all, whether as babies or as children or even as adults. Then we saw and heard Jesus, but we never have understood completely and we never will understand completely in this life. So we pray to see *and understand* what our Father is saying to us in Jesus. We link together seeing and hearing as Jesus has

The second half of Mark's gospel begins, and at this point Jesus begins to do two new things: he begins to tell his disciples that he, the Christ, must suffer, and he begins to say it openly. Up to now, there have been no direct references to the fact that Jesus will die; from now on in the gospel there are nearly twenty references to Jesus' death, references made between this time here at Caesarea Philippi, and the Last Supper. Even his very journey is a steady and direct journey south from now on, starting from Mount Hermon at his transfiguration and going straight to Jerusalem and death via Capernaum, the territory beyond the Jordan, and Jericho. In the first half of the gospel his journeyings criss-crossed and doubled back all the time. It is as if Jesus was waiting for Peter to be given the gift of faith, before he turned his face resolutely towards Jerusalem. (See the sketch maps on pages 135 and 136.)

Peter began something too: he began to rebuke Jesus for linking the Christ with suffering. If we imagine that the seed of faith has finally germinated in Peter, and begun to show over ground, so too we might say that the birds of the air are quick to swoop: 'Satan', Jesus calls Peter. The day will soon come when Peter is ashamed of Jesus and his words in the face of a hostile crowd. But we notice that Peter's faith survived in the end, and the Son of man is no longer ashamed of him.

SUGGESTIONS FOR PRAYER

Verses 1–9

Once we think of the feeding of the four thousand as a story to do with the bread of the Eucharist, and to do with manna in the desert, it becomes easy to pray. We place ourselves with the hungry people, and we tell Jesus that we have been with him now a long time; we have come a long journey through life already and we do not want to faint on the way home to paradise and the promised land. We call upon Jesus' compassion as the people wandering in the desert called upon Moses. (We remember that Peter, speaking at Solomon's Porch some time after the Resurrection, drew our attention to the likeness between Jesus and Moses, and to his belief that Jesus was the 'prophet like Moses' who Moses had prophesied would come.) The manna

Chapter 8

Providence is not a chance event, unpredictable. It happens every time, through Jesus. He is the one loaf uniting in himself all the grains of wheat. Nobody is to be left behind as being too faint, too weary, too sick, too much a sinner.

'Having eyes do you not see, and having ears do you not hear?' In Chapter 7 we prayed about the man who was deaf and had an impediment in his speech. The disciples now have ears but cannot hear, nor can they speak sense in answer to Jesus' questions. Next, here in Chapter 8, we have the story of the blind man of Bethsaida. He had eyes but he could not see, and even when he was given sight he still could not understand. I remember seeing in 1983 or thereabouts a television documentary film about a Scottish girl of eighteen or so who had been blind from birth. The doctors had in the meantime discovered a cure for her form of blindness, so at the age of eighteen she opened her eyes for the first time, with the camera watching and listening. She was filled with wonder about all sorts of things, but she was unsure what to call things right away. 'Ooh! is that a telephone?', I remember she said, when the telephone rang; 'I never knew a telephone looked like that!'

Up to this moment the disciples had been deaf to the true meaning of Jesus' words. In early life they did not hear his word; then they heard him but did not understand. In early life too they did not see Jesus; then they saw him but did not understand what they saw. They gave him the wrong name. As far back as the feeding of the five thousand, Jesus sent the disciples ahead to go to Bethsaida, but the wind was against them and they never reached their destination at that time. Now they have reached Bethsaida, and they are on the verge of a breakthrough in understanding.

Near Caesarea Philippi, Jesus asks his disciples who the people think him to be, then who *they*, the disciples, say he is. Peter suddenly has his ears opened *to understand*, his eyes opened better *to see clearly*, so that he can then *speak sense*. Jesus asks him to keep it secret for the time being: the time of proclaiming it is not quite yet.

This ends the first half of Mark's gospel, the gospel of Jesus (who is the) Christ.

*

a desert place, with nothing to eat. They have been with Jesus three days, and they are hungry. Some of them have come a long way. Jesus has compassion on them, he does not want them to faint on the way home. So he feeds them, there in the desert, with food whose source is a mystery, as if it were manna. In all of this, Jesus is clearly acting like Moses, but with more authority than Moses. The sign was clear enough, but in spite of what they had seen when the five thousand were fed the disciples could not foresee what Jesus was going to do. Thus for a second time they did not understand about the loaves, for their hearts were hardened.

As before, there are fish to eat, even though the scene is now away from the fresh-water sea and in a desert place. 'Fish born in living water' perhaps already by the time Mark wrote his gospel were seen as symbols of the Christian. Mark hints that this sign of the feeding of the four thousand happened in Gentile territory, since Jesus has been travelling through Tyre, Sidon and the Decapolis and has not yet returned home. In fact, Mark tells us that once Jesus sends the crowd away he goes with his disciples in the boat to Dalmanutha, a word which may mean *of his own house*.

The Pharisees then came and asked for a sign from heaven. According to Mark's gospel, Jesus has now given them two public signs, one saying he is the promised shepherd and the other saying he is the promised prophet like Moses. He will give them no more signs for the present, if they cannot see what he has already put before their eyes.

Next comes a discussion about 'one loaf' in which Jesus and his disciples are speaking at cross-purposes. The disciples were worried because they had only one loaf of bread among the thirteen or more of them in the boat. Jesus was talking about the leaven of the Pharisees and the leaven of Herod, which in the gospel we have lately seen in the story of John the Baptist's death and in the argument about clean foods. When Jesus sees how the disciples are firmly tied down to the earthly meaning of things, namely bread for dinner, he takes his lessons one stage further. This is a third misunderstanding about bread, again 'because their hearts are hardened'. If Jesus can feed five thousand with five loaves, and four thousand with seven loaves, and still have plenty over, he can certainly feed thirteen with one loaf. God's

Chapter 8

man, and begged him to touch him. ²³And he took the blind man by the hand, and led him out of the village; and when he had spit on his eyes and laid his hands upon him, he asked him, 'Do you see anything?' ²⁴And he looked up and said, 'I see men; but they look like trees, walking.' ²⁵Then again he laid his hands upon his eyes; and he looked intently and was restored, and saw everything clearly. ²⁶And he sent him away to his home, saying, 'Do not even enter the village.'

²⁷And Jesus went on with us, to the villages of Caesarea Philippi; and on the way he asked us, 'Who do men say that I am?' ²⁸And we told him, 'John the Baptist; and others say, Elijah; and others one of the prophets.' ²⁹And he asked us, 'But who do you say that I am?' I answered him, 'You are the Christ.' ³⁰And he charged us to tell no one about him.

*　*　*

³¹And he began to teach us that the Son of man must suffer many things, and be rejected by the elders and the chief priests and the scribes, and be killed, and after three days rise again. ³²And he said this plainly. And I took him, and began to rebuke him. ³³But turning and seeing his disciples, he rebuked me, and said, 'Get behind me, Satan! For you are not on the side of God, but of men.'

³⁴And he called to him the multitude with us, and said to them, 'If any man would come after me, let him deny himself and take up his cross and follow me. ³⁵For whoever would save his life will lose it; and whoever loses his life for my sake and the gospel's will save it. ³⁶For what does it profit a man, to gain the whole world and forfeit his life? ³⁷For what can a man give in return for his life? ³⁸For whoever is ashamed of me and of my words in this adulterous and sinful generation, of him will the Son of man also be ashamed, when he comes in the glory of his Father with the holy angels.' [*Note that verse 38 marks the end of the chapter, but not yet the end of the paragraph.*]

*　*　*

Next comes the story of the feeding of the four thousand in a desert place. Some commentators have suggested that this is another version of the same incident as the feeding of the five thousand. Mark clearly makes a quite different sign out of this story: the five thousand was about the coming of the promised shepherd; the four thousand is about the coming of the promised 'prophet like Moses' (see Deuteronomy 18:15f.). Here they are in

CHAPTER 8
*

I*N those days, when again a great crowd had gathered, and they had nothing to eat, he called us to him, and said to us,* ^{2}*'I have compassion on the crowd, because they have been with me now three days, and have nothing to eat;* ^{3}*and if I send them away hungry to their homes, they will faint on the way; and some of them have come a long way.'* ^{4}*And we answered him, 'How can one feed these men with bread here in the desert?'* ^{5}*And he asked us, 'How many loaves have you?' We said, 'Seven.'* ^{6}*And he commanded the crowd to sit down on the ground; and he took the seven loaves, and having given thanks he broke them and gave them to us to set before the people; and we set them before the crowd.* ^{7}*And we had a few small fish; and having blessed them, he commanded that these also should be set before them.* ^{8}*And they ate, and were satisfied; and we took up the broken pieces left over, seven baskets full.* ^{9}*And there were about four thousand people.* ^{10}*And he sent them away; and immediately he got into the boat with us, and went to the district of Dalmanutha.*

^{11}The Pharisees came and began to argue with him, seeking from him a sign from heaven, to test him. ^{12}And he sighed deeply in his spirit, and said, 'Why does this generation seek a sign? Truly, I say to you, no sign shall be given to this generation.' ^{13}And he left them, and getting into the boat again he departed to the other side.

^{14}*Now we had forgotten to bring bread; and we had only one loaf with us in the boat.* ^{15}*And he cautioned us, saying, 'Take heed, beware of the leaven of the Pharisees and the leaven of Herod.'* ^{16}*And we discussed it with one another, saying, 'We have no bread.'* ^{17}*And being aware of it, Jesus said to us, 'Why do you discuss the fact that you have no bread? Do you not yet perceive or understand? Are your hearts hardened?* ^{18}*Having eyes do you not see, and having ears do you not hear? And do you not remember?* ^{19}*When I broke the five loaves for the five thousand, how many baskets full of broken pieces did you take up?' We said to him, 'Twelve.'* ^{20}*'And the seven for the four thousand, how many baskets full of broken pieces did you take up?' And we said to him, 'Seven.'* ^{21}*And he said to us, 'Do you not yet understand?'*

^{22}*And we came to Bethsaida. And some people brought to him a blind*

Chapter 7

cannot have what we ask for, may we ask for a crumb of comfort: then perhaps you will be able to give us what we asked for in the first place.'

Verses 36 and 37

'Like Jesus, may we be modest and somewhat shy about being your children, Father. May we never give ourselves airs before others, who are after all your children just as much as we are.'

in truth God's children, with a place at his table and a share in the bread of the children. We could say that the character of the sacrament of baptism is that it gives us a place at the table. The place is given by God, so our place will never be removed from the table. I may be a long time coming home, but God my Father will never allow anyone else to sit in my place, nor to remove it from the table. From before the beginning of time my name was on my place, chosen for me as his adopted child by my Father. All this makes me immensely grateful: to the Father for choosing me, to Jesus the Son for not refusing to share the family table with the likes of me. I thank the Father, I thank the Son. I thank them both for giving me the Spirit, the spirit of adoption. I look forward to entering my inheritance and taking my place at the table in the banquet. I reflect that all others too are God's children, though so many do not realize it. I begin to have a new desire to share my blessings with those who do not know God as their Father.

Verses 31–35

We may notice and reflect on the fact that St Ignatius of Antioch, bishop of Antioch AD 69–107, once wrote that faith is the body of the Lord, and 'faith is the beginning', whereas love is the blood of Jesus, and 'love is the end'. Praying about the 'bread of the children' story, and then the cure of the deaf man, we may well think of the bread of the Eucharist. So far in Mark's gospel there is no mention of the blood, of the cup, but here in Chapters 6 to 8 'bread' and 'food' and 'banquet' appear, 'bread' many times. Another frequent theme is 'recognition': so we pray to recognize Jesus as the Christ present in the bread of the Eucharist. 'Open our ears, Lord Jesus, to hear your words as you say "This is my body" over the bread of the Eucharist. When we hear, let us understand; when we understand may we confess with our tongues that you are really there in the Eucharist, sharing with us your place at the table. You are the Son, so your body is the bread of the children, as we cease to be only who we were and become your sisters and brothers, one body, one family with you.'

The Syrophoenician woman was at first denied a whole loaf, so she asked for the crumbs. 'Jesus, inspire us too to keep on asking when you or your Father seem to say "No" to our requests. If we

Chapter 7

really understood him than crowds who only half-understood. Jesus alone already foresees the day when he will be killed and his disciples must carry on.

SUGGESTIONS FOR PRAYER

Verses 1–15

Reflecting on these verses we may pray to be delivered from the evils of spiritual deafness and blindness. We pray not to fall into the trap of making our religious customs and traditions more important than the greater things of conscience. At the time of writing of this book, the Catholic religion is fairly flexible compared with fifty years ago, but the temptation to freeze new customs and consecrate them is always there in human nature. Jesus reminds us to honour our father and our mother, so we search our consciences, ask pardon, make amends if we can. A clean conscience means a simple conscience: may we always obey our one Father in heaven, who speaks to us and invites us in our conscience ('what *I* think I ought to do in the choice before me'), and who will forgive us if we fail.

Verses 17–23

Jesus declared all foods clean. This is one of the declarations that set free the pagan world to become children of God. There was no longer any need for the simple people of the world to follow complicated rules and regulations about diet and about religious cleansing. As people coming from ancestors who were of the Gentile pagan world, we may give heartfelt thanks to Jesus for making his way so simple for us. We are children of God, and children know without asking anyone else or looking in a book what their loving Father wants. No need for complicated instruction books. No need for impossible customs.

Verses 24–30

Praying about the 'bread of the children' story, we may easily connect it with the Good News at the beginning of the gospel. We believe the Good News. We can say back to God our Father, 'I am your beloved child; with me you are well pleased'. And simply because (by God's gift) we believe Jesus, we find ourselves to be for in the first place, namely the bread of the children and a place at the table as one of the children. Such is the dramatic effect of faith upon a pagan. When the woman goes home she finds her child better, lying calmly on her bed. 'An unclean spirit' usually seems to mean a mental illness or handicap of some sort. Perhaps the child, with whatever handicap, had before been difficult to control.

Jesus then travels in a roundabout way back to the Sea of Galilee. Passing through the Decapolis, he cures a man 'who was deaf and had an impediment in his speech'. Almost certainly what was wrong was that the man had been born deaf. There was, however, nothing wrong with his lungs or his vocal cords. What made his speech imperfect was that he had never in his life heard other people speaking, nor could he hear his own vocal noises. A stone-deaf baby simply does not learn to speak properly even today without expert medical help and speech-training. Hence we have here in Jesus' cure of the man a double sign. At one and the same time the man's hearing is restored, and he can speak clearly. The second marvel, his speaking clearly, should normally have taken months or even years after the cure of the hearing. How did the man know what names to call things, when he had never yet heard the names? Who taught him to put sentences together? How was it that he not only heard clearly, but understood what he heard?

I think it is fair to say that in the whole of Mark's gospel so far, and indeed until after Peter's words of faith in the next chapter, there is very little stress given to 'do this; do not do that', as spoken by Jesus to the world at large. There are parables for the people, there are arguments with enemies, from which lessons may be drawn, but not what we might call regular sermons for everyone. The lessons for those closest to him are mainly about faith and recognition, about listening, looking, reacting to Jesus' actions, thinking over his parables. What Jesus seems to want of the disciples in the first half of the gospel is openness: '*Ephphatha*, that is, *Be opened*'.

Jesus asked for his cure of the deaf man to be kept a secret. Later in the gospel this desire for secrecy will be explained when Jesus is seen to be the Servant of God. Although he is Son of God, he empties himself to become the least of all and the servant of all. As for his mission, he would rather have a few disciples who

Chapter 7

blaming the Pharisees for twisting the word of God to suit their own pockets.

In the house, to a few of the disciples, Jesus speaks further about food, and Mark comments, 'Thus he declared all foods clean'. The Greek words Mark uses for 'clean' and 'unclean' are the same words, one of them quite technical and unusual, as those used by Peter in the description of one of his visions in the Acts of the Apostles. Peter was encouraged to baptize the first non-Jewish convert Cornelius because of the vision in which he was ordered to kill and eat animals the Jews thought unclean: 'What God has cleansed, Peter, you must not call unclean' (see Acts 10:14f.). This happened to Peter round about AD 48. If all foods were clean, there was no need for pagans of good will to become practising Jews before being baptized. We have here in this story of Mark's almost the first charter of our freedom to move straight from being pagans to being Christians, a charter ratified once and for all by the Council of Jerusalem in AD 49. Peter had his vision; he then saw a new depth of meaning in this story he had remembered about Jesus and the Pharisees; Mark in turn gets the story from Peter.

Then Jesus went away to the Gentile region of Tyre and Sidon. He often does withdraw after a major argument with the Pharisees or others who do not wish to understand him: he goes away somewhere quiet to teach or train his closest disciples. In this instance Jesus gives his disciples an object-lesson, and the gospel presents this next incident as another charter for the pagans, something for the disciples to ponder and digest. The story starts off with a strong Jewish flavour about it. Jesus wanted to be hidden, but a pagan woman of the district found where he was and begged him to cast 'an unclean spirit' out of her little daughter. Jesus replies that it is not right to take the children's bread and throw it to the dogs, until the children themselves are fed. Jesus was, by implication, on a mission to the Jews, the children, and they must be fed before the house-dogs under the table — the pagans.

But the woman takes up the metaphor and says in effect, 'Very well, I am like a house-dog; but now I am begging as house-dogs do for a scrap, for the crumbs, from the children's table'. So Jesus gives her, not a scrap or the crumbs, but exactly what she asked from within, out of the heart of man, come evil thoughts, fornication, theft, murder, adultery, [22]coveting, wickedness, deceit, licentiousness, envy, slander, pride, foolishness. [23]All these evil things come from within, and they defile a man.' [Note: *Other ancient authorities add verse 16:* 'If any man has ears to hear, let him hear.']

[24]And from there he arose and went away to the region of Tyre and Sidon. And he entered a house, and would not have any one know it; yet he could not be hid. [25]But immediately a woman, whose little daughter was possessed by an unclean spirit, heard of him, and came and fell down at his feet. [26]Now the woman was a Greek, a Syrophoenician by birth. And she begged him to cast the demon out of her daughter. [27]And he said to her, 'Let the children first be fed, for it is not right to take the children's bread and throw it to the dogs.' [28]But she answered him, 'Yes, Lord; yet even the dogs under the table eat the children's crumbs.' [29]And he said to her, 'For this saying you may go your way; the demon has left your daughter.' [30]And she went home, and found the child lying in bed, and the demon gone.

[31]Then he returned from the region of Tyre, and went through Sidon to the Sea of Galilee, through the region of the Decapolis. [32]And they brought to him a man who was deaf and had an impediment in his speech; and they besought him to lay his hand upon him. [33]And taking him aside from the multitude privately, he put his fingers into his ears, and he spat and touched his tongue; [34]and looking up to heaven, he sighed, and said to him, 'Ephphatha,' that is, 'Be opened.' [35]And his ears were opened, his tongue was released, and he spoke plainly. [36]And he charged them to tell no one; but the more he charged them, the more zealously they proclaimed it. [37]And they were astonished beyond measure, saying, 'He has done all things well; he even makes the deaf hear and the dumb speak.'

* * *

Three-quarters of this chapter is again to do with bread, with food, as was the last chapter. The final quarter is about recognition, a theme which also featured in the previous chapter. In Chapter 6 we saw 'the leaven of Herod'; in this present chapter we see 'the leaven of the Pharisees' as St Mark contrasts the teaching of Jesus about foods with the teaching of the Pharisees. They are concerned about rituals to do with food, whereas Jesus is more concerned with what comes from within people. In effect, Mark links 'food' with 'the word of God', and shows Jesus

CHAPTER 7

NOW when the Pharisees gathered together to him, with some of the scribes, who had come from Jerusalem, ²they saw that some of us ate with hands defiled, that is, unwashed. ³(For the Pharisees, and all the Jews, do not eat unless they wash their hands, observing the tradition of the elders; ⁴and when they come from the market place, they do not eat unless they purify themselves; and there are many other traditions which they observe, the washing of cups and pots and vessels of bronze.) ⁵And the Pharisees and the scribes asked him, 'Why do your disciples not live according to the tradition of the elders, but eat with hands defiled?' ⁶And he said to them, 'Well did Isaiah prophesy of you hypocrites, as it is written,

"This people honours me with their lips,
but their heart is far from me;
⁷in vain do they worship me,
teaching as doctrines the precepts of men."

⁸You leave the commandment of God, and hold fast the tradition of men.'

⁹And he said to them, 'You have a fine way of rejecting the commandment of God, in order to keep your tradition! ¹⁰For Moses said, "Honour your father and your mother"; and, "He who speaks evil of father or mother, let him surely die"; ¹¹but you say, "If a man tells his father or his mother, What you would have gained from me is Corban" (that is, given to God) — ¹²then you no longer permit him to do anything for his father or mother, ¹³thus making void the word of God through your tradition which you hand on. And many such things you do.'

¹⁴And he called the people to him again, and said to them, 'Hear me, all of you, and understand: ¹⁵there is nothing outside a man which by going into him can defile him; but the things which come out of a man are what defile him.' ¹⁷*And when he had entered the house, and left the people, we asked him about the parable.* ¹⁸*And he said to us, 'Then are you also without understanding? Do you not see that whatever goes into a man from outside cannot defile him,* ¹⁹*since it enters, not his heart but his stomach, and so passes on?' (Thus he declared all foods clean.)* ²⁰And he said, 'What comes out of a man is what defiles a man. ²¹For

forgetting that I possess all his love, and that I need never have worried, never have doubted.

Since in the story there are many disciples in the boat, we may also pray the incident with, or on behalf of, the group we generally worship with. Parish groups, prayer groups, religious communities, we all go through our times of distress when we seem to be getting nowhere.

Chapter 6

same day a letter from her signed 'With all my love, Mother', so the love of God is given to each of us completely. His love does not depend on whether our brothers and sisters give us a fair share of this world's goods.

We notice that at this stage of the gospel there are no instructions for the crowd, and no response is called for from us except to listen, to wonder, to receive with faith. There is bread and there is water, but as yet no wine, no chalice. The bread, and the teaching about God's love for us, are the truth upon which our response will be built in the second half of the gospel.

Verses 14–29

God's truth is real food. The kingdom of Herod, by contrast, is sheer poison. We may now go back briefly and compare Herod's banquet with that of Jesus our true king and shepherd. Do we really want to compete for a place at Herod's banquet, and not rather to accept a free place in Jesus' kingdom?

Verses 45–52

After the feeding of the five thousand comes the story of Jesus walking on the sea, when the disciples were distressed in rowing. At the end comes the unexpected comment: 'And we were utterly astounded, *for we did not understand about the loaves*, but our hearts were hardened'. This surely must mean that Mark sees the incident as having to do with the Eucharist. And when we take it that way, the story becomes easy to pray. How often in my life I seem to be rowing a boat against the wind, and I am in distress. Jesus sees my distress, and comes to me in the Eucharist. Can I believe that it is really he, and not some figment of the imagination? Can he really be walking freely over the waters of death, 2,000 years after Pilate certified him dead? Can he really be coming on purpose to help me in my distress?

Perhaps he makes as if to walk on by, but only to make me cry out as I suddenly recognize my need of him. Either he can save me or nobody can, this at least I know. So then he comes back and comes aboard my boat, saying those wonderful words, 'Take heart, it is I; have no fear'. He chides me gently for so soon place ourselves, in faith, within this family; we make here our home; we find here our brothers and sisters. Amen.

Verses 7–13

Jesus sent his disciples out to twos. I may ask myself, why? Perhaps to support each other. Perhaps because it is better to show what love looks like than simply to talk about it. Two apostles friendly to each other must be a better advertisement than one apostle working alone. We pray to be incurably friendly towards our family, and towards our companions in the faith. We do not want to be stand-offish with others not of the faith, but to love our fellow Christians so much that the warmth will spread.

'"When you enter a house, stay there until you leave the place." Help us, Jesus, to remain faithful to our old friends, to the ones who were the first to give us their support. May we not give them up when more attractive friends want to claim us. Thank you, Jesus, that you have never abandoned us for the sake of anyone else more attractive.'

Verses 30–44

Neither has Jesus ever said we were too many, or that we had come at an awkward time. We may best pray this story of the feeding of the five thousand as a communion-time prayer, thinking especially of the bread of the Eucharist, the body of Christ. As I come to the Eucharist, Jesus has compassion on me, and his pity is the pity a good shepherd has for his sheep or his lamb.

At any communion-time, I may in my imagination place myself at the outside edge of the crowd of five thousand, and wonder, 'Will there be any bread left for me?' And there always is, with plenty left over. It is shown to me sometimes in the following way: perhaps the minister has not enough hosts for one each per person. All he or she has to do is to break the host into smaller pieces. Then I receive a smaller piece of the divine bread, but I know it comes to me with *all* the love of Jesus. As when two children are separated from their mother, and each receives on the

Chapter 6

apostles to head for Bethsaida, but they do not manage to reach there. In fact, they do not reach Bethsaida till shortly before Peter's big confession of faith. The next chapter or two shows how much they still had to understand.

On the way across the lake they are struggling with the rowing, because the wind is against them. Strangely, Jesus has seen their difficulties and come on purpose to help them, but when he comes walking on the water he makes as if to pass them by. It only makes sense if the help he came to give them was faith. He does the same, we recall, with the two disciples at Emmaus, when he makes as if to walk on down the street, thus inviting them to call him back.

SUGGESTIONS FOR PRAYER

Verses 1–6

We too may praise the wisdom of Jesus. The early Church Fathers, looking in the Old Testament for hints of the mystery of the Trinity, used to call Jesus the Wisdom of God, ever with God. Here is the Wisdom of God contained in 'this man'! Here is a human life (itself therefore 'made by human hands') doing mighty works with his hands, works beyond the power of human hands. He himself in his body 'made by human hands' will be the bread who will feed our hunger. A carpenter makes things with his hands and mends things. How fitting that Jesus Son of God should be a carpenter, taking after his Father who makes all things and mends all things.

Next we may wonder along these lines: our faith in God as our Father places us as brothers and sisters of Jesus. Jesus is the only-begotten Son, we are the adopted children. But our Father, as a loving parent does, loves each of us adopted children as much as he loves his very own Son. And we share not just our Father with Jesus, but also our mother in Mary. Jesus is called 'the son of Mary', here in this chapter. Later on we shall hear him call God '*Abba*, Father'. We are not exclusively divine beings, with God for our Father *and* our Mother. We do not go beyond the Christ; we are other Christs. We are brothers and sisters of Jesus, with God for our divine Father and Mary for our earthly mother. We tell his disciples to beware of. In this chapter of St Mark the leaven of Herod and the bread of Jesus are placed side by side, and Herod's kingdom is shown to be a parody and a mockery of the true kingdom. Herod invites to his banquet only his courtiers, his officers and the leading people of Galilee; Jesus accepts anybody. Herod is tricked into stopping the mouth of the prophet John; Jesus starts his banquet by teaching his guests many things. Herod's birthday party combines adultery, lust, false pride, murder: on his plate comes the severed head of a good man. How very different, poles apart, is the atmosphere of the feeding of the five thousand.

The apostles come back, over-excited and over-tired, and Jesus goes with them in search of a lonely place. When he finds the crowds have got there first, Jesus shows compassion, not impatience. This story of the five thousand is told by St Mark in such a way as to show Jesus as the Shepherd promised in Ezekiel and elsewhere. 'You shepherds are feeding yourselves and neglecting my sheep. I myself will come and be their shepherd; my servant David will come. He shall feed them and be their shepherd.' The Shepherd would take the sheep away from their false shepherds, and lead them on to good pasture, make them lie down on the green grass by the running water, and there he would feed them. Their food would cost them nothing, and they would eat until they were satisfied. And here was Jesus with a huge crowd which had deserted the synagogues and their shepherds; he had compassion on them because they were like sheep without a shepherd; he fed their minds and hearts with truth; he made them lie down on the green grass by the fresh water of the lake; he fed them till they were satisfied, since there was plenty over; what should have cost 200 denarii (some thousands of pounds) cost them nothing. Mark even has time to admire the colours of the scene: the words he uses, translated above as *in groups*, in fact mean 'like so many flower-beds', with the green pathways in between the colourful groups for the Twelve to pass up and down.

The gospel of John tells us there was over-excitement at the end of this sign, with the crowds wanting to make Jesus king there and then. St Mark hints at the same, in the way Jesus packs off the Twelve into the boat while he dismisses the crowd by himself and then goes up into the hills to pray. Jesus tells the

Chapter 6

walking on the sea we thought it was a ghost, and cried out; [50] for we all saw him, and were terrified. But immediately he spoke to us and said, 'Take heart, it is I; have no fear.' [51] And he got into the boat with us and the wind ceased. And we were utterly astounded, [52] for we did not understand about the loaves, but our hearts were hardened.

[53] And when we had crossed over, we came to land at Gennesaret, and moored to the shore. [54] And when we got out of the boat, immediately the people recognized him, [55] and ran about the whole neighbourhood and began to bring sick people on their pallets to any place where they heard he was. [56] And wherever he came, in villages, cities, or country, they laid the sick in the market places, and besought him that they might touch even the fringe of his garment; and as many as touched it were made well.

* * *

Jesus leaves Capernaum and goes with his disciples to Nazareth, 'his own country'. He is looking always for faith, but he does not find much faith in Nazareth so he does not stay very long. The people there refer to Jesus as 'the son of Mary': it was most unusual for a man to be called son of his mother rather than son of his father. James and Joses who are mentioned here are presumably the same James and Joses mentioned later on, when Jesus is on the cross. Their mother also is called Mary, but she is quite obviously not Mary the mother of Jesus. The two Marys could only be cousins, not sisters. So James and Joses would seem to be second cousins of Jesus.

The people of Nazareth took offence at Jesus, so he withdrew. As always in Mark's gospel, the pattern seems to be that each time Jesus meets opposition he turns to concentrate on training his disciples. His own days are numbered, but they and those who follow them may go on for ever. This time Jesus sends out the Twelve. Through five chapters of the gospel we have seen Jesus healing: now he gives some of the same power and authority to his followers. They have been with him for some time; now they are to be sent out, on a trial mission, with temporary instructions which were changed later on, as we know from the other gospels.

From a story-teller's point of view, the story of John the Baptist and Herod neatly fills up the space between the sending out of the Twelve and their return. From a teaching point of view, the narrative illustrates 'the leaven of Herod' which Jesus will soon and the leading men of Galilee. ²²For when Herodias' daughter came in and danced, she pleased Herod and his guests; and the king said to the girl, 'Ask me for whatever you wish, and I will grant it.' ²³And he vowed to her, 'Whatever you ask me, I will give you, even half of my kingdom.' ²⁴And she went out, and said to her mother, 'What shall I ask?' And she said, 'The head of John the baptizer.' ²⁵And she came in immediately with haste to the king, and asked, saying, 'I want you to give me at once the head of John the Baptist on a platter.' ²⁶And the king was exceedingly sorry; but because of his oaths and his guests he did not want to break his word to her. ²⁷And immediately the king sent a soldier of the guard and gave orders to bring his head. He went and beheaded him in the prison, ²⁸and brought his head on a platter, and gave it to the girl; and the girl gave it to her mother. ²⁹When his disciples heard of it, they came and took his body, and laid it in a tomb.

³⁰ *We apostles returned to Jesus, and told him all that we had done and taught.* ³¹*And he said to us, 'Come away by yourselves to a lonely place, and rest a while.' For many were coming and going, and we had no leisure even to eat.* ³²*And we went away in the boat to a lonely place by ourselves.* ³³*Now many saw us going, and knew us, and they ran there on foot from all the towns, and got there ahead of us.* ³⁴*As he landed he saw a great throng, and he had compassion on them, because they were like sheep without a shepherd; and he began to teach them many things.* ³⁵*And when it grew late, we came to him and said, 'This is a lonely place, and the hour is now late;* ³⁶*send them away, to go into the country and villages round about and buy themselves something to eat.'* ³⁷*But he answered us, 'You give them something to eat.' And we said to him, 'Shall we go and buy two hundred denarii worth of bread, and give it to them to eat?'* ³⁸*And he said to us, 'How many loaves have you? Go and see.' And when we had found out, we said, 'Five, and two fish.'* ³⁹*Then he commanded them all to sit down by companies upon the green grass.* ⁴⁰*So they sat down in groups, by hundreds and by fifties.* ⁴¹ *And taking the five loaves and the two fish he looked up to heaven, and blessed, and broke the loaves, and gave them to us to set before the people; and he divided the two fish among them all.* ⁴²*And they all ate and were satisfied.* ⁴³*And we took up twelve baskets full of broken pieces and of the fish.* ⁴⁴*And those who ate the loaves were five thousand men.*

⁴⁵*Immediately he made us get into the boat and go before him to the other side, to Bethsaida, while he dismissed the crowd.* ⁴⁶*And after he had taken leave of them, he went into the hills to pray.* ⁴⁷*And when evening came, the boat was out on the sea, and he was alone on the land.* ⁴⁸*And he saw that we were distressed in rowing, for the wind was against us. And about the fourth watch of the night he came to us, walking on the sea. He meant to pass by us,* ⁴⁹*but when we saw him*

CHAPTER 6

H^E went away from there and came to his own country; and we followed him. ²And on the sabbath he began to teach in the synagogue; and many who heard him were astonished, saying, 'Where did this man get all this? What is the wisdom given to him? What mighty works are wrought by his hands! ³Is not this the carpenter, the son of Mary and brother of James and Joses and Judas and Simon, and are not his sisters here with us?' And they took offence at him. ⁴And Jesus said to them, 'A prophet is not without honour, except in his own country, and among his own kin, and in his own house.' ⁵And he could do no mighty work there, except that he laid his hands upon a few sick people and healed them. ⁶And he marvelled because of their unbelief.

And he went about among the villages teaching. ⁷*And he called to him the twelve, and began to send us out two by two, and gave us authority over the unclean spirits.* ⁸*He charged us to take nothing for our journey except a staff; no bread, no bag, no money in our belts;* ⁹*but to wear sandals and not put on two tunics.* ¹⁰*And he said to us, 'Where you enter a house, stay there until you leave the place.* ¹¹*And if any place will not receive you and they refuse to hear you, when you leave, shake off the dust that is on your feet for a testimony against them.'* ¹²*So we went out and preached that men should repent.* ¹³*And we cast out many demons, and anointed with oil many who were sick and healed them.*

¹⁴King Herod heard of it; for Jesus' name had become known. Some said, 'John the baptizer has been raised from the dead; that is why these powers are at work in him.' ¹⁵But others said, 'It is Elijah.' And others said, 'It is a prophet, like one of the prophets of old.' ¹⁶But when Herod heard of it, he said, 'John, whom I beheaded, has been raised.' ¹⁷For Herod had sent and seized John, and bound him in prison for the sake of Herodias, his brother Philip's wife; because he had married her. ¹⁸For John said to Herod, 'It is not lawful for you to have your brother's wife.' ¹⁹And Herodias had a grudge against him, and wanted to kill him. But she could not, ²⁰for Herod feared John, knowing that he was a righteous and holy man, and kept him safe. When he heard him, he was much perplexed; and yet he heard him gladly. ²¹But an opportunity came when Herod on his birthday gave a banquet for his courtiers and officers

wake up and find Jesus holding my hand and lifting me up? Did I hear him calling me? Why were my mother and father so amazed, and who were those three men over there, watching and amazed as well? Something was wrong, and this doctor knew right away what it was: I was so very hungry.

Going through the same story but this time pretending to be Jairus or his wife, we may well be reminded of what it is like to be present at a baptism, especially the baptism of one of our own children. Jairus's daughter could do nothing for herself, but the faith which saved her was that of her father and her mother.

Peter, James and John are like the witnesses for the Church at a baptism. They observe how Jesus responds to the faith of Jairus and encourages it under stress. They see this work of Jesus the physician, the doctor, as the summit of all his cures. By our becoming children of God in baptism through the work of the Son, Jesus as doctor not only heals disease of mind and heart and body, but defeats the last and greatest enemy underlying all disease, namely death. With Peter and the others we praise the Father who chose to adopt us, the Son who came to bring the news, and the Spirit of adoption who captures and frees our hearts.

Sharing the hunger of the little girl, we ourselves ask to be fed, now that we are feeling better.

Chapter 5

herd of swine go careering into the sea and drown, thinking rather of the many conflicting voices in my own heart which are powerless now that Jesus has set me free. Like Pharaoh's army they are drowned in the sea. They are drowned in the waters of baptism, by which God becomes our one Father.

Verses 18–20

Not every person rescued by Jesus is called to follow him in his travels. Sometimes he may give us a mission in our own neighbourhood, without calling us away. He esteems either kind of missionary just as much as the other. Any of us may hear Jesus saying to us, 'Go home to your friends, and tell them how much the Lord has done for you, and how he has had mercy on you'.

Verses 24–34

Next, how do I identify with the woman who had the haemorrhage? The story may suggest different memories to different readers, depending on their past lives. Maybe, when Jesus sets me free by calling me son or daughter of God, then I must fall at his feet and thank him for taking off me a burden that was too heavy to bear. Try as I might, for years I could not make myself worthy of God. Every effort was so full of faults, I seemed to go backwards instead of making progress. But once I am God's child, God takes my heart and my desires, but ignores my failures. What a great peace is there, and it comes of reaching out to touch Jesus as he passes by.

Verses 21–24, and 35–43

If I make myself one with the little girl twelve years old, the daughter of Jairus, then I can only imagine most of the story taking place at a distance from me, as I lie on the bed near to death and my father Jairus goes in search of this Jesus, this doctor who is so much more than a doctor. My mother stays with me, and a whole assortment of friends and relations are waiting anxiously out in the courtyard. Somehow I find I no longer want to keep up the fight with my sickness, and I begin to slip away into a deep sleep like a coma. The physician when he comes will say it was a sleep I fell into. What dreams did I enjoy, and what was it like to we would today. Finally, Jesus tells the parents to give the child (now seen to be about twelve years old, once she is out of bed and standing up) something to eat. In the three chapters that follow, there will be much about eating. After the cure comes hunger: the sons and daughters must be fed.

SUGGESTIONS FOR PRAYER

In this chapter the main prayers will centre round making ourselves one with the three special people: the man with the legion, the woman with the haemorrhage, and the young daughter of Jairus. In the latter story, we may also identify with Jairus and his wife, and with Peter or his two friends. We pretend, as the gospel by its nature invites us to pretend, that we are in some sense one with these people; and we discover that this is by no means a game.

Verses 1–17

How can we be one with a man who was inhabited by a legion of demons? We may not have suffered his symptoms in any extreme fashion — please God we have not. But milder forms of mental distress can afflict us all. Pretending myself into the gospel scene as if I were the man himself, I present to Jesus all the times I have ever been depressed or gloomy. I present my violent fits of temper when I have been provoked during depression. I present my moments, weeks, months of anguish from the past. I admit that when distressed or over-anxious I eat too much or smoke too much or in other ways cause myself bodily harm. I present the days when I have been tempted to throw away all restraints. I give to Jesus my sleepless nights.

Above all, I put before Jesus my divided heart. Pulled this way and that as I am by my many conflicting ambitions, I pray him to make me single-minded in my desire to seek and do the will of my Father in heaven. I ask him, may I never be tied down by guilt-feelings about the past, mistaking these for conscience. May I, instead, when all good advice has been taken, calmly do what I think I ought to do, since it is there in my conscience that my one Father speaks. If I wish, I may watch in my imagination the huge

Chapter 5

synagogue; but so many people follow Jesus that the place of celebrating the word comes to be wherever Jesus is. Jairus has enough faith in Jesus to believe that his little daughter is a daughter of God and will not die.

On the way to the ruler's house, a woman in the crowd touches Jesus' cloak and is healed. For twelve years she had been suffering from a haemorrhage. The book of Leviticus would seem to tell us of the misery this must have caused her as a Jewess (see Leviticus 15:19–30). Anyone she touched or who touched her any day in the past twelve years was automatically 'unclean' till the evening of that day. Any number of the things she touched or that touched her had to be washed immediately. We get the impression that she must have been confined to one corner of her house, afraid to come out and meet people lest she accidentally touch them and have them forever washing themselves. But she bravely made up her mind about Jesus, that if she touched *him* she would not render him unclean. In Jesus' eyes, she was a daughter of God with as much right to move in company as any other daughter or son of God. Her act of stretching out her hand to touch Jesus' garment must have had some such echo: 'In the strength you give me I believe I am not and never was really unclean'.

St Mark's words about doctors are included not to insult doctors but to point the contrast between Jesus the doctor and ordinary practitioners. In a moment Jesus can cure painlessly an ailment that has lasted painfully for ages; and he charges no fee. 'Daughter' (*of God*) 'your faith has made you well; go in peace, and be healed of your disease.' What many physicians in succession could not do, Jesus does alone.

As a climax to all these cures by Jesus the physician in the first five chapters of Mark, comes the raising of Jairus's daughter to life again now that she is no longer just sick, but dead. If in our prayers we think of these cures as examples of the power of Christian baptism, then the climax must be here in the raising of the dead to life. Death itself is now nothing but a sleep, from which Jesus will awaken us. We are children of the ever-living God. Jairus and his wife stand by, believing, and the three main disciples of Jesus are present as witnesses.

A small matter of interest: in the ancient world and certainly in the Greek language used by Mark, it would be more polite to say 'me and James and John' than to say 'James and John and me' as with an unexpected strength all attempts to restrain them, though nowadays with the help of powerful drugs they can be controlled. Inner anguish can lead to their calling out and shouting, whether their utterances mean anything or not to a casual listener. Inflicting damage on their own bodies is fairly common even among people not thought to be disturbed enough to need hospital. We discover later on that this man who ran and worshipped Jesus was naked: a reluctance to wear clothes is sometimes found in people who are seriously disturbed in mind. This poor sufferer cries out night and day, indicating that his mental state allows him no sleep at all worth the name. Sleeplessness does not have to mean mental illness, but the mentally ill are very often unable to sleep without drugs.

Above all, the gospel story underlines that the man in his frenzy calls himself Legion. A Roman legion at the time was a huge division of several thousand soldiers; the size of a legion is reflected in the thousands of pigs that go careering into the water and drown. With this sick man, as with many mentally sick people, there is the feeling of being pulled a thousand different ways, of wanting to do everything at the one time. Like a legion of soldiers, but with no one authority leading them, the strong feelings turn on one another or get in each other's way or cause panic. Jesus, by bringing to light the one authority of God, as Father whom every person in the world can find within themselves, stills the endless conflict in the human heart. Soon the Gerasene is sitting peacefully, clothed and in his right mind, at Jesus' feet. The cured man has found his true self (as *this* child of God), and no longer needs to listen to the thousands of voices telling him in thousands of contradictory ways what to do. He begs to come with Jesus as a disciple, but instead Jesus sends him on a mission, to prepare the people of his country for the day when the disciples would come back in future years — as indeed they did come.

Jairus, whose little daughter was at the point of death, was one of the rulers of 'the' synagogue beside the sea, the Capernaum synagogue. Jesus is by now pretty well excluded from the synagogues, but here is a ruler of the synagogue turning to him. The synagogue was the place for celebrating the word of God, as the temple at Jerusalem was the place for sacrifice. Jesus' version of God's word finds no place to take root and grow in the

Chapter 5

came one of the rulers of the synagogue, Jairus by name, and seeing him, he fell at his feet, 23and besought him, saying, 'My little daughter is at the point of death. Come and lay your hands on her, so that she may be made well, and live.' 24And he went with him.

And a great crowd followed him and thronged about him. 25And there was a woman who had had a flow of blood for twelve years, 26and who had suffered much under many physicians, and had spent all that she had, and was no better but rather grew worse. 27She had heard the reports about Jesus, and came up behind him in the crowd and touched his garment. 28For she said, 'If I touch even his garments, I shall be made well.' 29And immediately the hemorrhage ceased; and she felt in her body that she was healed of her disease. 30And Jesus, perceiving in himself that power had gone forth from him, immediately turned about in the crowd, and said, 'Who touched my garments?' 31*And we said to him, 'You see the crowd pressing around you, and yet you say, "Who touched me?"'* 32And he looked around to see who had done it. 33But the woman, knowing what had been done to her, came in fear and trembling and fell down before him, and told him the whole truth. 34And he said to her, 'Daughter, your faith has made you well; go in peace, and be healed of your disease.'

35While he was still speaking, there came from the ruler's house some who said, 'Your daughter is dead. Why trouble the Teacher any further?' 36But ignoring what they said, Jesus said to the ruler of the synagogue, 'Do not fear, only believe.' 37*And he allowed no one to follow him except me and James and John the brother of James.* 38*When we came to the house of the ruler of the synagogue, he saw a tumult, and people weeping and wailing loudly.* 39And when he had entered, he said to them, 'Why do you make a tumult and weep? The child is not dead but sleeping.' 40And they laughed at him. *But he put them all outside, and took the child's father and mother and us who were with him, and went in where the child was.* 41Taking her by the hand he said to her, 'Talitha cumi'; which means, 'Little girl, I say to you, arise.' 42And immediately the girl got up and walked; for she was twelve years old. *And immediately we were overcome with amazement.* 43And he strictly charged us that no one should know this, and told them to give her something to eat.

* * *

Again Jesus meets a man with an unclean spirit, and cures him. This time we can recognize many of the symptoms of severe mental illness. His living among the tombs must mean deep depression. People sick in mind are often violent and they resist

CHAPTER 5
---*---

WE came to the other side of the sea, to the country of the Gerasenes. ²And when he had come out of the boat, there met him out of the tombs a man with an unclean spirit, ³who lived among the tombs; and no one could bind him any more, even with a chain; ⁴for he had often been bound with fetters and chains, but the chains he wrenched apart, and the fetters he broke in pieces; and no one had the strength to subdue him. ⁵Night and day among the tombs and on the mountains he was always crying out, and bruising himself with stones. ⁶And when he saw Jesus from afar, he ran and worshipped him; ⁷and crying out with a loud voice, he said, 'What have you to do with me, Jesus, Son of the Most High God? I adjure you by God, do not torment me.' ⁸For he had said to him, 'Come out of the man, you unclean spirit!' ⁹And Jesus asked him, 'What is your name?' He replied, 'My name is Legion; for we are many.' ¹⁰And he begged him eagerly not to send them out of the country. ¹¹Now a great herd of swine was feeding there on the hillside; ¹²and they begged him, 'Send us to the swine, let us enter them.' ¹³So he gave them leave. And the unclean spirits came out, and entered the swine; and the herd, numbering about two thousand, rushed down the steep bank into the sea, and were drowned in the sea.

¹⁴The herdsmen fled, and told it in the city and in the country. And people came to see what it was that had happened. ¹⁵And they came to Jesus, and saw the demoniac sitting there, clothed and in his right mind, the man who had had the legion; and they were afraid. ¹⁶*And we who had seen it told what had happened to the demoniac and to the swine.* ¹⁷And they began to beg Jesus to depart from their neighbourhood. ¹⁸And as he was getting into the boat, the man who had been possessed with demons begged him that he might be with him. ¹⁹But he refused, and said to him, 'Go home to your friends, and tell them how much the Lord has done for you, and how he has had mercy on you.' ²⁰And he went away and began to proclaim in the Decapolis how much Jesus had done for him; and all men marvelled.

²¹And when Jesus had crossed again in the boat to the other side, a great crowd gathered about him; and he was beside the sea. ²²Then

Chapter 4

situation: the real helmsman of their enterprise is asleep on the helmsman's cushion. So in their alarm they wake him up. Calling upon Jesus to wake up and calm our storms is a step on the way to understanding who he is, because eventually peace and stillness come, and we know it has come because of his command. If I am in a storm myself at the present time, I may use the disciples' words to 'wake up' Jesus. As the Letter of James says of the man who asks for wisdom: 'But let him ask in faith, with no doubting, for he who doubts is like a wave of the sea that is driven and tossed by the wind' (see James 1:6). Faith, in Mark's gospel, is trust in Jesus that he speaks with authority about our being his Father's children.

we make a regular exercise of praying forgiveness and blessings on everyone else, we find in truth that our own burden is lifted.

But in their present context these two verses come to mean: 'Listen well to the good news'. If we refuse to listen to God-speaking-as-our-Father, then we condemn ourselves to the impossible task of *making ourselves* fit for heaven.

Verses 26–29

This lovely parable is found only in Mark's gospel. A gardener or a farmer does not keep on uprooting a plant to see how the roots are growing, nor is he constantly worrying about what stage his plants have reached. He has discovered by experience that most plants take him by surprise. So you or I need not be constantly worrying about how much progress we are making. God who speaks the word, God who created the plant, knows what he is about. The rest of us may safely 'sleep and rise night and day'. In my prayer I leave all to God.

Verses 30–34

'You are my beloved child; with you I am well pleased' is a tiny sentence, yet how enormous it can grow once it takes over our lives! And what a source of comfort to others, when they come for shade and shelter.

Verses 35–41

The farmer was sleeping; now Jesus is asleep in the boat. I can either continue to imagine myself as one of those in the boat, or I can stretch my imagination further and say, 'I am the boat, and though there is a storm, yet Jesus is asleep within me. If we sink, we sink together and all is well'. I may if I wish think of the Church as the boat, the unsinkable boat, and myself within the boat. Do I remember that the Church is unsinkable, even when Jesus appears to be asleep? If I choose to call the Church 'the barque of Peter', do I remember always that 'other boats are with Jesus' besides ours?

In the gospel story the disciples, perhaps unlike the gospel reader, do not yet know fully who Jesus is. They see the irony of the

Chapter 4

New Testament writings make clear that we were all chosen in Christ before the foundation of the world and adopted as God's children, a fact we celebrate in Christian baptism. So the word, the seed, to which I must open my ears and my heart is the word God is saying to me in Christ: 'You are my beloved son' or 'You are my beloved daughter'. And to show his love is permanent, like the love of any good adopting parent, he adds, 'With you I am (now and always) well pleased'. Can I believe this good news, this best of all good news?

This good news will live its own life in me, and will triumph in spite of apparent setbacks. Can I trust God, to do his own work in me? All this is the secret of the kingdom of God, and now is the time of sowing.

Some listeners hear right away. If everyone had heard right away, one may wonder if Jesus would have had to die at all.

Verses 15–20

We may save these verses from the allegory, and pray them later on down the gospel story.

Verses 21–23

As a lamp is not hidden long under a dark cover, but is brought out and put on a stand, so the seed does not stay put in the dark of the ground. Once it germinates, it soon comes up into the light of day. So the good news that we are God's children first of all dawns on the mind and heart, then has to be absorbed in secret for a while, before coming to the surface of our lives. Can I not feel this happening, either in the past or in the present? One day, if the day has not already arrived, I will be able to give consolation, light, comforting words, to others, because I know that God loves not just me, but all the rest of us as well.

Verses 24 and 25

Elsewhere these words are usually taken to mean that the more generous our forgiveness of others, the more our own hearts will be free, whereas the meaner we are in our forgiveness of others, the heavier the burden of guilt we ourselves will have to bear. If *word* of God was preached, not a place of sacrifice like the temple. Later on, there will be other commands of Jesus, for those who have once fulfilled the command to listen and been given the gift of faith in Jesus. The faith is the foundation; faith grows in a listener, and in the end becomes fruitful in love. As the Letter of James says, we must accept the word which has been planted in us and can save our souls. We must then do what the word tells us — but accepting the word comes first (see James 1:21).

Jesus then says to those in the boat with him, 'Let us go across to the other side'. To go further along the same coast would simply invite the crowds to follow on the land; so they go across the lake, and the other boats around go with them. Two details from the story of the storm on the lake might not be immediately obvious. First, when Jesus says to the sea 'Peace! Be still!' his actual words as given by Mark are more like 'Be quiet! Be muzzled!' as if the sea were like a wild animal. The second detail not immediately obvious is this, that the cushion Jesus rested his sleeping head upon was the helmsman's cushion: *the* cushion, not just *a* cushion.

SUGGESTIONS FOR PRAYER

Verses 1 and 2

As a setting for the whole chapter, I may imagine myself, as a local child or as a disciple or in any other role, being invited aboard the boat Jesus preaches from. What does his voice sound like? What is he saying? What do his words mean to me? I feel the gentle rocking of the boat.

Verses 3–14

Jesus is preaching parables about seed. Peter was there at the time, and the First Letter of Peter says in effect that Jesus was not talking about ordinary seed except as an example, but about the 'living and abiding word of God'. What is more, 'that word is the good news which was preached to you' (see 1 Peter 1:23ff.). So far in Mark's gospel the only word spoken by God has been the good news that 'You are my beloved Son; with you I am well pleased', spoken to Jesus at his baptism. Other passages in the

Chapter 4

crowds upon the shore. We are left with the impression that Jesus did indeed spend much time and attention in telling his disciples and the Twelve the secret of the kingdom of God, even though their hearts were slow to understand. Jesus must have known already that his days as a teacher were numbered, but he trusted to God's Spirit that his message would be recalled by his closest friends when he himself, the bridegroom, would be taken from them.

What, then, is the obvious and direct meaning of the parable of the sower? The meaning is, that the word of God will not return to God empty, but will produce fruit in plenty in spite of any obstacles or limitations in the soil. Isaiah had said much the same in prophecy (see Isaiah 55:10f.), but then Isaiah did not know what the word of God would one day turn out to be ('You are my beloved Son; with you I am well pleased').

'The sower sows the word . . .' We may take this first statement of the allegory (verse 14) and say that this early part of Mark's gospel is concerned with the *sowing* of the word. The rest of the allegory would apply later in the gospel.

With the parable about the lamp (see verse 21) we are back in the parables spoken to the crowd on the shore. The meaning the parables take on in the sequence chosen by St Mark may not be exactly the meaning they had in their original setting; but the sequence Mark was inspired to follow makes the parables say: 'The sower has sown the seed. It will be hidden, but only for a while. Seeds are sown to come to light; they are sown in secret, but designed to grow in the light of day. Opening your ears is like opening the ground to receive God's word; the more open your ears, and the more flexible your minds and hearts, the more you will be co-operating with the seed of God's word. Close your ears and you run the risk of being barren. Listening is all that you, for your part, can do. God gives the increase, while you are unaware: first the blade, then the ear, then the full grain in the ear. Such a tiny thing, the word of God when first sown in you; but in the end the seed will become — you yourself at full stature — a place of refuge for God's little ones.'

When Jesus speaks to the crowds in this first half of the gospel of Mark, the only command given to everybody is: 'Listen!' Jesus is being gradually forced out of the synagogues, and the crowds are coming with him. The synagogue was the place where the previously asked for. What started as crowds round the door of Peter's house has now become huge crowds on the seashore forcing Jesus and his disciples to sail away across the sea at the end of a day's teaching.

Thus Jesus begins to teach, in parables as always at this stage of his ministry. We need not think St Mark is trying to give us the whole of one day's teaching exactly as Jesus gave it on one occasion. These parables would have been preserved and given to Mark as a collection of parables of Jesus, and Mark fits them into his narrative at this point. But there is no reason to doubt that Jesus did preach mainly in parables during this early ministry in Galilee.

There is one 'stranger' among the parables given in this chapter: the explanation of the parable of the sower which Jesus gives to 'those who were about him with the twelve'. This explanation turns the parable into an allegory. A parable normally makes one main point very forcibly; an allegory takes every little detail of a story and gives a separate meaning to each detail. So in the present instance the seed, the path, the birds, the rocky ground, the thorns and thistles are all given a meaning for themselves. Biblical scholars seem to tell us that the simple, direct parable was Jesus' characteristic way of teaching, rather than allegory.

As for Jesus' suddenly finding space to be alone with a few disciples in the middle of a day's teaching, the scene painted by St Mark does provide space. We can easily imagine Jesus sitting in Peter's boat with all the Twelve; we hear a little later that other boats were with him that day. Nothing easier for Jesus than to lower his voice from time to time, stop speaking to the crowds on the shore, and see how those closest to him were taking his words. 'And when he was alone, those who were about him with the twelve asked him concerning the parables' (verse 10). If we ask, why do they ask about the *parables* when Jesus has only told one parable so far that day, then we may recall that Jesus already spoke in parables when he was last at home (see 3:23); but this is the first time Jesus is represented as giving a clearer version of his teaching to those closest to him.

We see some time later in the gospel that Jesus finds his closest disciples to be still 'seeing without seeing, hearing without hearing' and with hardened hearts, just like the people here in the

Chapter 4

be made manifest; nor is anything secret, except to come to light. ²³If any man has ears to hear, let him hear.' ²⁴And he said to them, 'Take heed what you hear; the measure you give will be the measure you get, and still more will be given you. ²⁵For to him who has will more be given; and from him who has not, even what he has will be taken away.'

²⁶And he said, 'The kingdom of God is as if a man should scatter seed upon the ground, ²⁷and should sleep and rise night and day, and the seed should sprout and grow, he knows not why. ²⁸The earth produces of itself, first the blade, then the ear, then the full grain in the ear. ²⁹But when the grain is ripe, at once he puts in the sickle, because the harvest has come.'

³⁰And he said, 'With what can we compare the kingdom of God, or what parable shall we use for it? ³¹It is like a grain of mustard seed, which, when sown upon the ground, is the smallest of all the seeds on earth; ³²yet when it is sown it grows up and becomes the greatest of all shrubs, and puts forth large branches, so that the birds of the air can make nests in its shade.'

³³*With many such parables he spoke the word to them, as they were able to hear it;* ³⁴*he did not speak to them without a parable, but privately to us his own disciples he explained everything.*

³⁵*On that day, when evening had come, he said to us, 'Let us go across to the other side.'* ³⁶*And leaving the crowd, we took him with us just as he was, in the boat.* And other boats were with him. ³⁷And a great storm of wind arose, and the waves beat into the boat, so that the boat was already filling. ³⁸*But he was in the stern, asleep on the cushion; and we woke him and said to him, 'Teacher, do you not care if we perish?'* ³⁹And he awoke and rebuked the wind, and said to the sea, 'Peace! Be still!' And the wind ceased, and there was a great calm. ⁴⁰*He said to us, 'Why are you afraid? Have you no faith?'* ⁴¹*And we were filled with awe, and said to one another, 'Who then is this, that even wind and sea obey him?'*

*   *   *

Again Jesus began to teach beside the sea. The previous time of teaching beside the sea was just before Jesus called Levi. The pressure from the crowds is all the time building up and increasing. Before, Jesus told his disciples to have a boat ready, as a means of escape from the crowds if they should block every other exit; now he climbs into the boat and preaches to the crowds from there. Some at least of the ancient manuscripts of the gospel of Mark imply that the boat is the same one Jesus had

CHAPTER 4

---
*

AGAIN he began to teach beside the sea. And a very large crowd gathered about him, so that he got into the boat and sat in it on the sea; and the whole crowd was beside the sea on the land. ²And he taught them many things in parables, and in his teaching he said to them: ³'Listen! A sower went out to sow. ⁴And as he sowed, some seed fell along the path, and the birds came and devoured it. ⁵Other seed fell on rocky ground, where it had not much soil, and immediately it sprang up, since it had no depth of soil; ⁶and when the sun rose it was scorched, and since it had no root it withered away. ⁷Other seed fell among thorns and the thorns grew up and choked it, and it yielded no grain. ⁸And other seeds fell into good soil and brought forth grain, growing up and increasing and yielding thirtyfold and sixtyfold and a hundredfold.' ⁹And he said, 'He who has ears to hear, let him hear.'

¹⁰And when he was alone, those who were about him with the twelve asked him concerning the parables. ¹¹*And he said to us, 'To you has been given the secret of the kingdom of God, but for those outside everything is in parables;* ¹²*so that they may indeed see but not perceive, and may indeed hear but not understand; lest they should turn again, and be forgiven.'* ¹³*And he said to us, 'Do you not understand this parable? How then will you understand all the parables?* ¹⁴The sower sows the word. ¹⁵And these are the ones along the path, where the word is sown; when they hear, Satan immediately comes and takes away the word which is sown in them. ¹⁶And these in like manner are the ones sown upon rocky ground, who, when they hear the word, immediately receive it with joy; ¹⁷and they have no root in themselves, but endure for a while; then, when tribulation or persecution arises on account of the word, immediately they fall away. ¹⁸And others are the ones sown among thorns; they are those who hear the word, ¹⁹but the cares of the world, and the delight in riches, and the desire for other things, enter in and choke the word, and it proves unfruitful. ²⁰But those that were sown upon the good soil are the ones who hear the word and accept it and bear fruit, thirtyfold and sixtyfold and a hundredfold.'

²¹And he said to them, 'Is a lamp brought in to be put under a bushel, or under a bed, and not on a stand? ²²For there is nothing hid, except to

Chapter 3

war against one another, so their kingdom cannot stand against yours. Set me free from their tyranny, since to serve you is freedom. You alone know my heart better than I do myself; you alone can direct me to the heart of my heart and open my ears to hear what it is the Holy Spirit says there.'

'We pray for anyone who is unwilling or unable to accept forgiveness from God or from you, Jesus, or from other people. I would be glad to let you, working in me, take out from them their heart of stone, to give them a heart of flesh instead (see Ezekiel 11:19), even if it means my being rejected as you were.'

Verses 31–35

Here Jesus says clearly for the first time in this gospel that those who do the will of God are his brothers and sisters. We try to take in this tremendous truth, that God has adopted us as his children, beside his only-begotten Son. 'Father, good parents try to love an adopted child as much as they love their own child. Do you really love me as much as you love my elder brother Jesus? I believe you do.' 'Father, to do your will is to do what you want, and what you want above all is that I call you "my Father". Everything else follows from that. If ever I lose my way, direct me back to my heart of hearts, where the Spirit is prompting me always to say "my Father" to you. I ask all this through Jesus whom you sent to do your will in us. Amen.'

'Mary, mother of Jesus, teach us what it means for us to do the will of God and thus be in our turn "mother of Jesus". Is it that we are *brother and sister* to all who have already accepted God's adoption, but *mother* to the life of Jesus in all the rest who do not know and love God's will? Share with us the joys as well as the pains of bringing your Son into our world. Amen.'

recognize Jesus for who he really is. Jesus does not say they are wrong, he only asks them to keep his secret for now.

Peter goes to fetch his boat, hoping that Jesus will come aboard soon. Jesus' presence within us is somehow like his being on board a boat of which we are master. We invite Jesus to be with us on our future voyage.

Verses 13–19

Jesus called the Twelve, to be his chief witnesses. But now Mark has put the story before us, and we in our own measure are called as well. 'Jesus of Nazareth, call me to you, from where you are in the hills. I know you desire me, to be with you and to be sent out. Just following this gospel of St Mark I feel privileged to be with you all the time. Peter and the others have opened up their own gift of being close to you, so that we can share what you all along meant to be shared. When you think I am ready, then please send me out; but for the time being may I simply enjoy being with you. The more I come to understand your word, the more I shall be fit to be sent out to others who do not know you yet, and the more I shall be likely to do good to those who are sick in mind or body.'

Jesus gives Simon the additional name of Peter (Rock). 'Jesus, your Father's love for us is the deepest Rock of all. Build us firmly on that everlasting and unshakeable love. Then we your brothers and sisters will become rocks of security ourselves for others to rely on. We will become like living stones in the spiritual house St Peter writes about' (see 1 Peter 2:5).

There is a new name which will one day be given to each of us, a name known only to God and to the one to whom it is given (see Revelation 2:17). We may well wonder what our own name will turn out to have been!

Verses 19–30

'Jesus, Son of man, your everlasting kingdom will never be divided against itself. I give you my house and all my possessions, that is to say my whole personality and inner life. I know you are stronger than the forces that still sometimes bind me: indeed they

Chapter 3

give way to his mother and his brethren. Catholic tradition has always understood these 'brethren' to be not brothers and sisters in the ordinary sense of the words, but cousins of Jesus. The Greek word can mean either. We notice that when Jesus says, 'Whoever does the will of God is my brother, and sister, and mother', he does not say, 'and my father'. Nor does he say 'is my son', nor 'is my daughter'. As far as Jesus is concerned, he has any number of brothers, any number of sisters, even any number of mothers — but no sons or daughters, and only one Father.

SUGGESTIONS FOR PRAYER

Verses 1–6

The right hand is, in most people, the hand of action and decision. Left-handed people will naturally think rather of what their left hand means to them. 'Jesus, Son of man, my will for doing good is withered. Convince me that I am your Father's beloved child. Then I will become decisive, since he who made me will love me whichever way I choose. If I choose badly, he will as gently as he can make it clear to me and set me off on the right course instead. Help me to trust in my own good will.' I imagine myself as the person with the withered hand — in the synagogue on a sabbath — with everyone watching — Jesus tells me to come to him — I come — at his request I stretch out my leading hand, withered as it is, and he heals it as I stretch.

We pray for all those whose hearts are hard, whose judgments upon us so easily wither our desire to do good. May they be greatly blessed, and their hearts be softened and set free.

Verses 7–12

I now imagine myself as one of the huge crowd, and I look within my heart to see what it is I would say to Jesus if I could get close enough to him. Whatever ailments or diseases I find hardest to live with in myself, I come forward and touch him, without having to explain or describe. If I am free from mental illness, I may give heartfelt thanks to God, but I notice that those with mental illness (those with 'the unclean spirits') are the first to coming on the clouds of heaven — at the transfiguration. The tax collector Levi the son of Alphaeus seems to have been left out of the Twelve, unless he is to be identified with Matthew the tax collector or with James the son of Alphaeus.

All the time Jesus and those with him are finding less time and space to themselves. In the early days, Simon's mother-in-law had served them with food once she was cured of her fever; Jesus later on was shown eating with tax collectors and sinners in Levi's house; next the disciples had to snatch a little to eat as they went along through the grainfields; now they have no time to eat at all, what with the pressure of the crowds who gathered again once Jesus and the Twelve came down the mountain. At present there is no time for eating: that time will come soon, but on Jesus' terms.

Jesus' friends come to rescue him from himself. Kindness is all very well, they must have thought, but he has no need to love all these people to distraction. The friends mentioned here are not the Twelve, nor the disciples: they must rather be old friends from Nazareth. The scribes coming down from Jerusalem take up the same refrain as the friends, but with a more sinister interpretation: 'he is possessed'. This is the first mention of enemies coming from Jerusalem: up till now the hostility has all been local; but recently the crowds have included people from Jerusalem (see 3:8). After answering these new enemies, and all his hearers, in parables, Jesus tells them that all sins *will be* forgiven, except that 'whoever blasphemes against the Holy Spirit never has forgiveness, but is guilty of an eternal sin'. We are justified by faith, faith in God's love for us as our Father. But anyone who refuses to be loved is stuck with that refusal. If anyone refuses to believe in God's love and forgiveness, how can that love and forgiveness get through to them? The Holy Spirit it is within us who makes us cry out 'Abba! Father!' to God. The Spirit is there in our hearts. If at Jesus' invitation we look into our hearts but then refuse to believe the evidence of our own hearts, then we are totally blind and helpless. We would in effect be calling the *holy* Spirit 'evil', calling the light 'darkness'. The writing is already on the wall for Jesus: his rescue of sinners will mean his dying willingly to save even those who are unwilling to be saved.

The friends who were concerned about Jesus' not eating now

Chapter 3

who were presumably partisans of Herod Antipas, the worldly king of the region and a puppet of the Romans. Later in Mark's gospel Jesus will use these two parties, of the Pharisees and of Herod, to show how *not* to find the kingdom of God. Jesus will say, 'Beware of the leaven of the Pharisees, and the leaven of Herod'; that is, 'Beware of their distortions of the truth' (see 8:15). Herod, of course, was the one who had arrested John the baptizer, though Mark has not yet said who arrested him. We notice, too, how Jesus is gradually being forced out of the synagogues, partly by the size of the crowds following him around, and partly by the hostility he provokes when he goes to synagogue. Even down by the seashore, which often forms a natural amphitheatre if the speaker stands with his back to the water, Jesus is in danger of being overwhelmed by the crowds drawing close to listen and to touch him. So Peter and the others are detailed to fetch one of their boats around behind Jesus, for an escape route.

From the many disciples who followed him, Jesus chose twelve for a special status. The understanding which the Twelve themselves later had of this choice, was that they were signs of the new kingdom of God being grafted onto the old kingdom of Israel (Israel being the other name of Jacob whose twelve sons were the patriarchs). By now there were four distinct groups of people following Jesus: the Twelve; the rest of the disciples; the crowds who came to listen or to be healed but not necessarily to become disciples; the enemies. Simon heads the list of the Twelve, and Mark says here that Jesus gave him the extra name 'Peter', which of course means Rock. Anyone wishing to put my version of Mark's gospel back into Mark's real version need only remember that up till here at 3:16 'I' or 'me' or 'my' stands for 'Simon' or 'Simon's'. But from now on to the end of the gospel 'I' or 'me' or 'my' stands for 'Peter' or 'Peter's'. Only Mark's gospel is so consistent about calling him 'Simon' to start with, then recording the added name and calling him by that name, 'Peter', for the rest of the story. Later on, Mark will record one occasion when *Jesus* called him 'Simon', but Mark himself always calls him 'Peter' from now on.

Jesus calls James and John 'Sons of thunder' — perhaps for their fiery temper, or perhaps because they would be with him on the mountain when he most clearly appeared as the Son of man house is divided against itself, that house will not be able to stand. ²⁶And if Satan has risen up against himself and is divided, he cannot stand, but is coming to an end. ²⁷But no one can enter a strong man's house and plunder his goods, unless he first binds the strong man; then indeed he may plunder his house.

²⁸'Truly, I say to you, all sins will be forgiven the sons of men, and whatever blasphemies they utter; ²⁹but whoever blasphemes against the Holy Spirit never has forgiveness, but is guilty of an eternal sin' — ³⁰for they had said, 'He has an unclean spirit.'

³¹And his mother and his brethren came; and standing outside they sent to him and called him. *³²And a crowd was sitting about him; and we said to him, 'Your mother and your brethren are outside asking for you.'* ³³And he replied, 'Who are my mother and my brethren?' ³⁴And looking around on those who sat about him, he said, 'Here are my mother and my brethren! ³⁵Whoever does the will of God is my brother, and sister, and mother.'

*   *   *

'Again he entered the synagogue ...' The first time of Jesus' entering the synagogue at Capernaum was told in Chapter 1; after that he went out in the country; in Chapter 2 Mark tells us he returned to Capernaum. On the first occasion of entering the synagogue there was a cure, but it was a curing of mental sickness in 'a man with an unclean spirit'. Besides, on the evening of that same day everyone waited until the sabbath was over, at sunset, before bringing their sick to Peter's house (see 1:32). Among the conflict stories we have already seen in Chapter 2 is the one about the Son of man being lord of the sabbath, and about people being more important than regulations. Here at the start of Chapter 3 comes the last of those early stories of conflict, in which Jesus heals the man with a withered hand, a physical cure, in the synagogue on a sabbath under the eyes of the local religious authorities. Jesus' question about 'to do good or to do harm, to save life or to kill' reminds me of the way the mob reportedly chose Barabbas at the trial of Jesus: chose a murderer rather than their saviour. As Peter would one day say, 'But you denied the Holy and Righteous One, and asked for a murderer to be granted to you, and killed the Author of life, whom God raised from the dead' (see Acts 3:14f.).

We notice that the Pharisees get together with the Herodians,

CHAPTER 3
✻

AGAIN he entered the synagogue, and a man was there who had a withered hand. ²And they watched him, to see whether he would heal him on the sabbath, so that they might accuse him. ³And he said to the man who had the withered hand, 'Come here.' ⁴And he said to them, 'Is it lawful on the sabbath to do good or to do harm, to save life or to kill?' But they were silent. ⁵And he looked around at them with anger, grieved at their hardness of heart, and said to the man, 'Stretch out your hand.' He stretched it out, and his hand was restored. ⁶The Pharisees went out, and immediately held counsel with the Herodians against him, how to destroy him.

⁷*Jesus withdrew with us his disciples to the sea, and a great multitude from Galilee followed; also from Judea* ⁸*and Jerusalem and Idumea and from beyond the Jordan and from about Tyre and Sidon a great multitude, hearing all that he did, came to him.* ⁹*And he told us to have a boat ready for him because of the crowd, lest they should crush him;* ¹⁰*for he had healed many, so that all who had diseases pressed upon him to touch him.* ¹¹And whenever the unclean spirits beheld him, they fell down before him and cried out, 'You are the Son of God.' ¹²And he strictly ordered them not to make him known.

¹³*And he went up into the hills, and called to him those whom he desired; and we came to him.* ¹⁴And he appointed twelve, to be with him, and to be sent out to preach ¹⁵and have authority to cast out demons: ¹⁶*me, Simon, he surnamed Peter;* ¹⁷James the son of Zebedee and John the brother of James, whom he surnamed Boanerges, that is, sons of thunder; ¹⁸Andrew, and Philip, and Bartholomew, and Matthew, and Thomas, and James the son of Alphaeus, and Thaddaeus, and Simon the Cananaean, ¹⁹and Judas Iscariot, who betrayed him.

Then he went home; ²⁰*and the crowd came together again, so that we could not even eat.* ²¹And when his friends heard it, they came out to seize him, for they said, 'He is beside himself.' ²²And the scribes who came down from Jerusalem said, 'He is possessed by Beelzebul, and by the prince of demons he casts out the demons.' ²³And he called them to him, and said to them in parables, 'How can Satan cast out Satan? ²⁴If a kingdom is divided against itself, that kingdom cannot stand. ²⁵And if a to punish us for getting along as best we can. We always *feel* guilty when we have to break a rule for the sake of a person's well-being: but this does not mean we are doing wrong. To follow one's conscience is to do what one thinks, here and now, to be the right thing. I pray for the strength of mind to do what I see to be right, no matter how others may criticize.

Chapter 2

that the likeness may grow ever stronger, but still in my own way of being like God.

Verses 15–17

Some people are afraid of going to the doctor when they are ill. Jesus is our physician, he tells us here, so we pray to be unafraid of going to him with all our ailments. I could list for myself all the things about my life that give me pain, and then bring them one by one to Jesus as to the doctor, and ask him to heal them. Many of our bodily sicknesses have their origin in our minds and hearts. In the end, Jesus the physician will heal them all, and we shall be as if we had never been hurt. We trust in his power, his skill, his will to heal us, his patience.

Verses 18–22

The presence of the Holy Spirit, making us sons and daughters of God, gives us an entirely new life, a completely different relationship with God from any previously known in history. There is no tax for getting into heaven, heaven is free, God loves us because we are his own children whether or not we fast or keep religious regulations or live unselfish lives. Once we have fully grasped and absorbed this astounding situation, we can then freely, if we wish to, do great things for God as a way of saying 'Thank You' for such generosity. Religious practices taken on without this total reliance on God can so easily grow into a spirit of pride and competition which can destroy us. We may pray, along those lines, to be like a totally new garment for Jesus to wear, or like a completely fresh wineskin to receive the divine wine without breaking. Or we may put the same thoughts in our own words and images.

Verses 23–28

King David made his followers free of the holy places and the bread of the Presence when they were in need (see 1 Samuel 21:1–6). I may if I wish imagine myself going through the cornfields with Jesus and the rest of his followers, and hear him defend the position that people matter more than regulations. Once God is our Father, he is no longer to be thought of as ready

Anyone who knows God as loving Father can at any time share with any other child of God (even one who does not yet know God) the forgiveness God has for our past, our present, our future. To those who are willing to listen, we can speak of God's forgiveness. Those who are unwilling or unable to listen, we can simply forgive in our own hearts, and try to treat them as children of God who are as dear to him as we are ourselves. We pray for our enemies, as Jesus taught us.

Jesus' discreet way of referring to himself as 'Son of man' rather than 'Son of God' reminds us to be like him in directing attention away from ourselves. 'May I be, in the secret of my prayers, ever your son (your daughter), but in my actions ever a child of the human race, at the service of those who do not yet know you as their Father.'

Verses 10–12

The Son of man, we recall, is also the promised liberator. We recall the promises of God's word, and pray for the coming of Jesus' kingdom as a liberty for the whole human race. 'Even if I should fall again in the future, my Father will forgive again, so I need not be afraid of falling. Free me, Father, from paralysing fear, through Jesus my liberator.' 'Jesus, say to my heart as you said to the paralytic, "Son (Daughter), your sins are forgiven".'

Verses 13 and 14

If the first four apostles were fishermen, that makes the fish an apt symbol for a Christian gathered in by the apostles, as we all are in the church of the apostles. So now if the tax collector is called to be an apostle, the coin with the image of *God* upon it is another apt symbol for us as Christians, who as images of God will be gathered into his treasury. We were created in the image and likeness of God, but now by Jesus the reason for that likeness is made clear: we are each of us like our Father, as children are like their parents. Yet that does not make us all in the exact same mould. Each of us is just like our Father, but in our own individual way.

I may reflect on the wonder of being *this* child of God, and pray

Chapter 2

physically, and then to many other forms of paralysis. People can be paralysed, unable to go forward in the service of God, for many, many reasons: anxiety, scruples, fear of an angry God, fear of what others will think, despair, undue ambition for success, indecision, enslavement to rules and regulations, being too busy judging other folk, being unable to break out of regrets over the past. Some people cannot cope with a competitive world, and simply freeze where they are; others need constant praise or they wilt. We can be so fascinated with the wonderful picture we have of ourselves that we cannot cope with the real person we turn out to be. Whatever our own particular paralysis, we allow ourselves to be presented before Jesus.

Jesus says to me in my frozen state: 'Son' or 'Daughter' — that is to say, 'God's son' or 'God's daughter' — 'God has forgiven your sins'. Even as I lie there unable to lift a finger towards my own forgiveness, God has already forgiven me, and forgiveness is his everlasting attitude towards me. So there is no need for anxiety, for scruples, no need for regrets, no need for any of the other fears or complications that bound us before. God is my personal 'first-generation' Father, and he is pleased with me just as I am, even if I should never lift a finger again in my life. If only I knew *that* in the depths of my heart, then I would no longer be afraid to get up, pick up my pallet and continue my pilgrim way towards home. So I pray for this reassurance, as a gift from Jesus. This reassurance has already been given, and celebrated, in my baptism many years ago. Nothing has changed since then, in God's love for his child. Those of us who were baptized as children may reflect that we too had to be carried to where Jesus became our brother and shared with us his Father and his Father's forgiveness. Those of us who were baptized as adults will also remember with gratitude friends who shared their faith with us and helped us to believe. Jesus himself must have been so fully aware of God's forgiveness that he never once froze in his tracks, but instead went *straight* — immediately — along his way.

Most of us do not have the gift of healing the physical or spiritual paralysis of others, except in small ways. But we can always do the easier thing for them, by telling them their sins are forgiven.

Jesus went out again beside the Sea of Galilee. As on his first walk to the sea in the first chapter, so here too Jesus finds a follower, Levi the tax collector. The tax office could well have been connected with the sea, a sort of customs office. Tax collectors were hated for making a rich living out of co-operating with the Romans, the current oppressors, at the expense of their own fellow-countrymen. Mark tells the previous occupations of only six followers of Jesus: the four fisherman, this tax collector, and last of all one blind beggar, Bartimaeus (see 10:46). But by the time Levi was called, there were many who followed Jesus. At the meal with the tax collectors and sinners, Mark takes the opportunity to give the followers of Jesus official status as *the disciples* of Jesus, calling them this for the first time. Many of them, as we know from other sources, had previously been disciples of John the baptizer.

We see the confident way Jesus compares himself and his disciples to the great King David 'and those who were with him' in the old days.

SUGGESTIONS FOR PRAYER

Verses 1 and 2
Like Peter, I can give Jesus the freedom of my own 'house', that is to say, all that I am. He can use my hands, my eyes, my ears, my mouth, my feet, my heart, all as his own base. From me he may, if he so wishes, bring his word and his healing to others. It will be a help, if I tell Jesus he is welcome. The word he brings to others through me is the same as the word he has already brought to me, the word of the Father saying, 'You are my beloved child; with you I am well pleased'.

Verses 3–9
As we read the story of the paralytic and his pallet, we may identify with the paralysed person, and imagine ourselves as the one on the stretcher. Just as the story of the leper referred first of all to leprosy and then to all other ailments having similar effects, so also this story can refer first of all to those who are paralysed

Chapter 2

invalid's sins? Is not paralysis sign enough, they think, that here is a sinner paralysed by his very sinfulness? Blasphemy is the first accusation levelled at Jesus in the course of Mark's gospel, as it will be the last, at his trial in Jerusalem. Doubtless nobody would have taken much notice if Jesus had simply gone around claiming to be God's son, without making friends with all the wrong people: he could have been treated as a harmless lunatic. But there he was, sharing his privileged position as child of God with the paralytic, who should 'by rights' have been excluded from God's mercy. The paralytic is forgiven by God because he is God's son, not for anything he had done or failed to do.

As to which is easier, to tell an invalid his sins are forgiven or to tell him to get up and get better, it is certainly easier to tell him his sins are forgiven, since this is the truth. God is permanently forgiving all his sons and daughters.

In all four gospels Jesus often refers to himself as 'the Son of man'. Scholars argue back and forth about the meaning of the title. From all the possible explanations I would take the following line: for Jesus to call himself 'the Son of man' is a hint to those who were really listening that his origin is from heaven, though the title sounds thoroughly human. The Book of Daniel, written about 165 BC, describes a vision of the prophet, in which 'there came with the clouds of heaven one like a son of man' before the throne of the Ancient of Days, and an everlasting kingdom was given to him (see Daniel 7:13f.). For the prophet Daniel himself this vision of the one like a son of man meant 'the people of the saints of the Most High' (see Daniel 7:27), who would, he predicted, rise in rebellion against the Greek oppressors and set the Promised Land free for ever. Sure enough, some twenty years later the war of independence came, and was successful; but the freedom lasted only eighty years instead of for ever. Others might have forgotten the everlasting promise contained in Daniel's vision, but not Jesus. Whereas for Daniel 'the people of the saints of the Most High' (i.e., the people of Israel) had a divine origin, coming on the clouds of heaven, Jesus knew that his own divine origin as God's Son would in time make divine the family of his brothers and sisters down through the ages, making them free for ever.

Mark strung together his stories and sayings of Jesus in a rather haphazard fashion, but the story of the paralytic let down through the roof could only fit into the overall pattern just here. If it came any earlier, during Jesus' first stay in Capernaum, there *would* have been room about the door, and no need to climb up on the roof; and on his only further return visit to Capernaum (see Mark 3:19) the crowds appear to be so large and so demanding that the four men with their paralysed friend would probably not have been able to get close to the house at all.

Mark makes the interesting comment that Jesus acted in response to the faith of the four men carrying the stretcher, without looking first for faith in the paralysed man himself. It seems somehow symbolic of the way a spiritually paralysed person cannot make the first movement back towards God; but for every one who cannot make a move there are four healthy friends to do the carrying. Jesus says to the paralytic, 'Son, your sins are forgiven', that is to say, 'Son, God has forgiven your sins'. The RSV here makes Jesus say 'My son . . .'; I have taken the liberty of dropping the word 'My', as do some of the other standard translations of St Mark. The evidence in the Greek manuscripts seems to me to be just as strong in favour of 'Son' as of 'My son'. The reason why I think it matters is that elsewhere in Mark's gospel and the other gospels Jesus makes clear that we have only one Father, and he is in heaven (see for example Matthew 23:9). To me it seems highly unlikely that Jesus would ever have called anybody 'my son' or 'my daughter', 'my child', or 'my children', since that would be to give them a second father and confuse his own teaching. 'Son', therefore, here means 'God's son'. Jesus is telling the sufferer that God has forgiven his sins, because God is his Father.

So far as I can see, Jesus never in any of the four gospels says, 'I forgive your sins'. He tells people, 'Your sins are forgiven', he treats them as if their sins are forgiven, he prays for forgiveness for his murderers, he refrains from condemning the woman caught in adultery, but he does not say, 'I am the one who forgives your sins'. Even so, the scribes sitting listening as he tells the paralytic his sins are forgiven think this is blasphemy enough, for who is Jesus to say whether or not God has forgiven this

Chapter 2

'Can the wedding guests fast while the bridegroom is with them? As long as they have the bridegroom with them, they cannot fast. [20]The days will come, when the bridegroom is taken away from them, and then they will fast in that day. [21]No one sews a piece of unshrunk cloth on an old garment; if he does, the patch tears away from it, the new from the old, and a worse tear is made. [22]And no one puts new wine into old wineskins; if he does, the wine will burst the skins, and the wine is lost, and so are the skins; but new wine is for fresh skins.'

[23]*One sabbath he was going through the grainfields; and as we made our way we disciples began to pluck ears of grain.* [24]And the Pharisees said to him, 'Look, why are they doing what is not lawful on the sabbath?' [25]And he said to them, 'Have you never read what David did, when he was in need and was hungry, he and those who were with him: [26]how he entered the house of God, when Abiathar was high priest, and ate the bread of the Presence, which it is not lawful for any but the priests to eat, and also gave it to those who were with him?' [27]And he said to them, 'The sabbath was made for man, not man for the sabbath; [28]so the Son of man is lord even of the sabbath.'

* * *

In this chapter and at the beginning of the next we find a series of incidents in which Jesus is in conflict with the local religious leaders. They are horrified that he tells a paralysed man his sins are forgiven; they complain about his eating with sinners and tax collectors; they criticize him for not making his disciples fast, for letting his disciples pick and eat ears of grain on a sabbath day as they walk through the cornfields; in the next chapter they will accuse Jesus because he heals a man on the sabbath. In each of these incidents Jesus turns the argument against his accusers. St Mark does not yet record any formal discourses or sermons of Jesus, but these short stories are in themselves a telling way of preaching the message of Jesus.

At the beginning of this chapter Jesus comes back again into Capernaum, not openly any more but hoping to keep his presence secret. When Mark tells us Jesus was 'at home' in Capernaum, this could be a reflection of Peter's way of telling the story. Jesus we know came from Nazareth, and Peter originally from Bethsaida (see John 1:44), but in these early days of his ministry Jesus seems to have made the house of Peter and Andrew in Capernaum his base. Some commentators suggest that St

CHAPTER 2
---*---

AND when he returned to Capernaum after some days, it was reported that he was at home. ²And many were gathered together, so that there was no longer room for them, not even about the door; and he was preaching the word to them. ³And they came, bringing to him a paralytic carried by four men. ⁴And when they could not get near him because of the crowd, they removed the roof above him; and when they had made an opening, they let down the pallet on which the paralytic lay. ⁵And when Jesus saw their faith, he said to the paralytic, 'Son, your sins are forgiven.' ⁶Now some of the scribes were sitting there, questioning in their hearts. ⁷'Why does this man speak thus? It is blasphemy! Who can forgive sins but God alone?' ⁸And immediately Jesus, perceiving in his spirit that they thus questioned within themselves, said to them, 'Why do you question thus in your hearts? ⁹Which is easier, to say to the paralytic, "Your sins are forgiven," or to say, "Rise, take up your pallet and walk"? ¹⁰But that you may know that the Son of man has authority on earth to forgive sins' — he said to the paralytic — ¹¹'I say to you, rise, take up your pallet and go home.' ¹²And he rose, and immediately took up the pallet and went out before them all; so that they were all amazed and glorified God, saying, 'We never saw anything like this!'

¹³He went out again beside the sea; and all the crowd gathered about him, and he taught them. ¹⁴And as he passed on, he saw Levi the son of Alphaeus sitting at the tax office, and he said to him, 'Follow me.' And he rose and followed him.

¹⁵*And as he sat at table in his house, many tax collectors and sinners were sitting with Jesus and us his disciples; for we were many who followed him.* ¹⁶And the scribes of the Pharisees, when they saw that he was eating with sinners and tax collectors, said to us, 'Why does he eat with tax collectors and sinners?' ¹⁷And when Jesus heard it, he said to them, 'Those who are well have no need of a physician, but those who are sick; I came not to call the righteous, but sinners.'

¹⁸Now John's disciples and the Pharisees were fasting; and people came and said to him, 'Why do John's disciples and the disciples of the Pharisees fast, but your disciples do not fast?' ¹⁹And Jesus said to them,

Chapter 1

Verses 40–45

This story is first and foremost about a leper, and about leprosy. But anyone praying the gospel may take the place of the leper. Probably most of us at one time or another have felt unwanted or rejected; perhaps we even have a persistent feeling of unease, as if we ourselves alone do not quite fit in, where everyone else seems to be at ease. Jesus reaches out and draws us into the circle: 'You are my sister', he says, or 'you are my brother. Do not be afraid. Join the circle. You are as good as anybody else.'

Verses 21–28

I reflect that now in me as in Jesus the prophecy of the new covenant is being fulfilled. I no longer need to ask anyone else what God is like, nor to look in a book. Everyone knows what his or her ideal Father is like, especially those whose own father was anything but ideal.

Next, I may pretend to be the man with the unclean spirit, being cured by Jesus. Now that I know from Jesus that God is none other than my own loving Father, there is no longer any need to hide my darkest secrets from him. I invite my Father to shine his light and warmth into every corner of my memory and my present day. As for the future, I reflect that my Father speaks to me in my conscience ('what I think I ought to do'), and therefore my conscience is a friendly invitation. He only invites me to take one step at a time; he will not reproach me for failure.

Verses 29–31

I identify now with Peter's sick mother-in-law. I imagine the kind of ways in which, once cured, I would serve Jesus and his followers. Several times in this chapter and other chapters Jesus wants it kept a secret that he is the Christ and the Son of God; instead he puts himself at the service of others. So too after our own healing adoption as God's sons or daughters, we should look to serve others rather than expect to lie back and be served.

Verse 35

A very valuable way of praying this gospel or any gospel is to take an empty exercise book and a pen and copy the gospel out in one's own hand, a few verses at a time. From the time of the writing of the gospels by Mark and the other evangelists, right down to the invention of the printing press, Christians who wanted a copy of a gospel usually had to copy it out for themselves, and those who did the copying found that they saw far more in writing out the gospel than they ever did by reading or hearing the same gospel.

Chapter 1

Verses 2–5

We acknowledge our need, as those people did who came to John. Without God we can never reach heaven, without hope we become even worse sinners. Without God we cannot know who God is or what he is like. We begin to listen, for unless he tells us about himself, we shall never know him.

Verses 9–13

First of all, I watch the scene as Jesus is baptized; I hear all that is said. Then I imagine that I am the next to be baptized, and as I come up out of the water, I see the dove come down over me, and I hear the voice of Jesus' heavenly Father saying *to me*: 'You are my beloved son; with you I am well pleased', or: 'You are my beloved daughter; with you I am well pleased'. The reply may be, 'Yes, I am your beloved child; with me you are well pleased'. This can be said with complete truth, anywhere, any time.

My heavenly Father is well pleased with me, so it follows that my sins must have been already washed away. He is not looking at them. Jesus his Son takes them away into the desert; they will never be seen again. Jesus shared his Spirit with us: we are at peace with God because now we know he is our constantly loving Father. We thank our Father, his Son and the Holy Spirit.

Verses 14–20

The first four disciples are called by Jesus, though not yet described as 'disciples' by Mark. St Mark extends the invitation to any reader or hearer of the gospel who wishes to follow Jesus — to anyone, not just to members of Christian religious orders or congregations, not just to the clergy. So we may pray like this: 'Jesus, I want to follow you, since you call me. These fishermen you turned into fishers of people — fishermen still, but in your cause. I offer you my dreams, my skills, my ambitions, for you to use and transform. I gladly take your Father in return for my father, of whom you will take good care. From now on your Father shall be my only authority, as I hear him in my conscience. Instead of having other people at my service, I wish only to serve, and to serve only my new-found Father, with you for my teacher.'

the mirror in whom we see ourselves as we really are in God's sight. The dove must be a reminder of the story in Genesis 8:6–12, where Noah sends out the dove once the waters of the flood recede. She comes back finally with an olive branch in her beak, signifying that the world is growing green again and all sins are forgiven. When Jesus is driven out into the wilderness by the Spirit, he is like the scapegoat who was loaded, so to speak, with all the sins of the people and carried them all away to be lost for ever in the desert (see Leviticus 16:20–22).

When Jesus comes to Galilee 'preaching the gospel of God' (verse 14) — that is, the good news from God — we may remember that the only news from God given so far in this gospel is that spoken by the Father's voice from heaven at Jesus' baptism: 'You are my beloved Son; with you I am well pleased'. *That* is the good news, which Jesus sets about preaching, but with discretion. *That* is the gospel we are invited to believe in. The people in the synagogue at Capernaum were astonished because Jesus spoke on his own authority, not quoting books or teachers for his message. In Jesus is the fulfilment of the new covenant as described by the prophet Jeremiah, where there is no longer need for one person to ask another about the Lord, but they will all know him, from the least to the greatest (see Jeremiah 31:31–34). The new covenant is written on their hearts. Once we know God as our *Abba*, our personal Father, then our hearts are clean: the unclean spirit departs, our conscience is clear.

Jesus does not put on airs because he is the beloved Son of God. On the contrary, he keeps his own identity a secret until the time will come to speak out. Instead, he treats all those to whom he has been sent as sons and daughters of God, showing in words and actions what his Father and theirs thinks about them, and how he feels for them.

SUGGESTIONS FOR PRAYER

Verse 1

A prayer of faith: 'Jesus of Nazareth, I believe you are the Christ, the Son of God'. A prayer to the Father: 'Lord God, open my eyes and my heart to the treasures hidden for us in your Son'.

Chapter 1

The gospel begins where the Old Testament prophecies said it would; it also begins where Peter said it must begin. In choosing a disciple to take the place of Judas as one of the Twelve, Peter insisted that it be someone who had 'accompanied us all the time that the Lord Jesus went in and out among us, beginning from the baptism of John' (see Acts 1:21f.). We have an example of Peter's preaching 'the good news of peace' to the centurion Cornelius and his household, and in it he begins 'from Galilee after the baptism which John preached' (see Acts 10:36f.).

The first verse of the gospel is also its title: the good news of Jesus Christ the Son of God. One of the earliest forms of the Christian creed is contained there: I believe that Jesus of Nazareth is the Christ (the promised Messiah) and is also the Son of God (authorized to invite the rest of us to be sons and daughters of God). St Paul mostly uses a slightly different wording: to believe that Jesus is the Christ, *the Lord*. Within the gospel of Mark there are two great prayers of faith. At the end of the first half of the gospel Peter says to Jesus, 'You are the Christ'; towards the end of the whole gospel the centurion in charge of the crucifixion of Jesus says, 'Truly this man was the Son of God' — he himself almost certainly not realizing the depths of what he said, but his words can be echoed with faith by the reader or hearer of the gospel.

The prophet Isaiah says the messenger will be sent on ahead to make the Lord's paths *straight* for him (see verse 3). John does the work of the messenger, and when Jesus comes he moves *straight* here, *straight* there, time and time again. Eleven times in the very first chapter, and over fifty times all told, Mark used this word meaning *straight*, though it is usually translated *immediately*. The implication seems to be that Jesus can travel in a straight line because John made the road straight in readiness for his coming. John's baptism was a request to God for the forgiveness of sins, an acknowledgement of need and of sinfulness; Jesus' baptism brought the Holy Spirit, and the gift of forgiveness.

The baptism of Jesus as it is described by Mark is not only a privileged watching of what Jesus saw and experienced, it is also a model of what happened in our own baptism, of what is still and always true in our relationship to God, and of what God is saying to every man, woman and child of the human race. Jesus is and they left their father Zebedee in the boat with the hired servants, and followed him.

²¹ *And we went into Capernaum; and immediately on the sabbath he entered the synagogue and taught.* ²²And they were astonished at his teaching, for he taught them as one who had authority, and not as the scribes. ²³ *And immediately there was in our synagogue a man with an unclean spirit;* ²⁴ *and he cried out, 'What have you to do with us, Jesus of Nazareth?* Have you come to destroy us? I know who you are, the Holy One of God.' ²⁵But Jesus rebuked him saying, 'Be silent, and come out of him!' ²⁶And the unclean spirit, convulsing him and crying with a loud voice, came out of him. ²⁷And they were all amazed, so that they questioned among themselves, saying, 'What is this? A new teaching! With authority he commands even the unclean spirits, and they obey him.' ²⁸And at once his fame spread everywhere throughout all the surrounding region of Galilee.

²⁹ *And immediately he left the synagogue, and entered my house (and Andrew's) with James and John.* ³⁰ *Now my mother-in-law lay sick with a fever, and immediately we told him of her.* ³¹ *And he came and took her by the hand and lifted her up, and the fever left her; and she served us.*

³²That evening, at sundown, they brought to him all who were sick or possessed with demons. ³³And the whole city was gathered together about the door. ³⁴And he healed many who were sick with various diseases, and cast out many demons; and he would not permit the demons to speak, because they knew him.

³⁵And in the morning, a great while before day, he rose and went out to a lonely place, and there he prayed. ³⁶ *And I and those who were with me followed him,* ³⁷ *and we found him and said to him, 'Every one is searching for you.'* ³⁸And he said to us, 'Let us go on to the next towns, that I may preach there also; for that is why I came out.' ³⁹And he went throughout all Galilee, preaching in their synagogues and casting out demons.

⁴⁰And a leper came to him beseeching him, and kneeling said to him, 'If you will, you can make me clean.' ⁴¹Moved with pity, he stretched out his hand and touched him, and said to him, 'I will; be clean.' ⁴²And immediately the leprosy left him, and he was made clean. ⁴³And he sternly charged him, and sent him away at once, ⁴⁴and said to him, 'See that you say nothing to anyone; but go, show yourself to the priest, and offer for your cleansing what Moses commanded, for a proof to the people.' ⁴⁵But he went out and began to talk freely about it, and to spread the news, so that Jesus could no longer openly enter a town, but was out in the country; and people came to him from every quarter.

CHAPTER 1
*

THE beginning of the gospel of Jesus Christ, the Son of God. ²As it is written in Isaiah the prophet,

> 'Behold, I send my messenger before thy face,
> who shall prepare thy way;
> ³the voice of one crying in the wilderness:
> Prepare the way of the Lord,
> make his paths straight —'

⁴John the baptizer appeared in the wilderness, preaching a baptism of repentance for the forgiveness of sins. ⁵And there went out to him all the country of Judea, and all the people of Jerusalem; and they were baptized by him in the river Jordan, confessing their sins. ⁶Now John was clothed with camel's hair, and had a leather girdle around his waist, and ate locusts and wild honey. ⁷And he preached, saying, 'After me comes he who is mightier than I, the thong of whose sandals I am not worthy to stoop down and untie. ⁸I have baptized you with water, but he will baptize you with the Holy Spirit.'

⁹In those days Jesus came from Nazareth of Galilee and was baptized by John in the Jordan. ¹⁰And when he came up out of the water, immediately he saw the heavens opened and the Spirit descending upon him like a dove; ¹¹and a voice came from heaven, 'Thou art my beloved Son; with thee I am well pleased.'

¹²The Spirit immediately drove him out into the wilderness. ¹³And he was in the wilderness forty days, tempted by Satan; and he was with the wild beasts; and the angels ministered to him.

¹⁴Now after John was arrested, Jesus came into Galilee, preaching the gospel of God, ¹⁵and saying, 'The time is fulfilled, and the kingdom of God is at hand; repent, and believe in the gospel.'

¹⁶And passing along by the Sea of Galilee, he saw me and Andrew my brother casting a net in the sea; for we were fishermen. ¹⁷And Jesus said to us, 'Follow me and I will make you become fishers of men.' ¹⁸And immediately we left our nets and followed him. ¹⁹And going on a little farther, he saw James the son of Zebedee and John his brother, who were in their boat mending the nets. ²⁰And immediately he called them;

Revised Standard Version (Catholic Edition), but whenever the text says 'Simon' or 'Peter', I have written 'I' or 'me' instead; and for 'they' or 'them' or 'the disciples' when it means Peter and the rest, I have written 'we' or 'us'. In each case I have written the altered sentence in italics, so that readers may be alerted and go to the proper text if it seems better to do so. My purpose, I need hardly add, is not to 'improve' on the gospel text, but to follow hints from saints and scholars about a possible way in to seeing more clearly the gospel as Peter saw it. Once these ways of praying are completed, I would expect readers to go back to the real text of the gospel.

The reason I have chosen the RSV text is this: the Revised Standard Version is a fairly literal translation, giving just what the original Greek text gives and not polishing it into better English. Polished, idiomatic English translations of Mark cannot so easily be switched to make Peter the speaker.

If anyone should ask 'For how long am I expected to pray following each of these suggestions?', again I would answer that readers must feel free. Many or even most of the prayer passages may take hardly longer to pray than they do to read. But at least one might read them prayerfully, and pause after each section of a few verses. Every now and then something may appeal to particular readers as being more precious, and then they would do well to stop and spend some time. One major tip I would give, and that is to read the book in the order in which it is written and not to dip into it at random here and there before the whole is read. And it would be much better to read quickly all through, and then come back to memorable passages, than to puzzle over a particular passage and never reach the end.

Mark is my own favourite gospel; so I hope that the love in this labour of love will make up for any shortcomings.

INTRODUCTION

When I was a child, there used to be any number of books available telling 'the life of Christ'. They were made up from a mixture of all four gospels. Nowadays the Church encourages us to take each of the four gospels separately, letting each tell the story in its own way.

This book is not a commentary on St Mark's gospel, but is designed to help people pray the gospel of Mark. I take the gospel chapter by chapter, give a short comment not for its own sake but for the sake of the prayer exercise that follows, then come the suggestions for prayer. These are simply offerings, suggestions, and are not meant to tie anybody down. I know they can be helpful because I have found them helpful myself, and so have many others to whom I have offered them over the past twenty years.

My own introduction to prayer owed almost everything to the methods of praying used in *The Spiritual Exercises* of St Ignatius Loyola. His favourite way of praying the gospel stories was to imagine he was there in the scene, looking on, helping out, taking part. Jesus is real and alive, the same yesterday, today and for ever, so to step into the gospel scene is not just a way of exercising the imagination, it is a way of coming into contact with the real Jesus who has never changed.

Perhaps it was because of my training in this method of praying that my attention was long ago caught by something that usually gets a mention in commentaries on St Mark: if the text of the gospel is read as if Peter were the speaker, it often runs more smoothly. The biblical scholar Cuthbert H. Turner drew attention to over seventy sentences in the gospel where this is true.

Now readers may easily find which text of St Mark's gospel suits them best. For this book what I have done is to take the

For Kevin Smyth

CONTENTS

Introduction	vii
CHAPTER 1	1
CHAPTER 2	8
CHAPTER 3	17
CHAPTER 4	24
CHAPTER 5	32
CHAPTER 6	39
CHAPTER 7	47
CHAPTER 8	54
CHAPTER 9	62
CHAPTER 10	71
CHAPTER 11	80
CHAPTER 12	88
CHAPTER 13	97
CHAPTER 14	105
CHAPTER 15	116
CHAPTER 16	125
Appendix 1: The Week of Re-creation	135
Appendix 2: Maps	134
1 'Through towns and villages teaching'	135
2 'Journeying toward Jerusalem'	136

Published in the United States of America by
Christian Classics, Inc.
PO Box 30, Westminster, Maryland 21157

Published in Great Britain by
Geoffrey Chapman, an imprint of Cassell Publishers Limited

© Trustees for Roman Catholic Purposes Registered 1990

All rights reserved. No part of this publication may be reproduced or transmitted in any form or by any means, electronic or mechanical including photocopying, recording or any information storage or retrieval system, without prior permission in writing from the publishers.

The gospel text is adapted from the Revised Standard Version Bible, Catholic Edition, copyright 1965 and 1966 by the Division of Christian Education of the National Council of the Churches of Christ in the USA, and used by permission.

First published 1990

British Library Cataloguing in Publication Data
O'Mahony, Gerald
Praying St Mark's gospel.
1. Bible. N.T. Mark. Devotional works
I. Title
242'.5

ISBN 0 87061 179 8

Typeset by Colset Private Limited, Singapore
Printed and bound in Great Britain by
Biddles Ltd, Guildford and King's Lynn

PRAYING
ST MARK'S GOSPEL

———————— * ————————

Gerald O'Mahony SJ

Christian Classics, Inc.
Westminster, MD
1990

By the same author from Geoffrey Chapman

THE OTHER SIDE OF THE MOUNTAIN

PRAYING
ST MARK'S GOSPEL